P9-DBQ-442

Handbook of Cooperative Education

Asa S. Knowles & Associates

HANDBOOK OF COOPERATIVE EDUCATION

Jossey-Bass Inc., Publishers
San Francisco · Washington · London · 1971

HANDBOOK OF COOPERATIVE EDUCATION
by Asa S. Knowles and Associates

Published in Great Britain by
Jossey-Bass, Inc., Publishers
St. George's House
44 Hatton Garden, London E.C.1

Library of Congress Catalogue Card Number LC 75-173854

International Standard Book Number ISBN 0-87589-112-8

Manufactured in the United States of America

JACKET DESIGN BY WILLI BAUM

FIRST EDITION

Code 7136

The Jossey-Bass Series in Higher Education

Preface

The widespread growth of cooperative education (nearly two hundred cooperative schools have developed during the past decade) clearly points to the need for a comprehensive description of its philosophy and objectives; the development and administration of its programs; its operating procedures; its relevance to special groups; and its academic, general, and financial administrative practices. The *Handbook of Cooperative Education* is designed to fill that need. Cooperative education combines periods of classroom instruction with periods of off-campus experience. In most instances the off-campus experience is paid employment related to the students' major fields of study.

The contributors do not propose to set rigid rules for the expansion or initial development of cooperative education programs. Since academic and administrative methods and policies vary considerably, each college and university must operate according to its own institutional goals and long-range objectives. The contributors do, however, discuss general policies and guidelines for the conduct of cooperative education programs. Those authors who were invited by me to contribute to this handbook were chosen on the basis of their broad experience and background in the field of cooperative education and their special competencies to deal with the various aspects of the subject.

The general purposes of the *Handbook of Cooperative Education* are as follows: To acquaint educators and the general public with the philosophy, purposes, and advantages of the cooperative plan of education. To inform educators about the organization and operation of cooperative education programs and to acquaint them with the significance of the system in serving those students who want more than the traditional educational offerings. To acquaint employers, businesses, industries, and health and government agencies with the advantages of cooperative education as a recruiting device; and to make clear the value of "coop trainees" as important sources of manpower. To illustrate the advantages of cooperative education to students from low-income families; it provides a head start on career objectives for many of these students and an inherent financial-aid feature for those who desire or need it. To show that cooperative education, once thought of as strictly vocational, effectively serves academic disciplines far beyond those considered technical or purely scientific. To show that cooperative education, through its built-in feature of relevance, has possible solutions to many of the problems of higher education in the years ahead. To show educators and employers how to make the most of cooperative education and how to combine their efforts in achieving a superior educational product.

I encouraged some duplication of content in the preparation of this work. Therefore, certain topics of discussion may appear under similar headings; the topics, however, are presented from entirely different viewpoints. For example, relations with public and private employers are presented in detail in two complete chapters; ways in which employers can be helpful to cooperative students are discussed in chapters on relations with students and on coordination and placement. Student relations are discussed from a different standpoint in the chapter on legal aspects of cooperative education.

All of the contributors to the *Handbook* sincerely hope that it will assist both existing and developing cooperative institutions in their efforts to augment a system that is destined to take its rightful high place in American higher education.

An undertaking of this scope can be accomplished only with the cooperation and assistance of many persons. Special acknowledgments must be made to certain of these individuals at Northeastern University. Roy L. Wooldridge, vice-president and dean of cooperative education, and James W. Wilson, research professor of cooperative education, were particularly helpful in suggesting appropriate persons to prepare materials and in advising on the contents of several chapters. Elizabeth H. Howkins, administrative secretary to the president, assisted in controlling and coordinating outlines, manuscripts, galleys, and page proofs. She also typed outlines and chapters, performed extensive editorial work, and assumed major responsibility for proofreading as well as for preparation of the index. Chester W. Storey, assistant to the president, and Joy W. Viola, editorial assistant to the president, edited several of the chapters and assisted in the preparation of others. Daniel J. Roberts, vice-president–finance, gave generously of his time to review portions of the chapter on general administration. William A. Lovely, assistant to the vice-president–business, also gave generously of his time to develop the presentation (in Chapter 20) of costs of conversion from a traditional college to a cooperative-plan college. Richard W. Bishop, dean of university relations, assisted in the preparation of materials for the chapter on academic administration and prepared some of the illustrations contained in the *Handbook*. Finally, several staff members of departments of cooperative education at Northeastern and other colleges and universities furnished materials for various chapters.

I dedicate this book to my son Asa and my daughter Margaret.

Boston
October 1971

Asa S. Knowles

Contents

TWO: DESCRIPTION OF PROGRAMS

FOUR: ADMINISTRATION

FIVE: RELEVANCY TO SPECIAL GROUPS

SIX: DEVELOPMENT OF NEW PROGRAMS

APPENDICES

Authors

Albert S. Barber, *director of coordination and placement, University of Waterloo (Ontario, Canada)*

Alvah K. Borman, *assistant dean of cooperative education and director of graduate cooperative education, Northeastern University*

John A. Chase, *director, Department of Cooperative Education and Placement, The Cleveland State University*

Stewart B. Collins, *executive secretary, Cooperative Education Association, and director, Department of Cooperative Education, Drexel University*

J. Dudley Dawson, *vice-president and dean of students emeritus, Antioch College, and consultant, National Commission for Cooperative Education*

Paul E. Dubé, *professor of cooperative education, Northeastern University*

Gilbert C. Garland, *dean of admissions, Northeastern University*

James Grant, *Academic Interchange, Newcastle upon Tyne Polytechnic (England)*

Donald C. Hunt, *director of cooperative education and placement, University of Detroit*

Asa S. Knowles, *president, Northeastern University*

Carole A. Lilley, *coordinator of cooperative education, Northeastern University*

Lena M. McKinney, *director of cooperative education program and summer employment, Morgan State College*

George H. Miller, *director, Cooperative Education Services, University of South Florida*

Thomas J. O'Toole, *Edwin W. Hadley Professor of Law, Northeastern University*

George E. Probst, *executive director, National Commission for Cooperative Education*

HAROLD P. RODES, *president, General Motors Institute*

CHARLES F. SEAVERNS, JR., *professor of cooperative education and director of training, Northeastern University*

RALPH W. TYLER, *chairman, National Commission for Cooperative Education, and consultant in higher education*

HARRIET P. VAN SICKLE, *coordinator of cooperative education, Borough of Manhattan Community College*

JAMES W. WILSON, *research professor of cooperative education, Northeastern University*

ROY L. WOOLDRIDGE, *vice-president and dean of cooperative education, Northeastern University*

Handbook of Cooperative Education

PART ONE

HISTORY AND PHILOSOPHY

I

Historical Development

James W. Wilson

Begun in 1906 on an experimental basis at a single institution, cooperative education—a plan of education that incorporates productive work into the curriculum as a regular and integral element—has grown until today 225 colleges and universities in the United States and six in Canada offer various patterns of cooperative education. The name, *cooperative education,* reflects the necessary cooperative relationship established between the institution and the agency providing the work situation. These programs are offered at junior colleges, senior colleges, and graduate schools. Estimates are that by the mid-1970s as many as five hundred colleges and universities will offer cooperative education programs.

The variations in the patterns, their organization, and their methods of operation are discussed in detail in subsequent chapters in this book.

Early Years

Cooperative education is in a period of very rapid growth, with most of the programs initiated during the past five to seven years. But cooperative education is not a new idea in American higher education. The first program was the inspiration of Herman Schneider, a University of Cincinnati engineering professor who was later dean of engineering and for a brief time president of the university. He brought the idea with him from Lehigh University in 1903 and was given authorization to institute the first program of cooperative education in 1906. Through this program Dean Schneider sought to solve two problems that he had observed. First, he had noted that many elements of most professions could not be taught effectively or at all in the classroom but rather required practical experience for their adequate mastery. Second, he had found that most students either needed or wanted to work sometime during their college careers; most of these jobs, he further observed, were menial and unrelated to the students' career goals. By means of his cooperative education plan Dean Schneider found a way of satisfying the needs of students for "state-of-the-art" experiences and for money (Park, 1943). His plan was to alternate two groups of students on a weekly basis between on-campus study of engineering and off-campus employment in engineering-related jobs in local industries. While one group of students studied on campus, the other group held productive jobs; and after one week the groups changed places.

This scheme to involve the student periodically in the work process was clearly consistent with the whole movement of higher education—a movement away from aloofness and isolation from the world to concern and direct engagement in the affairs of society (Harris, 1970).

It was not long before the benefits of the cooperative plan became manifest. Classroom learning was reinforced by job responsibilities. New knowledge, understandings, and skills were developed. Students were provided extraordinary opportunities for testing the appropriateness of their career choices, their interests, their abilities, and their temperaments. Students graduating from the cooperative program had greater confidence in their career choices and their potentials for success upon graduation. The conclusion drawn from these outcomes was that cooperative education has great value in the education of engineers and, generalizing, for the professions. It was further concluded that this contribution to career preparation was possible only if work assignments closely corresponded to the academic curriculum. Cooperative education was thought to be useful as an educational plan because and only because it was an extension, even though a realistic extension, of the college laboratories.

It was some years before the inadequacy of this examination of the values of cooperative education was fully realized. Not until research demonstrated other values, independent of career development, was it realized that the notion of cooperative education as but an extension of the campus laboratory was too specialized. It became increasingly clear that cooperative education experiences contribute to the developing sense of identity and sense of worth of the student, because, for perhaps the first time in his life, he relates to adults as an adult and because he learns important lessons about relating to other persons from many different backgrounds; that he typically achieves better in his academic program because—among other reasons—he changes his attitudes toward himself; organizes his time and work better, as a result of meeting work obligations; finds greater relevancy and hence greater motivation for his studies; is able periodically to have a change of pace from the lockstep of academic pursuits; and worries less about finances, which might distract him from his studies. The data now available about the impact of cooperative education upon students suggest a far more adequate explanation of the value of cooperative education than that ascribed early in its history. Because it places the student in new and challenging situations demanding of him new efforts and new modes of behavior, cooperative education makes a strong contribution to growth of the individual student in his personal development, his social development, and his career development.

Many educators today, reflecting upon the origins of cooperative education, consider Dean Schneider an inspired innovator in American higher education. If, however, his educational concept was revolutionary, its impact upon American higher education was indeed quietly revolutionary. No new program was begun for three years after the Cincinnati program was implemented. Then, in 1909 in

Boston, the Polytechnic School of the YMCA Evening Institute (which later became Northeastern University) initiated cooperative engineering courses. The program was patterned after Cincinnati's in that students alternated on a weekly basis between the classroom and employment in Boston industrial companies. By 1920 seven other baccalaureate institutions and one technical institute initiated programs of cooperative education. These institutions, together with the date they first offered cooperative programs, are listed in Table 1.

Table 1. EARLY ADOPTIONS OF COOPERATIVE EDUCATION PLANS

Institution	*Year Cooperative Education Initiated*
University of Cincinnati, Cincinnati, Ohio	1906
Northeastern University, Boston, Massachusetts	1909
University of Pittsburgh, Pittsburgh, Pennsylvania	1910
University of Detroit, Detroit, Michigan	1911
Georgia Institute of Technology, Atlanta, Georgia	1912
Rochester Institute of Technology (A technical institute until 1955), Rochester, New York	1912
University of Akron, Akron, Ohio	1914
Marquette University, Milwaukee, Wisconsin	1919
Drexel University, Philadelphia, Pennsylvania	1919
Massachusetts Institute of Technology, Cambridge, Massachusetts	1919

At each of these institutions the program was begun in engineering. The first nonengineering cooperative program was begun in business at the University of Cincinnati in 1919. Furthermore, all of these earlier programs of cooperative education were located in urban settings with substantial local industry. As a matter of fact, it was generally believed that a cooperative education program could not function effectively in any other setting. In 1921 the falsity of this conclusion was demonstrated, and the first break from vocationally oriented cooperative education came. In that year Antioch College, located in rural Yellow Springs, Ohio, inaugurated the first cooperative education program in a totally liberal-arts institution. To this point all programs of cooperative education were principally vocational and career oriented in their educational mission. Early proponents of cooperative education believed that the major, if not the sole, contribution of the cooperative plan was to the vocational preparation of students. The philosophy at Antioch, on the contrary, was that the cooperative experience is a valuable mechanism for general, liberal education in addition to career preparation. The following quotation from an Antioch publication gives clear perspective to the Antioch philosophy of cooperative education.

> *Whereas the popular impression of the cooperative work-study plan of education is merely that it aids the student in choosing a vocation and in preparing for it, Antioch as a college of liberal arts and sciences thinks of the plan also as contributing to liberal education. When the student leaves the sheltered environment of the campus for his regular work assignments, he is at least in a position to make direct observations about contemporary civilization.* If he receives some direction in this experience, *he may make distinctions between good ethics and bad not only in jobs but also in communities; he may see both tolerance and intolerance at work; he may appraise the effects of social planning or the lack of it; he may acquire greater sensitivity to beauty through exposure to art and music; he may learn the difference between a creative individual and a passive one; he may become sensitive to human beings both as individuals and in the mass. With this kind of first-hand knowledge about society today, students are in better position—Antioch feels—to comprehend the past and the various theories about human progress. They are also more likely to assimilate a liberal education in a way that means something in today's living. Thus liberal education can become more a constructive force in molding society, and less a badge of social prestige* [*Henderson and Hall, 1946, p. 85*].

Antioch remained the only liberal-arts institution with a cooperative program until 1932, when Bennington College initiated a field-work program which it continues to operate today. Between 1921 and 1930 five institutions in addition to Antioch implemented programs of cooperative education. These were Fenn College (now Cleveland State University), Cleveland, Ohio, in 1923; General Motors Institute, Detroit, Michigan, in 1924; Southern Methodist University, Dallas, Texas, and the University of Louisville, Louisville, Kentucky, in 1925; and the University of Tennessee at Knoxville in 1926. All of these were engineering programs. The General Motors Institute program is of particular interest because it is an industry-sponsored institution in which students alternate between on-campus study and work in General Motors plants throughout the country (see Chapter 7).

Between 1931 and 1945, which encompassed both the great depression and World War II, only five educational programs of cooperative education were instituted. Immediately following World War II, partly in response to large numbers of returning veterans, a relatively big growth rate occurred. By 1953 forty-three programs of cooperative education were in active operation. Thirty-five of these were in baccalaureate institutions, and eight were in community colleges and technical institutes (Armsby, 1954). By 1960 the number of baccalaureate institutions operating cooperative education programs had increased to sixty-one. Ten junior colleges, community colleges, and technical institutes had established cooperative programs by this date, bringing the total number of programs to seventy-one (Collins, 1970).

Problems in Implementation

In the history of cooperative education the period from 1906 to 1945 may be described as a time when solutions to various problems —the need to find suitable work assignments, resistance from labor unions and faculty; the effects of war and economic recession; and the struggle to find suitable work-study patterns—were sought.

NEED FOR WORK ASSIGNMENTS. Absolutely essential in the development of cooperative education have been the cooperative employers. Without them a good idea would have remained just that. In his early efforts to implement his plan, Dean Schneider initially found industrial reticence to the employment of students part time. Through his own enthusiasm for the idea, his conviction of its merit, and his persistence in seeking support, he convinced a number of Cincinnati firms to give it a try (Park, 1943). The students themselves validated the scheme and gave substance to Schneider's dream of "theoretical knowledge and first-hand experience be[ing] hitched together" (Park, 1943, p. 44).

Responsibility for development of cooperative work assignments rests with coordinators of cooperative education programs: they must identify prospective employers and potentially meaningful jobs; they must persuade employers of the advantages the plan holds for them; they must advise students regarding possible work assignments and assist in the placement process; and they must follow up with both student and employer to assure the needs of both are being satisfied.

Today's enthusiastic employer acceptance of cooperative education is amply demonstrated by the results of formal inquiry into their feelings, by the fact that they currently are providing over forty thousand cooperative jobs annually, and by their active participation in the professional societies of cooperative education. Just how many employers are providing cooperative work experiences for students is not known, but a conservative estimate places the figure at ten thousand. Northeastern University alone has 2,500 different employers.

In the very early days of cooperative education employers were always within commuting distance from the colleges. As noted earlier, the first programs were all initiated in urban institutions. Today, however, with the ease of travel the situation is quite different. Cooperative students may be found working all over the country and, increasingly, out of the country. Many of the newer programs being developed are some distance from metropolitan areas, and of necessity their students must leave the college community for their cooperative assignments. Some programs have policies which stipulate that students may not work in their home communities. Cooperative work assignments in foreign countries, for reasons of cost and complications in arranging work situations, account for a very small fraction of placements. Nonetheless, overseas assignments are made and increasingly so.

Historically, many employers have evidenced interest in cooperative education beyond providing jobs. They have written articles, given papers at meetings of professional societies, and worked with college people to strengthen programs. They continue today to give strong support to the national effort to extend and strengthen cooperative education.

EFFECTS OF RECESSIONS AND WARS. From time to time the country experiences economic disruption; and this, quite naturally, affects the operation of cooperative education. The nation experienced economic disruption in 1914 and again in 1921. But the most severe economic test for cooperative education came with the great depression of the 1930s. Mandatory cooperative programs nearly always experience a degree of unemployment for a variety of reasons, but that experienced between 1930 and 1939 was severe. At Northeastern University, for example, cooperative placements by 1932 were down to 54 per cent of the available students (White, 1933). At the University of Cincinnati the employment record was somewhat better; overall placement was 65 per cent in 1932 (Burns, 1934). Only one institution dropped the cooperative program altogether; and unemployment among cooperative students, although severe, tended to lag behind unemployment of full-time workers. Cooperative programs, then, fared comparatively well in hard times—probably for two reasons: first of all, because of the close relationships established with employers over the preceding years and the fact that students had demonstrated their value; second, because cooperative students were spread among a large number of different employers (Seulberger, 1932). At least two institutions (Northeastern University and The University of Cincinnati) devised on-campus programs for their unemployed students. At both institutions cultural and general education courses were provided on an optional basis at no tuition and for no academic credit. The plan was simply to provide an enrichment to the total educational experience of the students. In point of fact, although the situation was difficult, cooperative institutions were able to weather this severe unemployment and to do so with considerable enthusiasm and good morale on the part of all concerned.

Cooperative education also has survived two world wars. Only two institutions operating programs of cooperative education in 1918 are known to have suspended them. During World War II, thirteen institutions suspended operation of their cooperative programs (Smith, 1946). Most resumed the program after the war. The principal reasons for terminating the program temporarily were the need to accelerate the educational process and the drastic reduction of the male population of students except for military programs on campus.

RESISTANCE FROM LABOR UNIONS. The effects of economic disruption and war are serious, but they are temporary. Institutions gird themselves and weather the dislocations. The situation has been somewhat different with the organized labor movement in the country. Prior to 1935 there was relatively little difficulty in placing students on most kinds of jobs in most kinds of industries. After passage of the National Recovery Act in 1935, however, unions became stronger and strikes became more prevalent. Cooperative programs of necessity had to deal with the unions, and each institution had to develop relationships with each different union (Kapp, 1935). Some unions would excuse students from joining unions provided they were not classified as apprentices. Others would require students to become union members although they might suspend the initiation fee. Institutions adopted different positions. Most advised their students against joining unions if possible (SPEE, 1937). Some left the decision about joining a union or crossing a picket line entirely up to the student; others (for example, Drexel University) had a clear policy that if a strike occurred and as many as 40 per cent of the employees left their jobs, the students must also leave their jobs and report to the cooperative department (Kapp, 1935). At the local level relationships between cooperative departments and union officials have not always been cordial. The principal concern of the unions, of course, has been that cooperative students might take jobs away from full-time employees and that, if students were not members of the union, they could not be made to participate in a strike.

RESISTANCE FROM FACULTY. Another difficulty encountered by cooperative education programs has been the lack of support and occasional outright hostility on the part of some teaching faculty. Although most faculty members—particularly in professional curricula such as engineering, business administration, and accounting—appreciate the values of cooperative education and support it, faculty in liberal-arts curricula—especially in such fields as philosophy, history, literature, and language arts—find the programs more difficult to accept because, in fact, their students cannot invariably be placed in work situations that relate directly to their fields of study. However, with today's emphasis on relevance, the faculties are viewing cooperative education in a new light.

Although some faculty may never be persuaded, experience has shown that when a systematic effort is made to work with teaching faculty and to keep them apprised of what their students are doing at work, the relationships between the coordination staff and the faculty become very positive and faculty support for the plan is strengthened.

NEED FOR SUITABLE WORK-STUDY PATTERNS. Establishment of the cooperative calendar or pattern of on-campus study and off-campus work is another problem that cooperative programs have always had to face and must face today. Most programs, particularly those in professional curricula, use some kind of alternation pattern, so that employers can set aside full-time jobs for cooperative students with reasonable assurance that they will always be filled by pairs of students. When the first program was started in Cincinnati, the periods of alternation were one week. The programs that followed were also organized on this weekly changeover pattern. Over the years, however, the trend was to lengthen the periods, first to two weeks, then to four, then six, then ten, and finally to full twelve-week quarters or sixteen-week semesters. A few institutions use a six-month period, and one uses a full year. In addition, a few institutions have established what they refer to as a nonresident term. Their students do not alternate at regular intervals between school and work, but once each year leave the campus and spend about two months working with various business, industrial, and service organizations. Furthermore, a number of innovations are stemming from cooperative education, such as joint training-education programs conducted by colleges and industries, and intern programs in education and social work.

Most of the baccalaureate programs established prior to 1960 are five years in length, and a number of the early-established junior college programs were three years. The Cincinnati program was six years when Dean Schneider introduced it. The reason for extending cooperative programs is simply to ease scheduling of academic courses and to increase the number of possible cooperative periods. Most programs established over the past few years, however, have not extended the total length of the college program: baccalaureate programs continue as four years, and junior college programs as two. The reluctance of these institutions to add a year is based upon their concern that such a proposal would be rejected by both students and their parents. The consequence, of course, is that most newer programs provide fewer cooperative experiences.

Need for Affiliation

As cooperative education evolved, its practitioners sensed the need for an association to exchange ideas and share experiences. Since cooperative education began and initially developed in engineering education, it is not surprising that the first cooperative association to be formed was within the context of engineering education. The Association of Co-operative Colleges was formed in 1926 under the leadership of Herman Schneider. The first meeting was held at the University of Cincinnati with representatives from sixteen colleges and six industrial firms (Wohlford, 1971). In 1929 a group active in this association petitioned the officers and council of the Society for Promotion of Engineering Education (now the American Society for Engineering Education) to form a division of cooperative engineering education. The petition was approved, and the first formal meeting of the Cooperative Education Division was held at the society's summer convention in 1930 at Montreal, Canada (SPEE, 1930). The division exists today, meeting the needs of educators and employers concerned with cooperative engineering education. The 1971 membership of the division is 622. In September 1963 the Cooperative Education Association (CEA) was founded for the purpose of providing a forum for *all* persons involved and interested in cooperative education, irrespective of their fields of discipline or institutional type (Hunt, 1964). The membership of the CEA as of January 1971 was 979.

An Idea Finds Its Time

The contemporary period in the history and development of cooperative education began in 1957. At that time the colleges and universities of the country were deeply troubled about an anticipated onslaught of students and were seeking ways to meet the challenge. Charles F. Kettering, long-time Research Director of the General Motors Corporation, Chairman of the Thomas Alva Edison Foundation, and strong advocate of cooperative education, proposed that the Edison Foundation sponsor a conference of educators and representatives of business and industry to examine the cooperative plan as one solution. Representatives of some eighty colleges and one hundred industrial and business firms attended a two-day conference on "Cooperative Education and the Impending Educational Crisis" in Dayton, Ohio, on May 23–24, 1957. This conference made clear that over the years cooperative education had been adapted in a variety of ways to a variety of educational institutions. It also revealed that many kinds of businesses, industries, and professions were partners in cooperative education. Those experienced in cooperative education were enthusiastic about its potential but recognized that an objective investigation of its merits must precede any serious effort to expand cooperative education.

A request was made to the Fund for Advancement of Education to consider a grant for a systematic study of cooperative education. A grant of $95,000 was made available, a study committee was formed, and a staff was employed. A two-year national study was designed to appraise the claimed advantages and feared disadvantages of cooperative education. The findings of the study were reported both verbally (in June of 1960 at a two-day conference in Dayton, Ohio) and in print (Wilson and Lyons, 1961; Tyler and Mills, 1961). A major conclusion of the study committee was that "Cooperative education has important values for colleges and universities, for students and employers. These values should be given wide publicity and cooperative programs in American higher education should be greatly extended" (Tyler, 1961). (See Chapter 2.) Consistent with this recommendation, the Charles F. Kettering Foundation sponsored a conference in June 1961 at Princeton, New Jersey, "The Princeton Conference on Work-Study in Higher Education." This was a workshop conference where representatives of institutions could consult with persons experienced in cooperative education to discover how they might initiate programs. The Kettering Foundation invited the submission of a proposal for a plan to greatly expand cooperative education in the United States. The most direct outcome of this effort was the creation of the National Commission for Cooperative Education, with Ralph W. Tyler as Chairman and George E. Probst as Executive Director. The specific purposes of the National Commission were to give direct assistance to institutions planning to establish programs of cooperative education and to disseminate widely information about cooperative education.

Since its beginning in 1962, the National Commission has worked diligently to expand cooperative education and bring it to national attention. In addition to giving specific counsel, it has participated in television and radio programs, published papers and monographs, and sponsored state-wide conferences on cooperative education. In 1964 the commission turned its attention to Washington and sought to encourage legislation to support programs of cooperative education. As a result of these efforts, a provision of Title III of the Higher Education Act of 1965, entitled Aid for Developing Institutions, made funds available to qualifying institutions seeking to establish cooperative education programs. A further advance was made with the 1968 amendments to both the Vocational Education Act of 1963 and the Higher Education Act of 1965. Titles of both these acts provided support for institutions seeking to develop programs of cooperative education. The commission had no role in the Vocational Education Amendment; but, through testimony to the Congress of the United States and sponsorship of state-wide conferences, it played a significant role in the passage of Title IV, Part D, of the 1968 Amendment of the Higher Education Act of 1965. The commission continues to provide consultation and testimony to the Congress, on each occasion recommending a line item in the education budget consistent with the provision of the 1968 act. No money under this act has to date been appropriated; but some money has been made available through various appropriation acts, which have designated 1 per cent of college work-study funds for support of cooperative education. In fiscal 1970 this appropriation amounted to $1,540,000 and in fiscal 1971 to $1,600,000.

In the spring of 1965 the Fund for the Advancement of Education (FAE) made the first of a series of eleven grants to support the development of cooperative education. At the same time, it made a three-year grant to Northeastern University so that it might provide counsel for these institutions. In giving the grant to Northeastern, FAE indicated that consulting services could be granted to other institutions as well, so long as the service to the grantees was in no way impaired. Within this context Northeastern established the first Center for Cooperative Education. Although its initial purpose was to give specific aid to institutions planning programs of cooperative education, it shortly added a second purpose of providing training for coordinators already in the field and coordinators just starting. In 1967 FAE gave Northeastern a second grant, which, in this instance, was matched in equal amount by the university for the purpose of fully endowing a research chair in cooperative education. In 1968 James W. Wilson was invited to occupy this research professorship.

Since 1969 three other centers for cooperative education have been formed, each principally dedicated to training cooperative education coordinators. These centers are located at the University of South Florida, Virginia Polytechnic Institute, and the University of Detroit. In addition to the training provided through workshops at these centers, four institutions have operated summer institutes in cooperative education.

Cooperative education has had both a long and short history. It has had a long history in the sense that the idea was first propounded and implemented over sixty-five years ago. It has had a short history in the sense that only in the past ten years has the idea of cooperative education captured the imagination of hundreds of colleges and universities throughout the country. The number of cooperative programs established during this brief period has increased the total number by nearly fourfold, and by 1973 that figure might well be sixfold. This growth is occurring in every kind of institution—public and private, sectarian and nonsectarian, urban and nonurban, large multipurpose universities and small single-purpose colleges, coeducational colleges and all-men or all-women colleges, colleges serving affluent students and colleges serving low-income students, senior colleges and junior colleges. It is among the two-year junior and community colleges that some of the most rapid expansion of cooperative education is taking place. More than sixty-five programs are now in operation. Nearly half that growth has occurred within the past three years. By far the most dramatic growth is occurring in Florida, where nearly twenty junior colleges have initiated programs within the past two years and where the State University System of Florida has adopted a policy of implementing programs of cooperative education on every college campus in Florida. The cooperative plan has been viewed by community colleges as particularly appropriate, because they all have career-related curricula which can be greatly strengthened by a policy of off-campus work and because the cooperative plan helps to relate the college and the community much more closely.

Not only institutional adoptions but new curricula have grown. The number of different curricula offering the cooperative plan has increased from 46 in 1954 to 165 in 1970. Some of the newer fields of study include education (elementary, secondary, special, physical, recreational), law, actuarial science, and criminal justice. Within the last several years cooperative education has been applied to allied health fields—nursing, laboratory technician, physical therapy, medical assistant, and numerous others. The consensus is that cooperative education is applicable to all fields of study.

There is strong evidence that this growth will continue. In October 1970, when the U.S. Office of Education first funded proposals for the planning and implementation of cooperative education, the Division of College Support received 206 applications with requests totaling $8,500,000. In the second year of funding, 344 applications with requests for $12,300,000 were received. The requests have exceeded the available funds by 800 per cent. In the first three months of 1971 three separate reports on American higher education were issued (the Carnegie Commission on Higher Education Report, *Less Time, More Options;* the American Academy of Arts and Sciences report, *The Assembly on Goals and Governance;* and the *Newman Report on Higher Education*). Each recommends that many more colleges and universities of this country should seriously consider the introduction of some mix of study and off-campus work as an integral feature of their curricula.

Because cooperative education does respond to important issues of higher education, and because—as institutions throughout the country are now discovering—it is an extremely powerful tool for achieving the goals of education, cooperative education should continue to expand rapidly during the next several years.

II

Values and Objectives

Ralph W. Tyler

Many of today's college and university students, faculty, and administrators, convinced of the need for "relevance" in higher education, are offering proposals for involving students in activities beyond the cloistered campus walls. Some have suggested that students be encouraged to take "time out" from campus study for a year or more after the second college year in order to gain better understanding of the adult world and appreciation for the contributions of education before returning to complete the requirements for graduation. Others have argued for "community-work experience" as an option or a requirement to enable the student to participate in socially useful activities of the adult world. Numerous types of "colleges without walls" have been considered in an effort to free students from the adolescent isolation commonly characteristic of undergraduate education. The need for reducing or eliminating this isolation is clear, but the current proposals appear less effective educationally than a well-designed program of cooperative education.

Cooperative education guarantees for each student constructive work experience planned to relate to his campus study. Cooperative education gives him an opportunity to carry on an adult job and to be rewarded for successful performance on the same terms as adults who are not in college. He also learns to appreciate his own place in the employing institution and the place of the institution in the larger society. These features furnish a basis for the student to appreciate the relevance of his work and study that is not so easily provided by other current proposals.

Over the years, numerous reports have outlined the values of cooperative education. A few of these reports (Baskin, 1954; Coleman, 1934; Mosbacker, 1957; L. F. Smith, 1944) were based upon careful research; the majority, however, were reports of positive experience by personnel in the field. The most comprehensive evaluation of cooperative education was conducted over a two-year period from 1958 to 1960 (Wilson and Lyons, 1961). The researchers obtained from the literature and from interviews with persons active in the field a series of statements or beliefs about the advantages and disadvantages of the cooperative plan. In essence, their research supports the positive claims and lays to rest the feared disadvantages. Subsequently, other studies (Fram, 1964; Lindenmeyer, 1967; H. S. Smith, 1965; Stark, 1965; Yencso, 1970) have contributed further to our understanding of the significant values of the cooperative plan of education. The statements about the values of cooperative education that appear in this chapter are based upon the accumulated knowledge from all these reports.

Values to Students

Many students have developed an occupational goal before entering college; others expect to explore and develop their career aspirations through their college education. Cooperative education has enabled both groups of students to find meaning in what they are studying. They find meaning because the theories and principles learned in the classroom are reinforced and given concrete application on work assignments and because they increasingly perceive, as their experience continues, the relevance of what they are studying to the situations they encounter while off campus on the job. As students find meaning to their studies, they become more highly motivated.

A second source of motivation is found in cooperative education by students who are uncertain of their ability to succeed in college and who may lack confidence in other respects. Many of these students perform satisfactorily in their job assignments and thus gain increasing confidence in their ability to learn and to meet reasonable adult expectations. As they gain this confidence, they attack their studies with greater energy and assurance.

Cooperative education contributes to the career development of students in a number of ways. As noted above, opportunities are provided for them to practice the knowledge and skills learned in school. In addition, new knowledge and skills learned on the job further contribute to students' total understanding. Most of the jobs performed by cooperative students afford them opportunity to observe a range of vocations and professions actually being performed. Consequently, students can measure themselves against the requirements of the jobs they are in and those that they observe closely. They also gain a more realistic understanding of the tasks involved, the conditions under which they operate, and the kinds of rewards obtained in a variety of occupations. Furthermore, in large organizations the planned work experience provides for movement upward into jobs that require increasing skills, knowledge, and responsibility. Through these experiences, students can either confirm their earlier choice of careers or realize before too long that they have made an unwise choice. If they have made a wrong choice, they can replan their careers and the educational programs appropriate to them.

Many liberal-arts students, unsure of their vocational goals, specifically use cooperative education to explore and realistically test different career possibilities. They will first examine with the help of their cooperative coordinator their interests, areas of success and difficulty, and other conditions affecting career choice. Based upon this knowledge they will decide upon a job for the next cooperative period. Upon their return to school they and their coordinator will assess the job and its implications for a future career. If it seems to have potential, it will be followed up on the next cooperative term; if not, the information gained will be used to explore further.

Cooperative education also contributes indirectly to the career development of students, through its influence on many faculty members. As work programs are planned and developed, and as the students rotate from college to work and back to college again, the faculty is better able to keep in touch with business, industry, and some of the professions. In many of the colleges information gained through these contacts is used in planning the curriculum and in teaching, thus contributing greater educational vitality.

Cooperative education also can provide a superior opportunity for students to develop realistic social attitudes. Their work tasks frequently require cooperation with colleagues. In most jobs they must consider the feelings and ideas of their associates, and they are frequently involved in team responsibilities. These situations are not artificially devised by teachers, nor do they arise from undirected relations with fellow students; rather, they are necessitated by the demands of the work and therefore have a significance for the student that is often lacking in campus social contacts. Students in cooperative programs, then, do seem to develop attitudes of cooperation and the abilities required to get along with others, to adjust to work situations, and to function effectively as part of a team.

In a complex urban society, where adolescence is prolonged and maturation is slower than in earlier times, work experience affords opportunity for maturing that is not usually available in a social environment apart from the adult world. Cooperative students, on the job and in the socializing during work periods, associate mainly with adults. In these contacts, they can observe adults making decisions in various contexts; furthermore and of particular significance, they themselves have many opportunities to make decisions and to see their consequences. Greater self-confidence and independence result. Thus, work experience enables many students to develop into responsible adults.

Although some students attending college on the cooperative plan are involved in voluntary work programs, the great majority are paid. They are paid at the going rate for the jobs they perform. The money earned greatly assists students to meet the costs of their education. For many it makes the difference between being able to go to college or not. In addition, cooperative students have become a significant part of the work force in industry, business, the health agencies, and the civil service. The more than eighty thousand such students who were employed during 1970–71 earned in that year over two hundred million dollars in the work phases of their programs. Their work was equivalent to that of between forty and forty-five thousand full-time employees. As these students discover the extent of their contribuions to the labor force, they gain greater appreciation for their own work and their capabilities.

Values to Employer

Support from business, industry, government, and human-services agencies is obviously needed if cooperative education is to exist at all. That it has not only existed for sixty years but has grown is clear testimony that both the private and public sectors of our economy find value in having college students devote a portion of their time working. There are two principal reasons for their support. First, they have jobs that need to be done. They find cooperative students able and enthusiastic workers and eager to learn. Second, cooperative education is and has long been recognized by employers as a useful device for the recruitment of permanent personnel. On the average, 40 to 45 per cent of all cooperative students (including liberal-arts students as well as students in professional curricula), return to a cooperative employer as full-time employees on graduation or following graduate study. For students in professional programs only, the percentage is over 60. Studies of employment records consistently show that employees who worked for an employer as cooperative students typically remain longer and are better employees than those who had no prior connection with the company.

In very recent years employers have had difficulty with a small fraction of college-graduate recruits, who appear to have no real interest in their work but are primarily unhappy with the world in general and with American institutions, especially business and industry, in particular. Some of these recruits have caused disruptions and fomented dissatisfaction among other employees. Employers find that recruitment of permanent staff from their cooperative education students assures them of employees who are experienced in the company and have already established a record of constructive work.

The development of a cooperative education program with an industrial or professional employing agency can be, and frequently is, a first step in the evolution of a broader training-education partnership.

As industry and the professions have become more complex, as the body of relevant knowledge has sharply increased, the demand for continuing education and training at many stages in the careers of men and women has been growing. Many of these training programs are conducted within the employing agencies but often with the assistance of nearby colleges and universities. In fact, the more complex and advanced continuing education programs are often planned, staffed, and conducted and certified primarily by the educational institution. This can be a fruitful relationship, for the college as well as the agencies involved.

Finally, through cooperative education women and other minority groups can be introduced into jobs not usually undertaken by them (see also Chapters 18 and 19). The educational coordinator can help to analyze real requirements for a job and identify students who can qualify. He can also help the employing officers to perceive the value of opening jobs to all who can really qualify rather than to continue those traditional requirements that are not actually essential for successful job performance.

Values to Cooperative Institution

There are four major advantages of the cooperative plan to colleges. First, it has been used successfully to recruit able students to the college. Many high school students and their parents are interested in the opportunity to mix study and work and are attracted to colleges offering cooperative education.

Second, students bring back to the campus, the classroom, and the faculty up-to-date information on industrial and business practices and new technology. This feedback helps to keep the curriculum current and relevant.

A third advantage is that colleges are able to utilize their resources more economically and effectively. By using a rotation pattern, they can increase the student body substantially without any increase in the physical plant.

If a cooperative college is located in or near a metropolitan area and places its cooperative students with local employers, the college tends to become more closely allied with the community. As a result, in many communities positive cooperation has been substituted for the negative features of town and gown misunderstanding.

Values to Society

Most of the values of cooperative education that have been mentioned earlier in this chapter are social benefits in the broad sense. There are certain additional ones worthy of special comment.

Until recently, colleges and universities tapped only a small fraction of the youth from families where no one previously had enrolled in college. Now, there is wide concern for extending the opportunities for higher education to many more students from this background. Cooperative education, because of its connection with the world of work and the opportunity it affords for the student to earn a substantial part of his college costs, has a special appeal to these students. It provides a program in which students from working-class backgrounds can more easily understand the relevance of what they are learning in college and are more likely to make a success of their college work than if they were in contact only with academic situations. The proportion of students from working-class backgrounds is much larger in cooperative programs than others.

An additional social factor deserving special comment is the opportunity cooperative education furnishes to help the student deal constructively with the varieties of new situations and new experiences that educated men encounter. Because of the many different persons with whom they associate and because they undertake jobs in locations some distance from their homes, most cooperative students learn to adjust readily to new situations. Some of the employing officers have mentioned that cooperative students are able to adjust more readily to positions abroad, and acquire an understanding and appreciation for different cultures and customs they encounter.

Earlier in this chapter, the financial value of cooperative education for students was mentioned. From the standpoint of the public generally, the support of college education by earnings lessens the dependence on government grants or loans while adding to state and federal income through taxes paid on these earnings. This is a significant indirect value of this form of education.

The widespread emphasis on improving educational opportunities for youth from minority backgrounds makes the advantages of cooperative education for these students a matter of special comment. It is not enough to furnish a place in college for a minority student if he has small opportunity for placement after graduation in a position which utilizes his education. The cooperative program furnishes an avenue for his recruitment, orientation, induction, education, and placement in a position related to his educational development. Furthermore, most minority students want to enter occupations with opportunity for personal advancement and which are more a part of the mainstream of American economic life than has previously been possible. This strong motivation can be more effectively utilized in cooperative education than in programs where work, careers, and study have little direct connection.

One of the common obstacles encountered by minority college graduates in their employment after graduation is the wide gap between their previous work experience in nonprofessional and often menial occupations, and the conditions, customs, and behavior expected in the white-collar ones. The work-experience component of cooperative education furnishes a training ground for these students to acquire the understanding, attitudes, and skills needed for this adjustment.

Finally, of course, the earnings obtained from cooperative work provide a major part of the financial support for the education of minority youth.

In summary, cooperative education, by providing a bridge between the college and adult society, between education and full-time work, between the simpler world of youth associations and institutions and the interrelated, interdependent organizations and institutions of modern society, affords an effective way for youth to make the transition from adolescence to adulthood. It has special significance in modern post-industrial society.

PART TWO

DESCRIPTION OF PROGRAMS

Types of Programs

Stewart B. Collins

Today, the term *cooperative education* can refer to any one of a number of types of off-campus productive work. As a result, the umbrella of cooperative education sometimes covers almost any program involving classroom study and off-campus experience—programs variously designated as field experiences, internship programs, interlude programs, professional practice programs, experiential work, university without walls, industry periods, extramural term, cooperative periods, interval programs. In the vast majority of institutions, however, cooperative education is still conducted in accordance with the traditional definition. This definition requires that the following factors be adhered to as closely as possible: (1) The student's off-campus experience should be related as closely as possible to his field of study and individual interest within the field. (2) The employment must be a regular, continuing, and essential element in the educational process. (3) Some minimum amount of employment and minimum standard of performance must be included in the requirement for the degree or certificate presented by the school. (4) The working experience will ideally increase in difficulty and responsibility as the student progresses through the academic curriculum and, in general, shall parallel as closely as possible his progress through the academic phase.

There is also a certain amount of confusion concerning the meanings of cooperative education and the Federal Work-Study Program. Actually, as we have defined cooperative education, there is a great deal of difference between the two programs. The Federal Work-Study Program came into existence in 1965 to assist needy college students. Such students, after meeting financial-need requirements, work mostly on campus in part-time employment for a maximum of fifteen hours per week, with the federal government paying 80 per cent of their salary and the college paying 20 per cent. The funds may also be used for part-time work off campus in nonprofit organizations or for full-time employment in organizations participating in cooperative programs. These arrangements require a contract between the cooperating agency and the college. Again, the employing agency pays 20 per cent of the student's salary and the federal government pays 80 per cent. One advantage in using work-study funds in this manner is that it enables the students to work with certain desirable employers where salaries would not normally be paid. The funds can also be used to supplement salaries that are undesirably low.

Cooperative programs are found in 225 professional and liberal-arts curricula. Thirty per cent of the colleges and universities offering them do so in engineering and technology only, while 35 per cent offer them in nonengineering curricula only. The remaining 35 per cent offer both types. Three quarters of the institutions offering cooperative programs are four- or five-year colleges and universities, with junior colleges and technical institutes making up the remaining 25 per cent. Twenty-five per cent of the senior colleges also offer cooperative programs at the graduate level.

Mandatory, Optional, Selective

The extent to which the cooperative plan of education is part of the total educational program varies a great deal. In three quarters of the baccalaureate programs and 64 per cent of the junior college programs, cooperative education is optional in all curricula in which it is offered. Only 10 per cent and 9 per cent of senior and junior colleges respectively offer cooperative education as mandatory for all students in the institution. Among those institutions offering cooperative education on an optional basis, the choice is entirely with the student in 51 per cent of the baccalaureate institutions and in 58 per cent of the two-year institutions. In the remaining institutions, programs are selective.

MANDATORY PROGRAMS. Some colleges and universities have adopted cooperative education as a keystone of their educational thrust. All colleges and programs are conducted on the cooperative plan of education, and students must pursue this plan if they enroll. These institutions are said to have mandatory programs. Institutions wholly committed to mandatory programs are Antioch College, Wilberforce University, and Northeastern University. Those with mandatory programs in some of the colleges include the University of Cincinnati, Drexel University, the University of Detroit, and Rochester Institute of Technology. Students enrolled in mandatory programs are expected to complete satisfactory periods of work and off-campus experience as part of the total requirements for their degree. These institutions have a strong belief in the values of off-campus experience for their students.

OPTIONAL PROGRAMS. Some colleges offer cooperative education as a choice, in the sense that students may either attend college under the cooperative plan or under a full-time or traditional plan of study. Students who wish to pursue the cooperative plan of study are accepted or rejected on the basis of their qualifications and their interest in the program. Some colleges and universities require students to have their own job or off-campus experience determined and available before entering the program. Optional programs may involve only a small number of students in very large institutions and may be limited to particular departments of colleges or individual colleges within a university.

SELECTIVE PROGRAMS. Colleges and universities with selective programs enroll cooperative students on the basis of academic performance. Students usually are required to maintain a specified grade-point average to qualify for and remain on the cooperative plan.

Those who wish to pursue the cooperative plan apply and are offered the opportunity by appropriate administrative officers, faculty, or committees. Under such arrangements, the college or department usually offers a traditional plan of study with the cooperative plan as an alternative.

Organizational Variations

In more closely examining the various forms of cooperative education in existence around the United States and Canada, one encounters two-, four-, and five-year programs, transfer programs, junior-senior college linking programs, one-employer programs, consortium arrangements (colleges in partnership), company-based programs, and other variations.

Since the inception of cooperative education at the University of Cincinnati, the program has spread to all of the various levels of education. Its most recent growth has been in the two-year junior and community colleges, natural settings for the objectives of cooperative education. The number of master's and doctoral degree programs also has increased. Each program at each level is attuned to the level and background of the student, so that the fitting of academic and job level is compatible.

COMMUNITY AND JUNIOR COLLEGE PROGRAMS. Many community colleges practice a type of cooperative education known as concurrent, parallel, or shared-time programs, in which students attend classes for half of the day and work during the other half. Manhattan Community College has such a program. Necessarily, all students must be placed in the general vicinity of the college because of the commuting aspect. Some community and junior colleges, however, offer two-and-a-half-year or three-year programs with alternating quarters or semesters on the cooperative plan. All of these programs are discussed in greater detail in Chapter 4.

BACCALAUREATE FOUR-YEAR PROGRAMS. Four-year programs tend to predominate in the liberal-arts colleges, where off-campus work may be only one of a number of different activities that take place during an off-campus term. In addition, exposure to the practical side is lessened, in the interest of meeting a traditional four-year graduation date. Some institutions having a four-year cooperative program schedule their work periods so as to give the equivalent of one year of work experience (often during the summer months) prior to graduation.

Programs with limited off-campus assignments are provided at Keuka College, offering a single six-week experiential period in each of four years; at Bennington College, offering nine weeks per year; and at Beloit College, offering one term of fifteen weeks in the total program. Still other schools offer programs with limited work assignments of varying lengths of time. Some programs feature one period of working experience in a social service agency and another on an independent study project in their spectrum of off-campus relationships.

BACCALAUREATE FIVE-YEAR PROGRAMS. A type of cooperative program that has widespread acceptance at this time is offered by five-year baccalaureate-degree-granting institutions. These institutions have valued cooperative experience to the extent that they have added another year to the normal four-year curricula. The five-year period enables the student to have sufficient exposure to working situations to markedly affect his educational experience. These colleges have some of the oldest of the cooperative programs (which started, for the most part, in fields of engineering) and have served as the prototype for the many variations now present throughout the country. Colleges and universities offering such programs provide the basic patterns that give cooperative education its image and substance.

Under the five-year program, the cooperative student, at a predetermined time (usually at the end of the freshman or sophomore year), starts a regular alternation between college and the cooperative period. The students are paired so that one student is on the job while the other is on campus. Such programs enable the student to spend 30–40 per cent of his undergraduate time in the cooperative position while pursuing a fully accredited, unaltered academic program.

Baccalaureate programs on both a four-year and five-year basis are discussed fully in Chapter 5.

JUNIOR-SENIOR TRANSFER PROGRAMS AND CONSORTIA. Additional program variations include senior cooperative colleges which offer a two- or three-year academic program equivalent to the junior and senior years at a traditional college. Examples are the University of Michigan (Dearborn Campus) and the new universities of North and West Florida, which depend on transfers from other institutions. The University of Tennessee at Knoxville and its junior branch at Martin have an arrangement whereby the junior institution at Martin transfers the student to the senior college at Knoxville and the cooperative student maintains the same affiliation with the employer throughout his tenure at both schools. Broward Community College also has linking programs with senior colleges. A "one-employer" university, the University of West Virginia, has employment arrangements with the West Virginia Roads Commission, which serves as its sole source of cooperative work.

At least one consortium arrangement exists at present. Lees Junior College and Alice Lloyd College have one overall director with individual coordinators on each campus. North Carolina A & T University operates a consortium of colleges predominating in black enrollment. These colleges are interested in cooperative education as an intended major educational thrust. A more detailed discussion of these programs is found in Chapter 5.

GRADUATE PROGRAMS. Graduate cooperative programs also are on the increase. Many follow the same calendars established for the undergraduate programs, but in some instances special patterns have been developed for advanced-degree study. Master's degree programs are at a project level where the work is highly individualized and the continuity of students on the job of secondary consideration. Doctoral cooperative programs consist primarily of the writing of theses based on research conducted in industrial laboratories. The supervision of these theses is divided between a member of the university faculty and an industrial supervisor holding the Ph.D. degree. The subject is discussed further in Chapter 6.

COMBINED STUDY AND COOPERATIVE WORK PLACEMENT. Another form of cooperative education ties the student more closely to the academic institution by formally placing him near the college and requiring him to take evening courses in the interest of preserving stronger academic continuity. St. Joseph's College in Philadelphia requires this of students majoring in electronic physics. This situation closely parallels that of a regularly enrolled evening college student except that the cooperative student is still considered a full-time day enrollee who will return to the college on a full-time basis when his employment period is concluded.

Some colleges informally permit their students to take academic work while the student is in his work period if the job is located near the campus. This can be a convenience to the student, since it permits him to repeat courses, take advanced work, or enroll in courses of special interest, even though it is not the policy of the college to promote such arrangements.

The cooperative period also may provide the student with an opportunity to pursue academic study during nonworking hours on an independent basis. Certain course work lends itself to this system and permits the more mature student to move ahead on his own and still meet normal academic requirements.

If the student is placed on cooperative assignment some distance from a college, his school may permit him to enroll in a self-study course with a final examination to be given when the student returns to the campus. The truly talented student who utilizes the self-study feature may find it possible both to complete the work phase of his education and to graduate in five years with a master's degree. Such a program is available in electrical engineering at Drexel University.

COMPANY-BASED PROGRAMS. Most cooperative programs are college-based and require the cooperation of outside agencies to employ their students. At least one program, however, is based within the confines of the company. General Motors Institute, actually a college within a company, not only grants a baccalaureate degree but also places all of its students in the various plants and installations of the company for practical experience.

The United States Navy scholarship program for selected students guarantees the student employment for all of his working periods and also pays for tuition and books for specific years at the college. In return, the student is required to serve for a certain period as a permanent employee after graduation in accordance with the contract he has signed with the Navy.

Northeastern University has industry-sponsored programs in professional accounting, actuarial science, and power engineering. The industries provide scholarship assistance for students and guarantee cooperative work positions. In addition, the college and the industry collaborate in the selection of students. Any employer can set up similar arrangements as a result of the close relationship established through the cooperative program.

Industry-sponsored programs are treated at greater length in Chapter 7.

MISCELLANEOUS. Some cooperative students, primarily in the liberal-arts colleges, receive credit for periods of travel in foreign lands in recognition of the benefits of that experience. In such instances, the college usually requires that the student document his experiences or follow expressed directions from the college.

A few programs will be set up for an expressed purpose which is very narrow in scope. For example, an engineering or science major might be a cooperative student only if he is assigned a job as research assistant in his field; no other form of employment will be considered.

Relations with Cooperative Employers

Cooperative program arrangements between the college and the employing organization may be either formal or informal. In some cases, contracts are effected and a campus representative supervises the cooperative student and his work. In other cases, there are no on-site visitations by college personnel. Most colleges, however, ask employers to complete an evaluation form on each student, so that they and the student can be fully apprised of his performance and progress. Such a form also is useful in the counseling of the student when he returns to the campus.

Occasionally, an employer not only employs certain students for the cooperative period but, in addition, supports these students with a tuition-assistance program, calling it a scholarship, grant, or tuition remission. Such arrangements can be made either with the individual student or with the college directly.

IV

Community and Junior College Programs

J. Dudley Dawson

The educational world is well acquainted with the phenomenal growth of two-year colleges. There are now more than one thousand community and junior colleges in this country, with an enrollment in excess of 2.1 million students. A recent report by the Carnegie Commission on Higher Education has proposed that up to 280 additional community colleges be established during this decade, which would put one within commuting distance of 95 per cent of all Americans (Carnegie Commission, 1971).

Numbers and size alone, however, do not fulfill the pressing needs in community college education. As indicated in a current report (U.S. Department of Health, Education, and Welfare, 1971–a), the present expanded system of public education without major reform will not provide meaningful education for the ever broadening spectrum of entering students. Speaking to the demand for new curricula, the report goes on to say that many students have not had sufficient experience outside the educational system to know what a relevant education might be.

The two-year college is challenged not only by a new order of individual and social need for education but also by the demand for accountability which now faces all levels of education. The concept of accountability implies responsibility of the college to its students and to its public for an investment of time, energy, and money.

The responsibility is not just for instruction. It applies to those who leave as well as those who remain . . . to the dropouts as well as the stay-ins. It applies to both admissions and placement. If a school—especially a junior college—is not willing to accept responsibility for placement of a student when he leaves, then it should not admit him in the first place. And . . . when the dropout rates get too high, a school should be liable for its accreditation [*American Association of Junior Colleges, 1967*].

No better insurance exists for the two-year college in meeting these responsibilities than the use of cooperative work-experience programs.

Several features of the two-year college are similar to those of four- and five-year cooperative colleges. First, there is the widespread diversity of student interests, needs, and potential to be accommodated in the community college. This, in turn, calls for varied curricular programs that are both specialized and comprehensive and that integrate general with vocational or preprofessional education. Second, thousands of economically deprived students within the perimeter areas of community colleges are dependent upon these colleges for higher educational opportunities and for development toward meaningful occupations, further education, and purposeful citizenship.

Cooperative education with suitable adaptation can increase the appeal and vitality of the communtiy college. It can—through the use of work and other types of experience, integrated with teaching and counseling—better meet the objectives of community college students: enhance their self-development, self-confidence, sense of responsibility, feeling of worth, and economic independence; provide experience in choosing and preparing for a suitable career; add meaning to and facilitate understanding of classroom studies; supplement general education and give direction for desired further education; and, most important, supply for many the economic base and often the motivation for attending college. Furthermore, a well-developed cooperative education will reduce the numbers of failures and dropouts in a community college. It most surely facilitates the placement of students as they complete their college course.

For teachers and counselors, cooperative education can enliven the teaching-learning process, stimulate professional development, furnish a realistic framework for advising and program planning with students, and establish an active involvement with the community.

For cooperating employers, the engagement with cooperative students provides valuable productive assistance, extends their resources for long-range recruitment of personnel, and offers opportunity to participate with a college in educating and training human talent for their community.

For the community college itself, cooperative education becomes a positive asset in improving the quality of its teaching, counseling, and placement of students; strengthening the curriculum and possibly reducing some instruction costs; and enhancing the community services of the college by serving local personnel needs and by assisting in the development of the community's total resources.

Types of Programs

More than thirty two-year colleges have reported establishing cooperative programs (CEA, 1970; NCCE, 1970), but a much larger number have some form of cooperative education. Many make use of the Federal Work-Study funds, combined with a cooperative education program, to provide employment experience with nonprofit agencies for students of low income.

The great majority of cooperative or work-experience programs in community colleges are in the career or occupational curricula—in business and office services, in engineering, industrial and agricultural technologies, in the health occupations, and more recently in the social and public services. The shifting occupational needs and patterns in our society call for much more extensive development of cooperative education in the health occupations and human services.

Because of public interest and supplementary federal funding for the development of cooperative education in colleges and universities, two types of federally supported programs need to be delineated. Many of the work-experience programs in occupational education have been supported by the Vocational Education Amendment Act of 1968. These programs are known as cooperative vocational education programs, and the funding is administered by state offices of vocational education. Students in these programs usually alternate half-days of study with half-days of job experience, although other patterns of work and study periods can be supported. The distinctive features of the cooperative vocational educational programs are concisely described in Source Manual 71 of the Division of Vocational and Technical Education, U.S. Office of Education:

Cooperative vocational education is an interdependent combination of vocational instruction and employment related to that instruction. Employment under this arrangement is conceived to be an extension of in-school instruction, that is, a method of instruction which provides relevant laboratory experiences in a real-life setting. A cooperative vocational education program, therefore, is designed to serve an educational or training objective. Students participate in a cooperative program because they wish to acquire qualifications for a predetermined area of competitive employment. For them it is a career preparation.

Students entering cooperative vocational programs choose and follow a prescribed occupational curriculum, and these job experiences are carefully correlated with their academic course schedule. The student's cooperative education coordinator maintains well-defined working relationships with his employer or training station and also functions as a teacher-adviser with the group of students he places on jobs.

The more general type of cooperative education prevalent in four-year colleges and universities and in a number of community colleges has a similar but somewhat broader purpose, and normally alternates studies and work in separate blocks of time. In some programs, however, students may work on half-time jobs and study half time concurrently. Cooperative programs of this more general type may be given partial federal support under the Higher Education Act of 1968 as administered by the Bureau of Higher Education, United States Office of Education.

Each of these two types of cooperative programs have distinctive values and overlapping purposes while serving differing needs of students. The vocational cooperative programs respond to the needs of students for directed occupational education. The availability of specific vocational cooperative programs brings many students to community colleges and enables them to succeed in a meaningful career program. Enrollment in vocational cooperative programs is, however, unattractive to students who are uncertain of their goals and who desire greater breadth in general and vocational education. The more general type of cooperative education is less restrictive. Although care is taken to relate the work experience of the individual student to his interests, needs, and studies, there need not be a set structure of job placements for students by fields of study. A less structured cooperative program can be equally pertinent to students with well-defined career objectives, since these students can pursue a clearly focused goal through a general cooperative education program. Thus, they may confirm or modify their original plans as they proceed. There is the mistaken idea that cooperative education in community colleges is only for students in career or vocational programs. Students bound for further higher education may well find that cooperative education provides the needed sense of direction for going on with their education.

Spread of Two-Year Programs

Some examples will indicate the spread of cooperative education in community colleges across the country. Golden West College and Orange Coast College in Southern California have an impressive range of programs in vocational education, including applications of cooperative education principles in their adult continuing education. Los Angeles Trade Technical College is actively developing cooperative vocational education. Pasadena City College is initiating a new cooperative education plan in the human services for its college-transfer students along with other programs in the paraprofessional and other vocational fields.

In the Bay Area of California, the College of San Mateo has pioneered in the applications of cooperative education; and new programs in both general and vocational education are emerging at

Alameda College and Merritt College in Oakland. Southward, Mary Holmes College in Mississippi and Alice Lloyd and Lees Junior Colleges in Kentucky are developing comprehensive programs of far-reaching significance for their students, most of whom will transfer to four-year colleges.

In Florida there are numerous developments in cooperative education, as illustrated by the programs at Broward and at Miami-Dade Junior Colleges. Sinclair Community College in Dayton, Ohio, is redeveloping its long-established cooperative plan to include programs in both the general and vocational areas of its curriculum and to combine, where appropriate, qualified part-time employment with part-time study for individual students.

Several community colleges in the New York State University System are now establishing cooperative education programs, following the lead of the successful one in business administration at Manhattan Community College of the City University of New York. Mohawk Valley Community College, Utica, New York, has a long-established cooperative plan whereby students alternate study and work periods. Here two quarters of successful work experience are required for students enrolled in one of the seven or more departments offering cooperative education.

New Directions

Although extensions of the current types of cooperative education should certainly take place, modifications in the applications of experiential education should also emerge. If, for example, vocational cooperative education programs could be made more comprehensive and flexible in concept and in operation, many more students would be attracted to them, and perhaps more effective preparation for occupational life in our rapidly changing society would be realized. And if parents, counselors, and students could better understand the educational and vocational values of combining experience with education for those in general studies and college-parallel programs, many more students would enjoy the resulting benefits.

Other changes should be considered. Approximately 70 per cent of all community college students hold part-time jobs while attending school. Some carry up to full-time employment (often in order to get a suitable job) along with a full quota of studies. These students often have difficulties both on the job and in college and would be considerably better off if they were enrolled in a cooperative program, alternating periods of full-time study with periods of full-time employment. Since many students carrying part-time employment reduce their academic schedules and do not complete their college course in a two-year period, enrollment in the cooperative plan would not greatly extend the length of their course and would provide an opportunity for better-organized learning from work experiences as well as a better educational outcome.

There is another appropriate modification of cooperative education practices for full-time students who work part time. Many of these students have or could have half-time jobs that would qualify as excellent cooperative work experience and could be related to their educational program. In such cases the student would study half time and work half time concurrently, under the supervision of the college cooperative education department. Such a schedule is much the same as a plan of alternating study and work periods, and provides a desirable cooperative plan for students in particular jobs.

Community colleges might well consider the worth and benefits of investing more professional staff to advise and to place students in part-time employment. Job opportunities could thereby be upgraded and work experience could be better interrelated with teaching, advising, and eventual graduate placement of students.

Community colleges also serve large numbers of both young and older adults, who are enrolled as part-time students in the day or evening programs and who are usually partially or fully employed. An appropriately designed cooperative program, coordinated with employers and concerned with vocational and educational advising and with the upgrading of enrollment and placement of adults, would fulfill a critical community need.

Low-Income Students

Cooperative education can provide meaningful education for low-income students, most of whom look to the community college for higher educational opportunities. Many inner-city students cannot enter even a publicly supported college, much as they may desire it, without financial assistance. Since in many cases family assistance is nonexistent, the financial need goes beyond the cost of college fees, books, transportation, and incidentals to include clothes, medical services, and other personal expenses. Even with local and federal financial assistance, which is often inadequate if not unavailable, the student with no economic security is reluctant to incur indebtedness even if he could arrange to borrow funds. Cooperative education programs can enable low-income students to enroll in college and also can give them the sense of financial independence and the feeling of worth that comes from productive employment.

The educationally underprepared student, who rarely has a history of standard academic achievement, will usually at the start do better on a cooperative job than he will in his studies. Successful work experience may well add motivation for academic effort and accomplishment. The self-confidence that comes from well-designed cooperative experience adds to the student's will to succeed in college, especially when teachers and counselors help him to relate learning from work to academic planning and classroom studies.

The alternation of cooperative work experience between or within periods of study provides a "breather" for students who may "go under" with a full-time load of academic studies. Furthermore, cooperative job placements arranged to meet felt student needs (personal, academic, or vocational) will furnish learning situations which will enhance understanding and progress in these studies. Employers have a critical role in stimulating and in fostering learning on the job.

The counseling and self-guidance inherent in cooperative education are particularly significant for students from socioeconomically deprived backgrounds. These students enter college with little experience in making educational or career plans. A meaningful decision in this area usually requires some range of both academic and nonacademic experiences as well as some thought and counsel. If these elements are lacking, decisions are forced or made haphazardly. Cooperative education provides counseling and the stimulation for self-guidance critical to educational planning and a degree of freedom in career decisions.

Organizing Patterns

Programs of cooperative education can be developed around a number of different college calendars. Many of those in vocational cooperative education are on half-day alternation of study and work periods during the academic year, although there are numerous variations in the weekly employment schedules of students in these programs. They may also extend through the summer.

In the more general types of cooperative education, students usually alternate periods of study with periods of employment on the quarter, trimester, or semester calendar of the college. Under this plan of alternation the summer is used for study or work. The utilization of a twelve-month calendar for both work and study reduces the extension of the total time to complete the college courses and makes it possible to keep cooperative jobs filled on a year-round basis by pairs of alternating students. Depending on the amount of work experience and academic credit required, college cooperative programs extend the time of the total college course from three months to one year. Not all cooperative plans operate on the alternation principle. In colleges located near sources of employment, cooperative jobs may be arranged whereby students study half time and work half time concurrently on an individually arranged weekly time schedule under the supervision of the college.

Table 2. ILLUSTRATIVE STUDY AND WORK CALENDAR FOR A TWO-YEAR COLLEGE

Year in College	*Quarter of the Year*	*Summer Entrants*	*Fall Entrants*
First Year	Summer	Study	
	Fall	Study	Study
	Winter	Work	Study
	Spring	Study	Work
Second Year	Summer	Work	Study
	Fall	Study	Work
	Winter	Work	Study
	Spring	Study	Work
Third Year	Summer	Study	Work
	Fall	Work	Study
	Winter	Study	Work
	Spring	(Optional Study)	(Optional Study)

Opinions differ widely on the most desirable calendar for a cooperative plan. Many prefer the quarter system over the trimester or semester because of its greater flexibility for seasonal and short-run job placements, because of its adaptability to adding an equal summer term, and also because the quarter system provides a shorter break between study periods. Others prefer the longer periods because they allow more time for each study and work period and make possible better job opportunities in certain situations. In at least one college, students alternate their study and work on a yearly basis. In fact, students in some colleges now, with the sanction and assistance of their advisors, arrange irregular periods of work experience away from studies in order to serve their personal and educational needs.

Table 2 shows a time matrix based on a quarter calendar, which permits the most adaptable arrangements for cooperative employers and for seasonal job placement. It has multiple entry and exit points, provides optimum flexibility for variable schedule and length of courses, is readily modified for a trimester or semester calendar, and allows for graduation in three years or less.

CURRICULUM. An essential organizing principle for a cooperative plan is that the academic curriculum and schedule must take into account the sequential course needs of students in the program. In vocational cooperative programs academic offerings and schedules must be synchronized with the student's work experience. In other cooperative education programs, where there is less precise correlation period by period between studies and jobs, the course schedules must nevertheless be laid out systematically to accommodate students in the progression of their studies in alternate periods.

Difficulties often occur, especially in sequential courses, in colleges with optional cooperative programs because the curricula and schedule are planned for students in full-time study and cooperative students are expected to fit their course schedules into the conventional curriculum. If an institution wants to encourage students into cooperative education, it must establish a clearly visible academic schedule for cooperative courses.

Curricula for cooperative students should be so planned that these students will have adequate specialized courses early in their careers in order to provide elemental qualifications for appropriate job placement. Consideration should also be given to eliminating or waiving, for individual students, certain specialized courses ordinarily required of full-time-study students, based on their equivalent coverage through cooperative work experience. In short, those who plan the content of an academic cooperative curriculum should take fully into account the experiential phase of the student's program.

CREDIT FOR OFF-CAMPUS EXPERIENCE. If cooperative work experience is well designed and administered as an integral part of the educational program, then it merits recognition as part of the degree requirements. This recognition can be given in several ways. One way is to decrease the academic requirements for the degree, allowing the remaining credits to be earned through cooperative work. These credits can be allocated on the same unit basis as academic credit or on a separate system of credits. Because of understandable questions of giving *academic* credit for work experience, regardless of its educational value, perhaps simply *degree* credit rather than *academic* credit should be given for cooperative work on whatever unit basis seems appropriate. There are exceptions to this principle, however—particularly where intern or other work experience has a practicum relationship to a particular academic course, in which case *academic* crediting would be clearly justified.

College credit for cooperative work experience is usually awarded on the basis of the employer's report on the student's performance and a written report by the student which demonstrates the educational implications of his experiences. Perhaps in time college credits for cooperative education experience will be fully honored on transfer to a four-year college. At present, however, although a four-year college will undoubtedly admit a qualified community college graduate with cooperative credits, questions may be raised about the transfer of college cooperative credits (as happens for certain academic courses) toward the fulfillment of requirements for the baccalaureate degree.

Scope of Application

It is generally agreed that the full benefits of cooperative education are best achieved when an institution or a program is entirely on the cooperative plan. In this way all the students, faculty, and the total college are involved in the educational process. Greater economy is also possible in programs which are totally cooperative. This degree of totality, however, is not possible or feasible in many community colleges serving students of varying ages, maturity, and family responsibilities. Enrollment in well-developed cooperative education programs could well be *recommended* by the college but not necessarily *required*. As decisions are made regarding the establishment of programs, it would seem better for all students to have at least some cooperative work experience, even for a limited part of their course, than for a small number of students opting the cooperative program for a longer part of the course. Also, initiating a fully integrated program of study and work experience in one department may be a better way of introducing cooperative education into a college rather than by piecemeal methods in all departments.

Extending the length of the college course in cooperative education often poses a problem. Students bent on getting through formalized education as quickly as possible are often set against the cooperative plan because it may take an additional year. They do not realize that cooperative education might well be more stimulating and meaningful as well as serving to upgrade their occupational potential and employability. Students graduating from a cooperative program normally have an education which secures better and higher-paid jobs, which compensate for the longer time in college. For those going on with further education, the extra time given to cooperative work experiences may well provide needed motivation and a sense of direction for continuing with college.

Employers and Jobs

Interested employers and suitable jobs are an essential ingredient of a cooperative plan—fulfilling a most significant role in the education of students. The whole spectrum of jobs and employers can serve community college students in cooperative or in part-time employment. Business and industrial organizations, government and social agencies, and a wide range of professions employ community college students.

Cooperative students in general studies work for community agencies, hospitals, laboratories, libraries, news media, public services, and schools, according to their needs and fields of interest.

Business administration students hold jobs in accounting, data processing, office and secretarial work, marketing, purchasing, sales, and in a variety of mid-management positions in business, government, industry, and community agencies.

Engineering and technology students are employed as draftsmen, construction helpers, estimators, inspectors, laboratory technicians, and as engineering aids in industry, public services, and research organizations.

Because the purposes and values of cooperative education have a natural appeal to employers in all fields of endeavor, they desire, if possible, to have a part in the education and training of students, not only for their own benefits but for the benefits of their community. (See Chapters 12 and 13.)

Internal Organization and Commitment

Cooperative education will be successful in a community college to the extent that the president and administrative staff, teaching and counseling faculty, and students become deeply committed to its purposes. Among other things this means adequate financing and a competent staff of faculty coordinators to manage the program. Assuming substantial institutional support, the key to an effective program rests with the strength and leadership of the faculty coordinators. They must have imagination, administrative skill, and the facility for counseling and placing students, relating effectively and responsibly with employers, and enlisting the interest and involvement of the teaching and counseling faculty in their important roles in cooperative education. They should also actively utilize students as advisors in developing cooperative education and, if possible, as employed assistants in operating the program.

Locating the cooperative education department and its director or dean in the college administrative structure depends on local circumstances. Cooperative education is equally and intimately related to both the Dean of Academic Affairs and the Dean of Student Services. A Dean of Cooperative Education might well have an administrative status coordinate with these two deans in colleges sponsoring significant experiential programs. Regardless of its placement in the administrative hierarchy, however, the cooperative education department must have a close and unhampered working relationship with student counseling, financial aid, and other student placement (part time and graduate). Actually, cooperative education and other placement should be together in one administrative unit.

V

Baccalaureate Programs

John A. Chase

This chapter deals with some of the more common types of four- and five-year cooperative programs currently in operation in this country. It focuses also on some rather unique plans, particularly those at Kalamazoo, Bennington, Keuka, and Beloit Colleges.

Interspersed within the text are examples of the various types of cooperative calendars that may be used in four- or five-year programs. Other typical examples of four- and five-year cooperative calendars are shown in Appendix D.

Quarter System—Five-Year Programs

Most five-year programs are organized so that students will alternate quarters of academic study with quarters of cooperative work experience following completion of their freshman year of full-time study. Some of these programs are designed to provide experience

THE PROFESSIONAL PRACTICE PROGRAM

Five-Year Degree Program

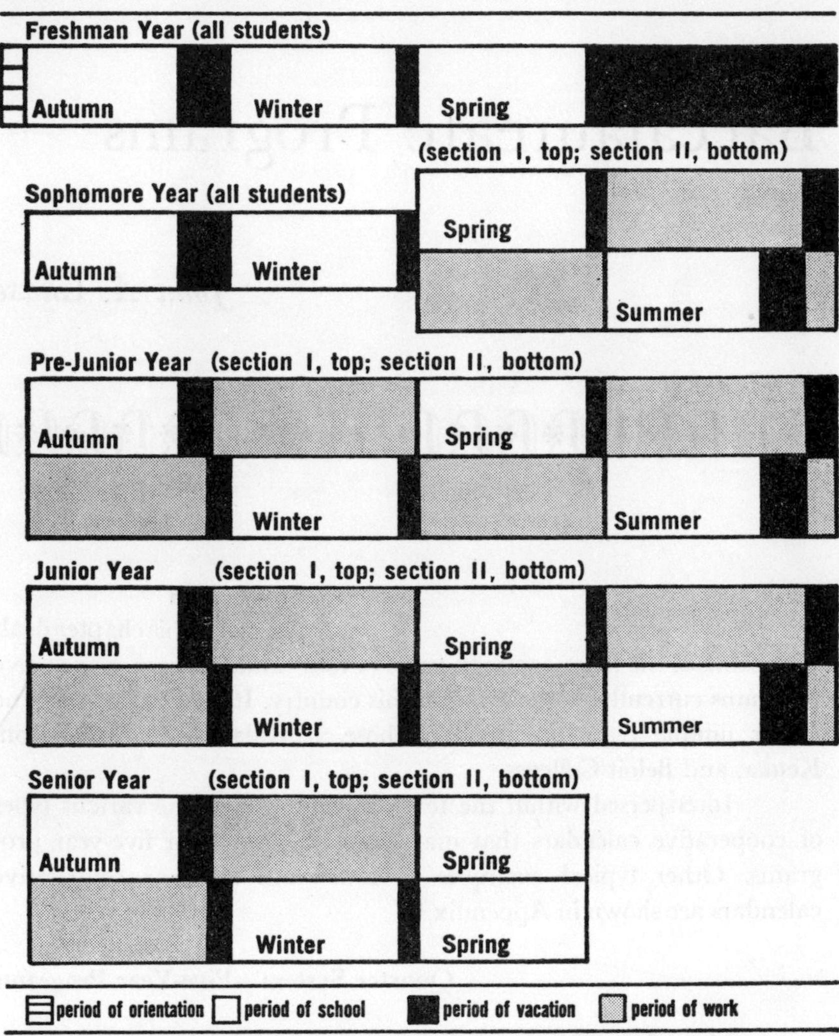

Source: *University of Cincinnati Bulletin,* 1971, p. 13.

FIGURE 1. University of Cincinnati Professional Practice Program.

related to the student's academic major in a very direct fashion so that he might become aware of the interrelationship between theory and practice, the responsibilities of professional practitioners in the field, and the responsibilities of members of society. Consequently, the student's six or seven quarters of work experience build upon relatively sheltered academic training to provide a sound and continuingly more responsible relevant education.

As most students move along the same major program track, they can be divided into two groups following the completion of the freshman year. This is clearly demonstrated by the Professional Practice Calendar followed by the University of Cincinnati's College of Business Administration. (See Figure 1.)

At Cincinnati, students enter the work phase of the program at the beginning of the spring quarter in the sophomore year and complete it at the end of the winter quarter of their senior year. Other colleges may begin the work phase in the fall quarter of the sophomore year and end it upon completion of the regular junior year. Each of these five-year programs covers the same number of academic quarters of study as do four-year programs. In some colleges, within specific majors, students may elect the cooperative program while others may not. For example, in the engineering curricula the program may be mandatory for all students, or it may be optional for engineering students and unavailable to students enrolled in the other curricula of the institution.

Only three of the University of Cincinnati's fifteen colleges make the Professional Practice Program available to all students. This is an unusual operation in that the degrees are offered both on a cooperative and noncooperative basis. There is an associate degree program which also offers cooperative work experience.

The following illustrative calendars simultaneously accommodate students in both an optional five-year cooperative program and a full-time traditional program. Divisions A and B are cooperative, while Division C is full time.

The calendar shown in Table 3 requires eleven study periods for all divisions and seven work periods for the two cooperative divisions (A and B); students in Division C have the option of using the spring quarter rather than the fall or winter quarter for study. This calendar also illustrates the "term reversal" system. Note that coopera-

Table 3. FIVE-YEAR QUARTER-SYSTEM COOPERATIVE PROGRAM AND FOUR-YEAR FULL-TIME-STUDY QUARTER-SYSTEM PROGRAM
Northeastern University

		Fall	*Winter*	*Spring*	*Summer*
Year 1	A	Study	Study	Study	Vacation
	B	Study	Study	Study	Vacation
	C	Study	Study	Study	Vacation
Year 2	A	Study	Work	Study	Work
	B	Work	Study	Work	Study
	C	Study	Study	Study	Vacation
Year 3	A	Work	Study	Work	Study
	B	Study	Work	Study	Work
	C	Study	Study	Study	Vacation
Year 4	A	Study	Work	Study	Work
	B	Work	Study	Work	Study
	C	Study	Study		
Year 5	A	Work	Study	Study	
	B	Study	Work	Study	

tive Division A students work two consecutive periods (summer quarter of year 2 and fall quarter of year 3) and also study two consecutive periods (summer quarter of year 3 and fall quarter of year 4). Cooperative Division B students study two consecutive periods (summer quarter of year 2 and fall quarter of year 3) and work two consecutive periods (summer quarter of year 3 and fall quarter of year 4).

The Georgia Tech plan, shown in Table 4, is selective as well as optional in that those who enter from high school must rank in the upper third of their class scholastically, and those who transfer to the program from other colleges or from the Institute's traditional four-year program must have a better than average scholastic record. Each of the three divisions is required to complete twelve study periods (note that cooperative Division B has five consecutive study periods just prior

Table 4. Five-Year Quarter-System Cooperative Program and Four-Year Full-Time-Study Quarter-System Program
Georgia Institute of Technology

		Fall	*Winter*	*Spring*	*Summer*
	A				Study[a]
Year 1	A	Work	Study	Work	Study
	B	Study[b]	Work	Study	Work
	C	Study	Study	Study	Vacation
	A	Work	Study	Work	Study
Year 2	B	Study	Work	Study	Work
	C	Study	Study	Study	Vacation
	A	Work	Study	Work	Study
Year 3	B	Study	Work	Study	Work
	C	Study	Study	Study	Vacation
	A	Work	Study	Work	Study
Year 4	B	Study	Work	Study	Study
	C	Study	Study	Study	
Year 5	A	Study	Study	Study	
	B	Study	Study	Study	

[a] June registration.
[b] September registration.

to graduation). Cooperative Division A must complete eight work periods, as opposed to seven for cooperative Division B. Note that each cooperative division is on campus during the senior year.

The preceding illustrations indicate the flexibility and variability of the cooperative system. Individual calendar arrangements are numerous, as other calendars presented subsequently will attest. However, large institutions that repeat courses regularly need not adopt a new calendar to accommodate students when converting to the cooperative plan. When on campus, these students can usually arrange a program of study, particularly if substitutions are allowed for required courses. Although larger institutions may need to offer some repeat or "trailer" courses in order to enable students to meet specific degree requirements, smaller schools offering optional or selective programs should make definite plans to offer such courses to meet the needs of their cooperative students.

Students who pursue optional or selective programs may complete their degree requirements in less than five calendar years. They can do so by carrying overloads while in school, or by off-campus or independent study projects while on work assignment. They may also be able to take correspondence courses or courses at institutions in the vicinity of their cooperative jobs.

Other examples of unique five-year cooperative calendars are shown in Table 5 and 6.

Table 5. FIVE-YEAR QUARTER-SYSTEM COOPERATIVE PROGRAM
Northwestern University Technological Institute

Year	*Fall*	*Winter*	*Spring*	*Summer*
1	Study	Study	Study	Vacation
2	Study	Study	Study	Work
3	Study	Study	Work	Work
4	Study	Work	Study	Work
5	Work	Study	Study	

The calendar shown in Table 5 provides about eighteen months of industrial employment. Most of the student's work experience, as shown, is during the latter half of his education, and he has a vacation of one or two weeks at the end of each quarter in school.

The very unusual calendar shown in Table 6 may be the only one of its exact type in the nation.

Quarter System—Four-Year Programs

A rather different scheme pertains when the cooperative program is offered within a degree-granting period of four years. The

Table 6. Five-Year Cooperative Program
Requiring twelve months of work and study alternation,
Tennessee Technological University

Year 1	Full-time study on campus
Year 2	Full-time employment in industry
Year 3	Full-time study on campus
Year 4	Full-time employment in industry
Year 5	Full-time study on campus

Kalamazoo plan is an excellent example of this type of program. Here the students take three courses each quarter and engage in study for three of the four calendar quarters each year. (A similar calendar arrangement is possible when the usual quarter system of twelve to fifteen class credits applies.)

While the Kalamazoo plan requires only one "work experience" each quarter, the calendar structure would permit year-round coverage if experience in depth were a part of the program.

"The Kalamazoo plan is a unique interrelationship of on-campus academic offerings and off-campus foreign study, career-service, and individualized projects for the student interested in the challenges found in the small liberal-arts college" (*Kalamazoo College Bulletin,* 1969, p. 2). An unusual but extremely worthwhile cultural experience for all students is built into the plan through the inclusion of foreign studies. As Table 7 shows, the study and off-campus pattern is designed to maintain some balance of classroom enrollments throughout the year.

The career-service quarter of the Kalamazoo plan is that which is deemed "cooperative education." However, other colleges would include their foreign study and/or senior individualized project as part of a cooperative program. The stated developmental objectives of this program focus on the individual career, self-reliance, independence, responsibility, and understanding of the role of business in society.

Table 8 illustrates Drexel University's Business Administration and Home Economics programs. There are eleven quarters. Students

Table 7. THE KALAMAZOO PLAN

KALAMAZOO COLLEGE QUARTER PATTERN (A)

	Fall	Winter	Spring	Summer
FRESHMAN	On Campus	On Campus	On Campus	Vacation
SOPHOMORE	On Campus	On Campus	Career-Service	On Campus
JUNIOR	Foreign Study		On Campus	On Campus
SENIOR	On Campus and Senior Individualized Project		On Campus	

KALAMAZOO COLLEGE QUARTER PATTERN (B)

	Fall	Winter	Spring	Summer
FRESHMAN	On Campus	On Campus	On Campus	Vacation
SOPHOMORE	On Campus	On Campus	Foreign Study	On Campus
JUNIOR	Career-Service		On Campus	On Campus
SENIOR	On Campus and Senior Individualized Project		On Campus	

Source: *Kalamazoo College Bulletin,* 1969, p. 6.

are not allowed to begin work earlier than the third quarter of the second year or later than the fourth quarter of the same year. The last possible quarter that students are allowed to work is the first quarter of the senior year.

Semester System—Four-Year Programs

A semester-system program is most often found in a college that offers the four-year baccalaureate degree, since these colleges have available for study the equivalent of three summers normally used for

Table 8. Four-Year Quarter-System Cooperative Program
Drexel University Business Administration and
Home Economics Programs

Year	Sept.-Dec. *Fall*	Jan.-Mar. *Winter*	Mar.-June *Spring*	June-Sept. *Summer*
1	Study	Study	Study	Study
2	Study	Study	Work	Study
3	Study	Work	Study	Study
4	Work	Study	Study	

vacation periods. Whether the program is mandatory or selective, students who participate in this program are required to attend classes on a year-round basis.

At Alderson-Broaddus College, for example, students operate on a year-round calendar which requires two terms of off-campus educational experience for graduation. Some of the programs require work related to the major, while others do not; all students, however, must engage in field experiences. Included among the options are voluntary service, study abroad, or independent research, with paid employment considered the only "cooperative education" activity as such.

All students receive counseling to help them establish a program for wise utilization of time during the off-campus period. These needs range from financial and personal to travel, professional, occupation exploration, social, etc. An experience directly related to certain majors is required in nursing, medical technology, radiologic technology, physician's assistant program, education, and social work. (See Chapter 15.)

Since the establishment of this program in 1964, the College has expanded the number of majors participating in the work-experience phase and has established new degree programs as well. It is significant that the students may have no required work experience in several programs, may include one or two in others, but are required to have three in the physician's assistant program.

At Alderson-Broaddus, cooperative students generally work three to four months during each academic year. Work periods are staggered so that each class is off campus at a different season. Students have the option to use the first two off-campus periods as vacation periods. Table 9 shows the basic Alderson-Broaddus calendar.

Table 9. FOUR-YEAR SEMESTER-SYSTEM COOPERATIVE PROGRAM
Alderson-Broaddus College

Year	*Fall*	*Winter*	*Spring*	*Summer*
1	Study	Study	Study	Work
2	Study	Study	Work	Study
3	Study	Work	Study	Study
4	Work	Study	Study	

Trimester System—Four-Year Programs

Four-year cooperative programs on the trimester system are not common and usually operate on a year-round basis. Sequences of work and study periods, as with other plans, are variable. Table 10 shows two examples of calendars in effect at Wilberforce University. A five-year trimester cooperative program may simply add another year of some form of work and study alternation.

Short-Term Programs

A great many colleges have long offered a brief period of work experience during the student's senior year of study. These programs entail some scheduling difficulties but are tailored to meet the individual needs of students. Those colleges offering 4-1-4 programs utilize the one-month period for this purpose (usually in January); others arrange the schedule so that all seniors in specific majors may be off campus for an extended period following the Christmas holidays. As a result, there is additional study pressure on students engaged in these released-time internships. Often these internships are included in

Table 10. FOUR-YEAR TRIMESTER COOPERATIVE PROGRAM
Wilberforce University

EXAMPLE 1

Year	Sept.-Dec. *Fall*	Jan.-April *Spring*	May-Aug. *Summer*
1	Study	Study	Work
2	Study	Work	Study
3	Work	Study	Work
4	Study	Study	Study

EXAMPLE 2

Year	Sept.-Dec. *Fall*	Jan.-April *Spring*	May-Aug. *Summer*
1	Study	Study	Study
2	Work	Study	Work
3	Study	Work	Study
4	Work	Study	Study

accounting majors' programs. Then all seniors participate in a structured internship in a professional accounting office. Such internships could be the culmination of a program arranged according to the Keuka College "Field Period" or the Bennington College "Non-Resident Term" models, although they are not part of these two colleges' programs.

For many years these two liberal-arts colleges have required all students to engage in off-campus activity in order to complete graduation requirements. Their purposes appear to be quite similar, although the activities may vary considerably.

The Bennington College program is largely structured by the student but must be approved by the program director. Nine-week field-work periods are scheduled between the fall and spring semesters of each of four successive years. Each work period, which is jointly

Table 11. THE BELOIT COLLEGE PLAN

Sept.-Dec. *Fall Term*	Credit Term Two Weeks Vacation		**UNDER-CLASS YEAR**
Jan.-April *Winter Term*	Credit Term Two Weeks Vacation		The *Under-class* year, involving three consecutive 15-week terms, is standard for all students. Vacation periods, of two weeks each, follow the fall and winter terms. A vacation period of approximately three weeks is scheduled at the end of each summer term.
May-Aug. *Spring-Summer Term*	Credit Term Three Weeks Vacation		
Sept.-Dec. *Fall Term*	☐ Two Weeks Vacation	Vacation Term Credit Term Field Term Vacation Term Credit Term	**MIDDLE-CLASS PERIOD**[a]
Jan.-April *Winter Term*	☐ Two Weeks Vacation	Vacation Term Credit Term Field Term Vacation Term Credit Term	The *Middle-class* period is highly variable—in many ways the most exciting part of the Beloit plan. These five terms are spent in one of more than 30 possible combinations of on-campus study, off-campus field experience, overseas work or study, and vacation. Stu-

Period	Vacation	Options	Description
May-Aug. *Spring-Summer Term*	Three Weeks Vacation	Vacation Term Credit Term Field Term Vacation Term Credit Term	dents must earn college credit during two of the terms—at Beloit or off campus—perhaps at Argonne Laboratory, or in Washington, D.C., or at an overseas university. One of the remaining three terms will be spent in a carefully selected work experience arranged by Beloit's Field Placement staff, and two terms are free for vacation. The five terms can be arranged in any way that makes sense. For example, the field term and vacation terms can be combined to provide a full year off campus. Counselors help students work out schedules most appropriate to their individual programs and interests.
Sept.-Dec. *Fall Term*	Two Weeks Vacation	Vacation Term Credit Term Field Term Vacation Term Credit Term	
Jan.-April *Winter Term*	Two Weeks Vacation	Vacation Term Credit Term Field Term Vacation Term Credit Term	
May-Aug. *Spring-Summer Term*		Credit Term	UPPER-CLASS YEAR
		Three Weeks Vacation	This *Upper-class* sequence is standard for most students. In some cases, however, the field term might come during this year rather than during the Middle-class period. A student electing off-campus activity during the final year ordinarily would have completed three credit terms during the Middle-class period. Students graduate together at the end of the winter term in April.
Sept.-Dec. *Fall Term*		Credit Term	
		Two Weeks Vacation	
Jan.-April *Winter Term*		Credit Term	

[a] Students who wish to accelerate to graduate in three years rather than four can do so by eliminating the two Middle-class vacation terms.

Source: Beloit College Catalogue, 1968.

evaluated, may be varied in content and may be in a business, social agency, or social service setting.

At Keuka College, a five-week work period follows each fall quarter. Freshmen are expected to perform a social service in a recognized agency. Sophomores may study one of the fine arts, or a topic of individual interest, independently or in seminars. During the junior and senior years the activity is directly related to career and major-field interests. The sophomore-year activity may take place abroad, particularly if it involves the study of history or culture.

An unusual feature of the Keuka program is the direct granting of academic credit for the field experience. Freshmen and sophomores may earn one credit for a minimum of 120 hours of activity; juniors and seniors may earn two for 200 hours. The field experience may be repeated to a maximum of ten academic credits. (See Chapter 15.)

Another program is that developed by Beloit College. The Beloit plan is designed to relate the total college program to prior educational experience, to career plans, and to the changing demands of contemporary society. All students at Beloit must have at least one four-month "field term" of work experience; but students have the option of combining one or both "middle-class" vacation terms to increase the length of the experience to eight or twelve months, or to alternate vacation and study with classes to meet individual needs and interests.

Table 11 illustrates the Beloit plan.

Planning New Programs

An effective program of cooperative field experience cannot be organized and implemented without considerable effort on the part of students, faculty, trustees, and administration. As mentioned, a large university with a wide variety of offerings need not establish a new calendar when converting to an optional or selective cooperative program; however, the university may need to offer trailer (repeat) courses or allow substitutes for required courses to enable students to meet degree requirements. (See Chapter 20.)

It may be beneficial at this point to see how a particular scheduling problem was solved at Cleveland State University's Departments of Chemistry and Biology, a problem caused by the number of enrollees. (See Table 12.)

In this illustration, chemistry or biology students may not—because of course scheduling—be able to engage in the work situation on a year-round basis. Consequently, seasonable or short-term research activity must be found, or the employer must be willing to find other means for accomplishing his work, or (on occasion) students with other majors may be scheduled. In this specific illustration, all of these resolutions are possible. Where the enrollments are much larger and classes can be economically offered with greater frequency, these problems may not arise.

Academic Credit

Much discussion has developed over the years regarding the granting of academic credit for the off-campus experience. (For more detailed information on this subject, see Chapter 15.)

Junior-Senior Transfer and Consortia Programs[1]

Two interesting arrangements for implementing cooperative education have developed within the last few years in response to specialized needs. Both are instances of intercollege cooperation. The first is the establishment of transfer arrangements between junior and senior colleges that both have cooperative programs. The second is the creation of consortia, the coming together of two or more institutions to plan, implement, and operate cooperative education programs.

TRANSFER ARRANGEMENTS. Initially, only students and staff of junior colleges were concerned about the transfer process; but as increasing numbers of young people have planned their education around this two-step plan, senior colleges have also sought ways to reduce the "transfer trauma." One effort being tried currently among a few cooperative education colleges is a plan for continuity of cooperative employment. The plan calls for a formal agreement between the junior college and the senior college whereby the senior college

[1] The author gratefully acknowledges this contribution to this chapter by James W. Wilson, research professor of cooperative education, Northeastern University.

Table 12. Chemistry-Biology Schedule
Cleveland State University

Year		*Freshman*				*Sophomore*				*Pre-Junior*				*Junior*				*Senior*			
Quarter		F	W	Sp	S	F	W	Sp	S	F	W	Sp	S	F	W	Sp	S	F	W	Sp	S
	A					4	C	5	C												
Group		1	2	3	V					6	C	C	7	C	8	9	C	10	11	12	
	B					C	4	C	5												

1, 2, etc., refer to academic quarters of study.

C refers to period of cooperative work experience.

Groups A and B both enroll for on-campus study during quarters 1, 2, and 3, and 6 through 12. During the "pre-junior," junior, and senior years, all take the same professional courses together.

places transferring students on the same cooperative assignments they previously had. The anticipated advantages to the student are two. First, even though he must adjust to a new institution, a new curriculum, and a new faculty, there exists an important element of continuity, which should ease the adjustment process. Second, in contrast to students who attend senior cooperative colleges from the start, transfer students rarely have the opportunity to develop a three- or four-year relationship with a single employer; the transfer agreement between junior and senior cooperative colleges gives them this opportunity.

It is too soon to know how effective this scheme will prove to be. Some senior colleges will surely disdain any formal agreement, asserting that they will provide their own cooperative assignments in light of students' interests and needs. There is even some feeling that senior colleges will be reluctant to turn cooperative assignments back to the junior college when students graduate, as is called for in the agreement—since, after working with a given employer for two or three years, coordinators may tend to view the jobs as their own. Further, some coordinators feel that many students should not spend every cooperative term with the same employer but, on the contrary, should try different kinds of experience. They argue that this plan for continuity is really an opportunity for the student to become too comfortable and thus subverts one of the potential values of cooperative education. However, this criticism would apply to many situations in senior colleges as well. Perhaps one of the greatest potential values of this transfer-agreement plan is that it will pave the way for additional intercollegiate efforts to ease the burden of transfer.

CONSORTIA. State departments of education and the federal government have strongly encouraged cooperative arrangements among colleges and universities—mainly because such arrangements are economical and provide opportunities to emphasize the unique strengths of a given institution. The vehicle of cooperation might be as simple as two institutions agreeing to offer particular courses to the students of both, or it might be as complex as establishing an educational television network.

The first cooperative arrangement for the purpose of implementing a cooperative education program was established in 1969. Under a federal grant for developing institutions five junior colleges in

Kentucky constituted a consortium for attacking several different problems. Each institution was free to decide whether to participate in any given consortium project. Two of the colleges—Lees Junior College and Alice Lloyd College, both located in eastern Kentucky and serving youth of the Appalachian Highlands—became interested in the possibilities of cooperative education. The Kentucky Highlands Cooperative Education Program was created. Through the consortium a director was employed. For the first year he alone served both colleges in planning and starting the programs. He worked with faculty groups at both colleges to work through curriculum patterns and to establish educational policies to support the programs; he developed cooperative jobs for students at both colleges; and he counseled and placed students at both colleges. After a year each school employed its own coordinator with the director acting as overall supervisor.

Even before the Kentucky Highlands program was begun, representatives from a group of sixteen predominantly black colleges in the South began meeting to investigate possibilities of their developing cooperative programs in concert—because, they felt, such an approach would be more efficient and the programs would be better received by the community. This group incorporated in North Carolina as the Corporation for Experiential Learning Programs in February 1970. In July 1970 this educational nonprofit agency received a grant from the U.S. Office of Education enabling it to provide substantive services to each of the member institutions. To date, the services have consisted principally of making funds available to member institutions so that they may proceed with efforts to plan and implement programs. The money available is insufficient to fund programs, but it is used to bring consultants to the colleges, to enable representatives of the colleges to attend cooperative education workshops and conferences, and periodically to assemble all the members to share experiences, discuss problems, and exchange ideas for solving problems. It also encourages the members to seek unilateral funding for their programs and assists in the preparation of proposals. In its original proposal for support, the sixteen-college consortium sought enough money to be able to establish a computer-based job bank, which would be available to all members. This will have to wait, however, for substantially greater funding than currently appears possible.

The principal advantage of the consortium arrangement, at

least at the outset, was economical. One person could effectively develop cooperative programs at two institutions, at a saving to both institutions. A second advantage reported was that the director had a larger pool of students for possible placement on a given job than he would have if each college operated independently. Thus, it was argued, employers could be better served.

The Office of Education has also funded as consortia two other agencies seeking to establish cooperative education programs. They are not consortia in the sense described above—of independent institutions coming together to strengthen one another. They are both state educational agencies providing support, guidance, and supervision to institutions within the state. Every public institution of higher education in Florida is being encouraged to make cooperative education available to its students. Leadership for this rests directly in the State Education Department. In Minnesota, the Board Office of the State Junior College System coordinates all financial matters for its eighteen junior colleges, including the cooperative education programs being developed in eight colleges and all formal arrangements with off-campus agencies. Coordinators in each college, however, report to their own line officers. Aside from fiscal and off-campus arrangements, they have no obligations to the Project Office.

It is too early in their history to evaluate the soundness of these consortia. A parent organization for support and guidance appears eminently reasonable. However, a centralized job bank—as hoped for by the consortium of sixteen colleges and as the Kentucky Highlands consortium, in effect, has—might have practical difficulties, including institutional competition for jobs. Whether this is simply cynicism or potential difficulty will not be known until more experience is gained. In any event, considering the rationale given for establishing consortia, their goals should include their own eventual demise; for after the participating institutions have developed strong viable programs, they would no longer need support from the consortium.

VI

Graduate Programs

Alvah K. Borman

A recent survey of cooperative institutions showed that fourteen were conducting graduate cooperative programs in the fall of 1970. An additional six institutions reported that programs are in existence, but no students are currently enrolled. (See Table 13.) All of these institutions reported full-time academic periods alternated with periods of full-time professional employment.

Advantages and Disadvantages

Many of the advantages of undergraduate cooperative education apply with equal validity to graduate cooperative programs. Additional benefits result because of the professional aspects of the program.

THE STUDENT. In addition to the usual benefits that the student obtains from any cooperative plan of education, such as exposure to the world of work, practical experience, and financial assistance, the

Table 13. GRADUATE COOPERATIVE STUDENT ENROLLMENT, SEPTEMBER 1970

Institution	*Total Enrollment*	*Engineering*	*MBA*	*L. A. Science*	*Other*	*First Program Started*
Adelphi	4		4			1964
U. Arizona Tucson	(1)					
U. Cal. Berkeley	100	100				1947
U. Detroit	10	10				1959
Drexel University	23			23		1963
Indiana State	2			2		1969
Iowa State	(1)					
Lehigh University	1	1				1970
Mississippi State	2	1			(2) 1	1970
MIT	39	36			(3) 3	1916
Northeastern	417	78	81		(4) 258	1956
Rensselaer	44	40		4		1945
U. Sherbrooke	75		75			1966
Texas A & M	(1)					
U. Texas Austin	(1)					
Union College	3				(5) 3	1970
Virginia Poly.	(1)					1965
U. Waterloo	(1)					
U. Washington	2	2				1969
U. West Florida	8		4	3	(6) 1	1970
Total	730	258	174	32	266	

(1) Programs organized but no students enrolled.
(2) Banking and Finance.
(3) Doctoral candidates in Chemical Engineering.
(4) Pharmacy 21, Actuarial Science 44, Professional Accounting 48, Law 145.
(5) Industrial Administration.
(6) Psychology.

graduate program offers such additional professional advantages as (1) the opportunity to work directly with qualified professionals in his field in a professional situation, (2) the opportunity to develop a professional reputation in the employing company, (3) exposure to the latest theoretical concepts of his profession in both the academic and practical worlds.

The major disadvantage is that the normal program usually requires nine to twelve more months of time than the traditional program, but this extra time is offset by the experience gained. The student may have to be geographically mobile in order to take advantage of the best possible professional opportunity. This requirement may create housing problems, especially for the married student.

THE EMPLOYER. The greatest advantage to the employer is the possibility of attracting highly qualified students. The potential also exists of integrating the academic program with a company training program to develop superior professional talent. The combination of academic training and on-the-job training produces a fully trained individual with an advanced degree at the end of the program. Experience shows that 90 per cent of the graduate cooperative students remain with their employers upon receiving a degree.

The program also helps to develop a strong relationship between the academic institution and the employer. Frequently expert advice becomes available to participating organizations through the faculty member who serves as thesis advisor to a student conducting a research project associated with his employment.

If the program is to be successful, the employer must develop meaningful job assignments and provide adequate supervision, which requires effective planning and management support. The employer may be inconvenienced by the alternating work periods. Admittedly, it is difficult to alternate graduate students in a position because of the small numbers available and their varied fields of professional interest.

THE INSTITUTION. The major advantage to the college or university is its ability to offer a superior educational program and graduate better qualified students. Industry often refers exceptionally well-qualified graduate students to the institution. The intimate and continuous relationship which exists between the institution and industry helps to keep courses up to date and often leads to the development of new courses to meet anticipated needs in the professional field. Faculty members often find that consulting opportunities develop as a result of their contact with industry through graduate students. Frequently the institution-industry relationship results in funds and grants being made available to the institution which normally may not be available.

The major disadvantage develops in the scheduling of classes. Sometimes the same course must be given twice in a year to accommodate two different groups. If the program is sufficiently large or can be arranged carefully, this problem can be eliminated. The institution also is required to supply personnel to coordinate the program, and this function may involve one or more full-time coordinators or the release time of a faculty member. In addition, some funds must be made available for the travel expenses of the coordinator visiting cooperating companies.

Employer Participation

Employers may seek to participate in graduate cooperative programs by four general methods.

First, a professional position may be established and the coordinator asked to furnish a qualified student to fill it. The job is usually one that will lead eventually to a higher position requiring advanced theoretical background.

Second, a company may recognize the need to develop or update a current employee. The institution is then approached to admit the employee as a graduate cooperative student.

Third, a condition of employment may be that the student be accepted for and complete a graduate cooperative program.

Fourth, the company may use the graduate cooperative program to attract new personnel in its recruiting program. The better qualified undergraduate students recognize the need for further education as well as an entry into the professional field. The company can then offer a training program which combines orientation to the company with advanced theoretical training.

In each case, however, the coordinator must be responsible for

Table 14. Northeastern University
Graduate School

FORM OF AGREEMENT

Concerning Possible Patent Rights Arising from Research Carried on at an Industrial Plant

1. In accordance with regulations established by the University Committee on Patents which were approved by the Executive Council on November 17, 1960, the undersigned hereby waives any and all patent rights for any invention that may result from research in the conduct of his thesis undertaken as a Graduate Cooperative student at his place of employment.

....

Name of Industrial Organization

Signed: ....
Graduate Cooperative Student

2. The undersigned, in the capacity of University Thesis Supervisor, hereby waives any and all patent rights for any invention that may result from the research in the conduct of the above student's thesis.

Signed: ....
University Thesis Supervisor

3. The .... Corporation hereby agrees to permit ...., an employee of the company, to carry on research in its laboratories in connection with his thesis, with the understanding that any and all patent rights for any invention that may result from this research shall be wholly the property of the Corporation.

Signed: ....
For the Corporation

4. Northeastern University agrees to permit ...., a graduate student, to carry on research incident to his thesis at the plant of the .... Corporation and hereby waives any and all claim to any patent rights for any invention that might result from this research. The completed thesis, however, will become the property of Northeastern University when it is submitted as part requirement for the degree of ....

Signed for the University

..............................., *President*

Date:

maintaining the liaison between the company, the student, and the institution.

Academic Requirements

Academic requirements are normally determined by the faculty involved in a specific program. In addition, students must perform in an acceptable manner on their professional assignments.

THESIS IN INDUSTRY. Since the student will be working as a professional in his field, a suitable thesis topic may be developed with his cooperating employer. The concept of a thesis in industry is unique. It permits the employer to get a specific job done and also gives the student the advantage of access to specialized equipment and research data.

When a student does his thesis in industry, the university coordinator is responsible for setting up the necessary liaison channels among the student, faculty advisor, and company supervisor. In order to protect proprietary information that may result from the student's work, an agreement should be concluded among the employer, student, and university. (See Table 14.)

ADMISSIONS. Admission requirements are essentially the same as those for any graduate program. In addition, however, the student must have capabilities and personality traits deemed desirable to enter the professional world for which he is preparing. Each applicant should be reviewed by a committee consisting of the director of the graduate school, the chairman of the department in which the student is planning to take his work, and the coordinator who will be responsible for placement. A personal interview is particularly important, since the success of the program will depend upon the demonstrated competence of the student in his cooperative assignment.

Scheduling

The faculty determine the number of class terms necessary to meet the academic requirements for the degree and the work terms necessary to meet the professional-experience requirement. The cooperative program usually requires nine to twelve months more than a

Table 15. TYPICAL QUARTER-PLAN CALENDARS

	First Year				Second Year			
	Summer	*Fall*	*Winter*	*Spring*	*Summer*	*Fall*	*Winter*	*Spring*
Standard Engineering with alternate divisions								
Division A	W[a]	S	W	S	W	W	S	X
Division B	W[a]	W	S	W	W	S	W	S
Engineering—one division	W[a]	S	W	S	W	W	S	X
Modified Engineering / Mechanical Engineering }	W[a]	S	S	W	W	S	S	X
Business Administration		S	S	W	S	W	W	S
Professional Accounting	S	S	W	S	S			
Law—1st two years		S	S	S	W	S	W	S
3rd year	W	S	W	S				
Actuarial Science[b]		S-10	W-16	S-10	W-15	S-10	W-17	S-10

W—Professional-experience period.
S—Academic period.
X—Period in which academic requirements have been completed but formal degree-granting exercises have not yet taken place. Student is normally on full-time employment.

[a] Optional employment period.
[b] The ten-week academic periods are keyed to the examinations given by the Society of Actuaries.

traditional program. Scheduling is usually based on the normal academic calendar of the institution, although the number of terms may also be based on the specific requirements of the program. Table 15 shows some of the calendars in existence at one institution.

Placement

The placement of graduate cooperative students in professional positions is the responsibility of the coordinator, who must have a broad knowledge of the academic programs offered, a wide acquaintance with professional employment opportunities, and an intimate knowledge of the qualifications and needs of students to be placed. The ratio of potential positions to anticipated number of students in a program should be at least three to one.

Students must be matched with available positions. For company-based (those in employ of company) students, matching is the responsibility of the company, with the coordinator acting as liaison. For institution-based students (those who do not have an affiliation with a company prior to matriculation), the coordinator is responsible for the matching process. He must analyze the aptitudes, abilities, qualifications, and goals of each student and match these qualities with one or more positions. He then arranges for the student to meet the employer. If the match is satisfactory, the student is hired.

A number of external factors tend to interact with the placement process. In periods of economic expansion, the student is in a position to pick and choose among jobs. Theoretically, he should choose the one that offers the greatest opportunity for professional development. He may, however, wish to choose on the basis of financial advantage, convenience of location, or some other factor irrelevant to the educational process. Experience has shown that many students prefer to work in the area near the university, even when superior positions are available at more distant locations. The coordinator should attempt to overcome the student's self-imposed limitations and work toward the most advantageous placement situation.

In periods of economic depression, the job market shrinks. If the coordinator has done an adequate job of convincing employers that graduate cooperative education is "an investment in the future," positions will be available, but the student's choice will be limited.

The question of salary is always important. No specific figures can be stated. Generally the student should be paid the same rate as new full-time employees coming into an oragnization with the same background and experience. Salary rates are usually set as the result of an agreement between the student and the employer, with the coordinator acting as a resource person.

Supervision

The student's immediate job supervisor oversees the professional assignment. Overall supervision of the program is provided by the coordinator. The expertise and effectiveness of these two individuals are the key to a successful program.

The supervisor of the professional-employment phase of the program is often referred to as an extramural member of the faculty of the college or university. His role as an effective teacher depends upon his education, experience, leadership ability, professional attitude, and management responsibilities. A supervisor who does not have the necessary qualifications can waste the time and funds of the company as well as the time and energy of the student.

The coordinator's job does not end with the placement of the student. He must continue to monitor the student's progress, maintain liasion with the company supervisor, be alert to new developments in the company, act as advisor to his faculty and institution, and serve as a counselor and advisor to his students.

VII

Industry-Sponsored Programs

Harold P. Rodes

Although most cooperative education programs are sponsored by colleges and universities, with the cooperative student employed on work assignments by participating companies, some few programs are sponsored directly by industrial concerns or governmental agencies. These cooperative programs are of several types: (1) complete sponsorship and support by a single corporation (example: General Motors Institute); (2) sponsorship and support by industry or government of special cooperative programs at existing institutions (example: Northeastern University); (3) sponsorship and support of a graduate program by a single corporation or industry (examples: Chrysler Institute of Engineering and Northeastern University).

Support by Single Corporation

General Motors Institute (GMI), located in Flint, Michigan, conducts five-year cooperative programs in mechanical, industrial, or electrical engineering, and in industrial administration. The mechanical engineering curriculum offers upper-division options in automotive, materials science, mechanical-electrical, plant engineering, and process engineering; the industrial administration curriulum offers options in production management, marketing, and production and material control. These programs provide General Motors Corporation with a nucleus of college graduates who are well qualified and highly motivated to assume positions of responsibility and leadership, primarily in engineering and management.

GMI is incorporated in the state of Michigan as a nonprofit institution of higher learning and is accredited by the North Central Association of Colleges and Secondary Schools to grant the bachelor's degree. Its primary purpose is to develop and offer educational and training programs which are expected to be different, better, or less expensive to General Motors than could be obtained from any other source. Approximately 60 per cent of all of the graduates of the GMI program, dating back to 1928, are still employed by the General Motors Corporation; 40 per cent are employed by other companies or colleges or have gone into business for themselves.

Since the common characteristics of cooperative education are described elsewhere in this book, only the distinctive features of GMI's program are presented here.

SELECTION OF STUDENTS. The cooperative students enrolled at GMI are selected jointly by GMI and the sponsoring units of the General Motors Corporation. Applicants for admission are recruited primarily in secondary schools by GM plant representatives or the GMI admissions staff. They must then be approved academically by the GMI faculty admissions committee on the basis of their secondary school courses and grades as well as test scores and recommendations. Once approved, an applicant is invited to select, in order of preference, four of the 135 GM sponsoring units throughout the United States and Canada. Since every GM unit projects each year the number of new students it wishes to appoint to GMI, the size of the freshman class is determined by this total projection rather than by the number of qualified applicants.

The applicant information is reviewed by the GM sponsoring unit of his first choice. If that sponsoring unit is interested, the applicant is invited to the plant for a personal tour and interview, at which time a local selection committee determines whether the candidate has the motivation, maturity, and other leadership qualities they are seeking. If he does, the applicant is then officially appointed to the cooperative program by the sponsoring unit. If he is not appointed by the sponsoring unit of his first choice, his folder is forwarded to the unit of his second, third, or fourth choice for further consideration.

Since 1946, General Motors Institute also has enrolled selected students from GM Overseas Operations in special one- or two-year cooperative programs. The GMOO Scholarship Plan enrolls students from nineteen different countries that have General Motors plants. Students selected for this program must have completed at least two years of college or university study in their native country and must have been employed by their GM overseas plant for at least two years. Students come to GMI under the sponsorship of their respective GM overseas divisions. Their courses at GMI are selected on the basis of their anticipated field of specialization with their GM unit when they return home. Since these students obtain work experience at GM plants in the United States on the same cycle as other cooperative students, there are no unusual scheduling problems.

ACADEMIC CALENDAR. Students at GMI begin their cooperative work experience with the sponsoring unit at the beginning of the freshman year. In fact, half of the freshman class will have spent at least six weeks working in the sponsoring unit prior to beginning any classes on the campus. The academic calendar includes forty-eight weeks, with classes not held during the Christmas holidays and the "down period" of two or three weeks at the beginning of August. The student body is divided into two groups, Section A and Section B, so that only half of the student body is on campus at a given time.

In comparison with other cooperative programs, the six-week periods of alternation between study and work are unusually short. The advantages of this cycle include the following: (1) There is greater opportunity to relate the academic experience in the classroom and laboratory with the work experience, particularly in the upper-division courses after the student has selected his option in engineering or industrial administration. (2) The six-week break for work experience in the middle of each course gives the student an opportunity to devote some time to self-study in courses which might be particularly difficult for him. (3) The work periods provide a refreshing change of pace and can provide the motivation to continue a rigorous educational preparation. Moreover, because the student obtains this work experience at the outset of his collegiate career, he can decide more immediately whether he really wants to spend the rest of his life in industry. (4) The change from campus to plant provides an outlet for some of the boredom and frustration that many college students occasionally feel. (5) The student has more income and receives it more often than if the work periods were longer or started later. In the five-year program, students should be able to earn enough on their coop jobs to cover most, if not all, of their college and living expenses.

TUITION AND SALARY. Although the education of GMI undergraduate cooperative students is subsidized by the GM Corporation, each student pays tuition currently at the rate of $950 per year. This figure is established annually by a long-standing policy of the Board of Regents that the tuition rate should be approximately 20 to 25 per cent of the average earnings of the freshman class. Accordingly, the annual tuition has risen in recent years, because the average earnings of students have increased. The philosophy behind this unusual tuition policy is that a GMI student should make some sacrifice and contribution toward the cost of his education, particularly since he is free to use his education following graduation in any way he wishes. As is true at most colleges and universities, the tuition charged by GMI covers only a portion of the total cost of the student's education.

Students in the GMI cooperative program are "hourly-rate" employees during the work periods of their first two years. Thereafter, they become salaried employees. Working on an hourly basis during the first two years gives students a greater understanding of the contributions and responsibilities of hourly workers, including punching the time clock. However, students are not required to join any of the unions with which General Motors has contracts, since cooperative students are not used on production work to replace union employees, and since union leaders recognize the advantage to their membership of having future engineers and managers who have worked closely with them in the plant.

THESIS. General Motors Institute is one of few American colleges requiring a bachelor's thesis for graduation. In the second term or semester of the fifth year, just prior to graduation, GMI students are employed on a full-time basis by their sponsoring unit. However, during this time they are required to undertake a "fifth-year project" related to a major problem confronting the sponsoring unit. This project must be reported in the form of a written thesis, after which the student also gives an oral presentation, including his recommendations, to the management of his sponsoring unit.

On the basis of surveys made of GMI graduates, faculty project advisors, plant project advisors, and plant managers, the fifth-year project and thesis provide a number of benefits. First of all, the student obtains valuable educational experience, which gives him a preview and preparation for other engineering and management problems he will encounter in the future. Moreover, since many of the fifth-year projects are related to improved policies, procedures, and processes, the projects frequently result in cost savings and improved earnings for the sponsoring unit. Finally, serving as advisors to students on the fifth-year projects can be an educational and stimulating experience for faculty members and gives them an excellent opportunity to upgrade and update their own knowledge. This carries over into their classroom and laboratory instruction and counseling on the campus.

BACHELOR-MASTER PLAN. The only exception to the requirement of a fifth-year project and thesis for graduation occurs in the unique Bachelor-Master plan. This plan originated at the Massachusetts Institute of Technology in 1957, when several GMI fifth-year students near the top of their class academically were admitted to full graduate standing and completed the requirements for a master's degree at MIT instead of undertaking the normal fifth-year project in their sponsoring GM units. Upon meeting the requirements for the master's degree at MIT, these students were subsequently awarded the bachelor's degree from General Motors Institute. The GMI Bachelor-Master plan has become so popular that it now includes forty-two leading graduate schools throughout the United States and Canada, and students in the top 10 per cent of their class at GMI are eligible for participation.

Many bachelor's degree-granting colleges and universities have sooner or later extended their educational programs to the graduate level. However, there appears to be little need for General Motors Institute to do so, as long as its students have access to the faculties and facilities of so many outstanding graduate schools in North America.

ADMINISTRATION. The administration, organization, and operation of General Motors Institute is not nearly as complex or cumbersome as might be imagined. The policy-making and fund-raising activities of GMI are centered in the Board of Regents, consisting of fifty-one members and including all of the general managers, vice-presidents, and group vice-presidents of the General Motors Corporation, with an executive vice-president of the corporation serving as Chairman of the Board. Since the Board of Regents normally meets only twice a year, at which times major decisions concerning policies and budgets are made, the president of GMI reports between board meetings to the executive committee of the board or to the vice-president in charge of personnel staff of the corporation.

Although all members of the GMI faculty and staff, as well as other employees, are hired by General Motors Institute, they are granted by the Board of Regents the same job classifications, salary ranges, and fringe benefits as are received by all salaried employees of the General Motors Corporation. Accordingly, policies and procedures related to personnel administration are determined by the Corporation; and whenever changes or improvements are made, employees of GMI automatically receive the same.

ADVANTAGES AND DISADVANTAGES. There are some academic advantages which accrue to the faculty and staff of GMI, and subsequently to the student body, from the close relationship with one corporation. For example, it is relatively easy to obtain the time and talents of technical and managerial experts throughout General Motors to serve in an advisory capacity for the development of courses, curricula, and instructional aids. Since these men are the prime employers of the cooperative graduates and prime users of the educational services, they have a self-interest in seeing that GMI receives the best possible facts and advice in evaluating current programs and developing new ones. Moreover, this relationship gives the faculty and staff access to proprietary data and research activities which could not be made available to those "outside the family." The same is true, of course, for cooperative students who are employed on work assignments that may involve classified information.

One characteristic of a cooperative college or program sponsored by a single corporation could be considered a disadvantage: When all of the students are appointed and employed by one company, what happens when economic conditions require cutting costs and laying off employees? Fortunately, General Motors Institute has two safeguards against this. First, with the company's wide diversity of operations, it is not likely that all phases of the business will be down at the same time. Second, the top officials take the position that appointment to GMI involves an obligation on the part of the sponsoring unit to see that each student has an opportunity to complete his undergraduate education. Enrollment may fluctuate from year to year, depending upon the anticipated future needs of GM divisions and staffs, but it tends to remain relatively constant for the total five-year program.

Support by Industry or Government

Although the sponsorship of a complete undergraduate cooperative college by one corporation is most unusual, many programs are sponsored and supported by industry or government at existing institutions of higher learning.

Northeastern University, for example, has engaged in a variety of special cooperative programs to meet the occupational needs of organizations and industries for highly qualified and experienced personnel to become power systems engineers, navy engineering and science specialists, and health professionals.

POWER SYSTEMS ENGINEERING. In 1963, with the scholarship and matching-fund support of members of the Electric Council of New England (a regional group of investor-owned electric utilities), Northeastern University established a program in power systems engineering on the cooperative plan of education. Fourteen electric utilities and power-equipment manufacturers now sponsor this program, which leads to a master's degree in six years, with a bachelor's degree awarded at the end of five years. Students have the option of terminating at the end of the undergraduate phase.

Northeastern and the power companies agreed to the following commitments when the program was initiated: The university agreed to update the curriculum when expedient; to apply the cooperative plan of education at both degree levels; to select highly qualified students based on scholastic merit and residence location; to provide quality instruction and direction to the program and to add new power faculty as warranted; to improve and update power laboratories; to participate in the activities of a power-program advisory committee. The industry agreed to provide scholarship grants to students, to be applied to first-year tuition and expenses; to employ each of its sponsored students in a well-planned program of cooperative work following the freshman year; to contribute to Northeastern for each of the students to aid in program implementation; to make final selection of those qualified students to be sponsored; to be represented on a power-program advisory committee.

NAVY ENGINEERING AND SCIENCE TRAINING. The Department of the Navy has joined with several colleges of engineering operated on the cooperative plan of education to sponsor training programs in engineering and science. Among the colleges involved in these programs are Virginia Polytechnic Institute, Drexel Institute of Technology, and Northeastern University. The most active employers of coop students are the Philadelphia Shipyard, Portsmouth (N.H.) Naval Shipyard, the Naval Research & Development Laboratory in Annapolis, the Naval Research & Development Center in Washington, D.C., and the Naval Ammunition Depot in Crane, Indiana. In these programs the student is offered financial assistance by the Navy and guaranteed coop employment during upper-division years. In return for these benefits, the student obligates himself to remain with the Department of the Navy following his graduation for approximately the length of time (generally eighteen months) for which he has received scholarship assistance.

NURSING. When Northeastern's College of Nursing was established in 1965, an agreement was made with five Harvard teaching hospitals (Massachusetts General, Beth Israel, Children's, Peter Bent Brigham, and New England Deaconess) giving them exclusive use of the nursing coop students. In turn, the hospitals provided funds for financial aid and facilities for clinical instruction, and took an active part in the development of nursing curricula. The college initially offered a three-year program leading to an associate degree; later, a five-year baccalaureate-degree program was introduced. Presently, the college has become one of the largest in the country, with eight hundred students enrolled in the two programs. Students are now placed in more than twenty hospitals and industrial clinics on their coop assignments.

Support of Graduate Programs by Industry

Graduate programs of cooperative education are also sponsored by corporations or industries.

CHRYSLER CORPORATION. The Chrysler Corporation in Detroit provides a two-year cooperative graduate program through the Chrysler Institute of Engineering and participating universities. The program leads to the master's degree and subsequent employment by Chrysler as a professional engineer. Candidates for the program must complete the requirements for a bachelor's degree in engineering from an accredited school and be acceptable to a participating university for admission to their graduate school. In addition, candidates are selected by the Chrysler Institute of Engineering on the basis of such characteristics as automotive interest, maturity, demonstrated ability to work with other people, and potential for assuming executive responsibilities in engineering.

Students in the Chrysler two-year cooperative graduate program must complete noncredit automotive courses presented by members of the Chrysler staff; a minimum of six work assignments (each assignment lasting three months) in various departments at Chrysler over the two-year period; and the normal academic courses required for the master's degree by a participating university in which the student is enrolled.

Significant features of the Chrysler Institute of Engineering Graduate Program include the following: (1) The Chrysler Institute noncredit courses meet for approximately six hours a week during working hours and provide a comprehensive coverage of automotive engineering principles as they are applied in the Chrysler Corporation. (2) The student is given a variety of three-month assignments in various engineering departments of the Chrysler Corporation. His status is that of a regular salaried employee. (3) No tuition charges are made for the orientation courses offered by the staff of the Chrysler Institute of Engineering. Moreover, the company pays the tuition for all courses taken by the student at his participating graduate school. (4) Each engineer in the program has a counselor from the Chrysler organization who follows his progress during the two-year period and is available for consultation, visits to his university, and evaluation of his performance. (5) Upon successful completion of the two-year cooperative graduate program, the engineer receives his master's degree from the participating university and is then ready for placement on a permanent job.

GROUPS OF COMPANIES. Cooperative graduate programs are also sponsored by groups of companies in a related industry. Northeastern University offers such graduate programs in actuarial science and professional accounting.

Cooperative students in the two-year actuarial science program, which leads to the degree of Master of Science in Actuarial Science, are full-time employees of their sponsoring companies. Their tuition is paid in full by the company. Internship periods are fifteen to seventeen weeks in length, during which time students may expect to earn a minimum of $7,000. Financial grants are also normally provided by the employer.

Another Northeastern University program, the Graduate School of Professional Accounting, was established in 1965 with the support of ten large national accounting firms. This program, intended specifically for liberal-arts and other nonaccounting majors, leads to the degree of Master of Science in Accounting. Designed to prepare students to write the C.P.A. examination, as well as to serve as the foundation for future advancement in the profession, the program is fifteen months in length, including a three-month internship with a public accounting firm. During the internship period, students earn enough to cover tuition for the entire course. In addition, financial grants by the firms enable most students to receive substantial scholarship aid; a limited number of fellowships are also available on a competitive basis.

VIII

Cooperative Education in Canada

Albert S. Barber

The philosophy of cooperative education was adopted in Canada in 1957 in the Faculty of Engineering at the University of Waterloo, Waterloo, Ontario. Prior to the establishment of this program, representatives of government, the university, and industry visited and consulted with several United States colleges that had operated professional programs for several years. Through these consultations, the Canadian representatives hoped to learn the basic operations of such programs, so that the most applicable of these operations could be used to formulate a program acceptable to the Canadian academic, industrial, and economic climate.

Differences from United States Programs

When the Canadian program was initiated, it followed very closely the pattern set by professional programs at Northeastern University, the University of Cincinnati, Drexel University, and the

University of Detroit. As the program was developed, however, some significant differences appeared.

TRIMESTER SYSTEM. The Waterloo program at first operated on a quarter basis, with students admitted at the beginning of each term. However, the quarter program presented a number of problems: academic resistance (because teaching terms were considered too short), high student travel cost to job assignments, and reluctance on the part of industry and government to employ and train students for such a short period of time. In addition, the heavy work load imposed on the coordination department, the registrar's office, and the business office was unacceptable. Consequently, a complete restudy of the operation was made and a form of trimester adopted, with freshman students registering at the beginning of the fall term (September) only and with streaming (the division of the freshman class into two groups) to take place after four months. This streaming provided a four-month academic term, with half the students attending classes for four months and then going to their work assignments while the remaining half attended classes for eight months and then went on their work assignments. Each half completed six four-month work terms and came together for their last academic term, graduating in the spring, four and two-thirds years after commencing the course. (See Table 16.) This new timing was much more acceptable to all participants (faculty, students and employers).

The transition period was difficult, particularly for the students. Some students were required to spend three terms at school, and several were required to spend two terms at school; all of these students suffered a loss of earnings, and the university was required to subsidize them with loans. In addition, some students were required to spend two terms on work assignments, which again was disruptive. If this difficult transition had not been undertaken as early in the program as it was, with a relatively few students, it would probably have been impossible to accomplish.

This version of the trimester system at the University of Waterloo proved viable and became the accepted Canadian pattern for subsequent programs started in 1966 at the University of Sherbrooke (engineering and business administration); in 1969 at the Memorial

Table 16. ACADEMIC CALENDAR, FACULTY OF ENGINEERING
University of Waterloo

	1971 *Fall*	*Winter*	*1972* *Spring*	*Fall*	*Winter*	*1973* *Spring*	*Fall*
STREAM A	First Term 1A	Second Term 1B	*Work Term 1*	Third Term 2A	*Work Term 2*	Fourth Term 2B	*Work Term 3*
STREAM B	First Term 1A	*Work Term 1*	Second Term 1B	*Work Term 2*	Third Term 2A	*Work Term 3*	Fourth Term 2B

	Winter	*1974* *Spring*	*Fall*	*Winter*	*1975* *Spring*	*Fall*	*1976* *Winter*
STREAM A	Fifth Term 3A	*Work Term 4*	Sixth Term 3B	*Work Term 5*	Seventh Term 4A	*Work Term 6*	Eighth Term 4B
STREAM B	*Work Term 4*	Fifth Term 3A	*Work Term 5*	Sixth Term 3B	*Work Term 6*	Seventh Term 4A	Eighth Term 4B

University of Newfoundland (engineering) and at the Regina Campus of the University of Saskatchewan (engineering); and in 1970 at the Nova Scotia Technical College at Halifax (architecture). By mutual consent of the schools offering cooperative programs, the actual calendar dates are timed to correspond as closely as possible, in an attempt to give students and employers an opportunity to change from one university to another.

FREE-CHOICE JOB PLACEMENT. In addition to this common approach, all of the Canadian coop programs give students free choice of job assignments and also give employers free choice of students. Employers are asked to forward a complete description for each job opening, and the students are asked to read the descriptions carefully and then to select jobs that interest them. Employers in turn receive a very complete history of each student who has expressed an interest in the jobs offered. The employers are encouraged to interview these students on the campuses. Each student is permitted interviews for eight jobs. At the completion of all interviews, they then rank their preferences. Employers are asked to do the same, and the student and employer choices are matched by computer. This method of free choice must be credited for much of the acceptance of the cooperative programs by employers. In addition, it makes students less likely to complain of bias and favoritism by coordinators, fostering a much better student-coordinator relationship than when students are "placed" by the coordinators.

LOCATION OF COORDINATOR. Because most of the coop schools are located far from the high-density industrial areas, a coordinator usually is located many miles from the university rather than based at the school. Since approximately two thirds of his time is spent developing new jobs and visiting the students for whom he is responsible on their work assignments, this location reduces travel time and cost. In addition, he becomes well known to the employers of his area and is available for consultation on short notice.

Extent of Programs and Trends

There has been very limited growth of cooperative programs at other than newly founded universities in Canada, primarily because most universities (as well as many of the community colleges that have been or are being established in Canada) operate on the conventional timing, from mid-September to mid-May. There appears to be little likelihood of many changes from this traditional pattern. Of the few schools on the trimester pattern, a small number are experimenting or have experimented with coop programs. Their reluctance appears to stem from lack of commitment either in time or money to provide a viable program.

Within the universities presently operating cooperative programs, there has been a gradual broadening into new areas. For example, at the University of Waterloo coop programs are now offered in engineering, applied physics, applied chemistry, mathematics, kinesiology, recreation, and architecture, with some 4,800 students (approximately 50 per cent of the total undergraduate enrollment) participating. A study is presently being made to consider the feasibility of introducing coop programs in the faculty of engineering at the graduate level.

Location of Jobs

Because most of the coop universities are located in areas remote from businesses and industries large enough to provide sufficient jobs, many of the participating students must travel long distances to their work assignments. Approximately 85 per cent of the cooperative students on work assignments from the University of Waterloo are employed in southern Ontario. Many of these students are located within a hundred-mile radius of Waterloo, and the maximum distance would be about 350 miles. Other significant areas of employment are northern Ontario, 6 per cent; Quebec, 4.5 per cent; western Canada, 2 per cent; and United States, 1 per cent. The University of Sherbrooke places most of its students in the province of Quebec; Memorial University and Nova Scotia Technical College are concentrating initially on the Atlantic provinces; and assignments for students of University of Saskatchewan are principally in western Canada.

From the point of view of the student, cost of travel is one of the principal considerations in a job located a long distance from campus. In some instances, employers help students to pay travel costs, especially to remote locations not readily accessible by regular transportation facilities. In other situations, higher wage levels at isolated sites may compensate the student for the additional expense incurred in reaching the job.

Administrative Organization

The administrative organization of cooperative programs in Canada is similar to that in the United States. The smaller programs are usually responsible to the faculties with which they are associated. The larger and more diversified programs are administered through a separate department reporting to the academic vice-president.

At the University of Waterloo the administrative structure has evolved with the growth in the cooperative programs. The director of the Department of Coordination is responsible for the policies, structure, and budgeting of the department. Within this framework two assistant directors and two senior coordinators manage the operations of the various programs. In the largest program (engineering) an assistant director, Engineering Faculty Liaison, handles the special problems of communication between the department and faculty and students. Since most of the coordinators are based outside the Waterloo area, provision must be made for several staff members in the office to maintain liaison with coordinators and to provide points of contact for on-campus students.

A general office meets the extensive clerical needs of the cooperative programs. Certain members of the staff are assigned to specific programs, but others are available to carry on functions common to all programs and to assist with peak work loads.

Employers' advisory councils have been established in connection with a number of the Canadian cooperative programs. Members of these organizations represent the employers associated with a particular program and have a keen personal interest in cooperative education. These councils do not enter into the academic planning of the programs, but they do provide direction on many aspects of the operation of the work terms. They bring to program administrators their concerns and suggestions for improvement and offer advice on changes proposed in cooperative programs. In the early stages of a program, a council may also play an important role in the encouragement of employer participation.

Academic Calendar

As mentioned, the standard cooperative program in Canada is on a trimester system, with streaming taking place after the first four months. At the University of Waterloo, however, a number of exceptions to the standard program have been designed, either to effect economies in the academic portion of a program or to conform to special characteristics of the employment situation.

The kinesiology and recreation program operates on a single stream, with first-year students spending two terms on campus and going out for their first work assignment in the spring term. This pattern was adopted because it provided for the most effective use of faculty in terms of the number of students anticipated in the first year of the program, combined with the opportunity to teach students in two terms on campus the skills that would contribute to their initial employment.

The option in chartered accounting (mathematics) operates on a single stream, with the fall term on campus and the first work term in the winter. This calendar was selected because chartered accountants are very busy in the winter term and can utilize students effectively, while suitable work for inexperienced people would not be available in the spring term.

In applied physics the two streams are amalgamated at the beginning of the third academic year to overcome problems of very small senior classes. The option in cooperative mathematics for prospective high school teachers becomes cooperative in the second year to give students some additional maturity and academic training prior to their first school assignments.

In the Canadian cooperative programs, there has been little substitution of alternative experiences for the regular course-related work term. Most exceptions have been for travel as a replacement for one work term, and employers have usually been very understanding in making any necessary adjustments.

Earnings

Salaries paid to cooperative students are determined by employers within their own wage structures. Employers are asked to complete confidential questionnaires on student earnings for each work term, and averages obtained from these surveys are made available to employers and prospective employers to assist them in reviewing or establishing salary scales.

It is impossible to arrive at any numerical assessment of the importance of student earnings in meeting the costs of education. A brochure prepared by the Student Advisory Council to the Department of Coordination at University of Waterloo for the information of students considering enrollment in cooperative programs makes the following comment: "It is perhaps easier to manage economically because school terms are financed in four-month stretches, rather than eight."

Many students who have problems in financing a university education feel that they do receive additional assistance from work-term earnings, compared to that available from summer employment in regular university programs.

Faculty

Academic appointments in the cooperative programs carry an explicit commitment and responsibility for two terms a year, a total of almost eight months. These terms are devoted to lecturing, scholarly work, academic supervision of students, setting and marking of examinations, and general participation in university affairs through the work of councils and committees. For the remainder of the year, faculty members are expected to pursue activities of a scholarly or professionally developing character.

A benefit of the cooperative system, where a significant amount of instruction is given in the spring term, is the possibility of combining, in a two-year period, four terms of regular service and two consecutive uncommitted terms. Every encouragement is given for a faculty member to spend this period from time to time in industry, business, government establishments, or at another university. For those who wish to remain on campus during uncommitted periods, to continue their personal research or to supervise graduate students, some faculties have established systems of research stipends. In many programs, salary increases and promotions are influenced by the activities of academic staff members through the entire academic year, not just through the eight-month period explicitly committed.

Future

Since the introduction of cooperative education in Canada in 1957, its underlying precepts have been strongly endorsed by employers and the academic community. The continuing interest in cooperative education would point to a moderate further development in Canada. The timing of future growth, however, is hard to forecast, since it will be closely related to the expansion of the Canadian economy. There is a reference to this relationship in the report "Ring of Iron—A Study of Engineering Education in Ontario." After outlining the development of the cooperative engineering program at Waterloo, the report states (Lapp, Hodgins, and Mackay, 1970, p. 526):

New Cooperative programs are being introduced in other provinces, which may cut into the employment market for Ontario university students. In times such as the present, with some scarcity of employment opportunities, the market for cooperative students will become saturated. For these reasons, we recommend that Waterloo continue to be the only engineering school offering a cooperative program in Ontario throughout the 1970s and that its engineering be limited to this type of program.

Although the philosophy of cooperative education has been accepted, certain factors appear to preclude any great expansion in the universities in the next ten years. The established universities are on the traditional pattern, and the present close scrutiny of educational expenditures does not encourage the founding of new institutions. In addition, universities on tight budgets recognize that the proper operation of a cooperative program is not a money-saving device.

The community colleges are showing a great deal of interest in cooperative programs, and it is expected that they will contribute substantially to the growth of cooperative education in Canada in this decade.

Sandwich Plan in England

James Grant

It is primarily within an industrial context that the sandwich plan in England must be approached, since its roots go back to the realization that mere schooling in the early years is not enough to produce a person sufficiently developed to make a significant contribution in an industrial complex.

The mainstream of traditional education is scholarship, the pursuit of knowledge and understanding. The selection processes for admission to schools at various academic levels have been based on assessing the students' ability to conceptualize and work with abstractions. Until recently, those not amenable to these processes learned in "the school of hard knocks." They taught themselves by observation and experiment. For such people relevance still remains the principal driving force. Understanding and knowledge come first through common sense rather than through abstractions. For example, they must start with automobile engines and proceed to the study of thermodynamics, since the study of dynamic theory itself seems pointless to them.

The sandwich plan provides these students with a good education, which can lead them to goals more commonly achieved through the old traditional routes. Industrial exposure leads to an appreciation of relevance, an understanding of concepts, and a desire for conceptualized knowledge. The results of the sandwich course so far have been most encouraging, and a growing willingness to experiment with such courses is developing.

Since 1903, when the first sandwich course in England was started at Sunderland Technical College (now Sunderland Polytechnic) in the main branches of engineering and in naval architecture, employers have recognized the value of the sandwich course, not only as a marriage of theory and practice but as a scheme that eases the transition from the academic educational world to the rough and tumble of industry and commerce. Although much of the pioneering work in sandwich training took place in the fields of engineering and technology, the sandwich principle recently has expanded into business and commerce.

Specific Features

A full-time traditional course entails attendance at a college generally for thirty hours or five days per week for an academic year of usually thirty-three to thirty-six weeks. In a sandwich course, on the other hand, full-time study is broken by a period or periods of industrial, commercial, or professional vocational training. This training is part of an overall course of two, three, four, or five years' duration.

A feature of the sandwich course is the integration of the periods of training in industry with the periods of education. Thus, excluded from the definition "sandwich" are those courses in which a student spends a limited time in industry before embarking on a full-time course; also excluded are courses where there is no direct contact during the industrial period between the firm and the college. Courses involving short periods of vocational experience are also excluded unless there is evidence that an integrated approach is adopted.

Similarly, the length of time of industrial training limits the types of courses that can be described as "sandwich." Some sandwich degree courses must involve a total of at least eighteen months spent in industry; others normally demand twelve months. Generally a two-year course requires six months to be spent in industry, a three-year course needs one year, while a four-year course demands eighteen months.

This time element excludes a wide range of courses—most notably, courses that involve attendance at college for one day a week throughout the year; those that involve only three or four months of study at college during a one-year course; and those apprentice courses where the first year comprises off-the-job integrated education and training and the remaining years are composed of one day's study a week at college.

Types of Courses

There are chiefly two types of sandwich courses: "thick" and "thin." In the former, the periods of time spent in college (C) or industry (I) are relatively long. For example, a four-year thick sandwich degree course could have the pattern C–C–I–C; a five-year course, I–C–C–C–I. In a thin sandwich course, the periods spent alternately in industry and college are shorter. Table 17 shows the variations that may be found in courses even of the same length.

CNAA DEGREE COURSES. A major and relatively recent development has been in sandwich courses at the first degree (B.A., B.S.) level. This development was encouraged when the National Council for Technological Awards (NCTA) was set up in 1955. NCTA was superseded in 1964 by the Council for National Academic Awards (CNAA), which has continued to encourage sandwich degree courses in the new polytechnics and in eight or nine other colleges, in subjects ranging from applied sciences and business studies to languages, urban and regional planning, nautical studies and, of course, various branches of engineering.

In September 1970, seventy-one CNAA first-degree programs were offered. Of these, forty-five were of the sandwich type. Of these forty-five, two were five-year courses, and five were four-and-a-half year courses; thirty-eight were four-year courses. The CNAA has, of course, many other proposals for first degrees before it.

Table 17

	YEAR 1			YEAR 2			YEAR 3			YEAR 4			YEAR 5		
1st Term	*2nd Term*	*1st Term*	*2nd Term*	*3rd Term*	*3rd Term*	*1st Term*	*2nd Term*	*3rd Term*	*1st Term*	*2nd Term*	*3rd Term*	*1st Term*	*2nd Term*	*3rd Term*	
I	I	I	C	C	C	C	C	C	C	C	C	I	I	I	THICK
C	C	C	I	I	I	C	C	C	I	I	I	C	C	C	THICK
C	C	C	C	C	C	I	I	I	C	C	C	THICK			
C	C	C	I	I	I	C	C	I	I	C	C	THICK/THIN			
C	I	I	I	C	C	C	I	I	C	C	C	THICK/THIN			
C	C	C	I	I/C	C	I	I/C	C	I	I/C	C	THIN			
C	C	C	I	I	I	C	C	C	THICK						
C	C/I	I	C	C/I	I	C	C	C	THIN						
C	C	I	I	C	C	THIN									
C	I	I	I	C	C	THICK									

C—Periods spent in college.
I—Periods spent in industry.

The philosophy, syllabi, curricula, and aim of a proposed CNAA degree course of three, four, or five years' duration, honors or ordinary, sandwich or full-time, are assessed by critical panels and committees. The CNAA and its committees and subject boards include representatives of university teachers, college teachers, and industry and commerce. The council does not approve a degree course submitted by a college until it has carried out a rigorous examination both of the proposed course (content and approach) and of facilities and accommodation at the college, and is satisfied that they meet the high standards required. Teaching accommodations, staff, library facilities, equipment and laboratories, student accommodations, academic and administrative structures, staff research—all are assessed. CNAA degree-granting powers are granted for a five-year period, after which a statutory CNAA inspection takes place.

Many feel that the CNAA degree approach allows for and encourages greater variety, originality, and flexibility than many university degree courses. Moreover, the CNAA degree man is held to be far more ready for industry than is his university equivalent; for, apart from technological and industrial experience, a built-in feature of the CNAA degree is that it contains significant areas of study contrasting to the main tenor of the degree. For example, the student reading for the CNAA Bachelor of Science degree in Mechanical Engineering has socioeconomic and general studies as integral parts of his total course.

HND COURSES. The sandwich plan is not, however, confined to degree-level courses. The Higher National Diploma (HND), which is slightly below degree level, is awarded after either a two-year full-time or a three-year sandwich course. The sandwich course is available in thirty-four separate subjects—among them, agriculture, computer studies, applied science subjects, various branches of engineering, hotel and catering administration, mining, and printing.

HND courses are administreed by joint committees, each made up of representatives of the professional bodies for the subject, the Department of Education and Science, and members of the teachers' associations.

OND COURSES. In addition, Ordinary National Diploma (OND) courses are available on a sandwich basis. OND is roughly equivalent to the General Certificate in Education (GCE), Advanced Level, and is accepted as an educational entrée to degree courses at polytechnics and a number of universities. (Students applying for a degree course need at least two GCE Advanced Levels or an OND in an appropriate group of subjects.) Thus the OND holder can be seen as the equivalent of a good high school graduate.

Enrollment

Between 1952 and 1965, when they became universities in their own right, Colleges of Advanced Technology (CAT) became the spearhead of full-time and sandwich-course expansion. In 1966 it was announced that a group of sixty or so of the leading colleges—colleges of technology, colleges of commerce, colleges of art—were to be formed into thirty new polytechnics. Most of these polytechnics have since come into being; the total at the time of writing is twenty-eight, with the remaining two still under discussion. These new polytechnics now have something in the region of 15,000 students taking sandwich degree courses. Another 12,000 take HND sandwich courses in seventy-five other colleges; over 2,500 take OND sandwich courses; and 4,000 take a variety of professional and technical courses on a sandwich basis. Thus, approximately 35,000 students in England and Wales (about 2,500 of them women) are enrolled in some form of sandwich degree course.

There is no fixed ratio of men to women enrolled in sandwich courses. In such courses as a first degree in mathematics, statistics, or computing the ratio can be ten men to one woman. In information science, it can be five men to one woman; in chemistry, fifteen men to one woman. But when a course involves such a field as fashion technology, then understandably the women intake is much higher. Ultimately, the ratio depends upon supply and demand in industries and professions.

Specific Programs

To illustrate the workings of the sandwich type of program in England, two specific programs are described here in some detail.

HIGHER NATIONAL DIPLOMA IN BUSINESS STUDIES/FASHION (MAINLY FOR WOMEN). The course is of three years' duration. In the first and third years, the student's time is divided equally between business studies and fashion studies.

In the second year, a total of seventeen weeks is spent in placement in industry. These seventeen weeks are divided into two periods of twelve and five weeks. The twelve-week placement is spent in a firm where practical experience is concentrated on business management. The period of five weeks is spent in an organization where the emphasis is on fashion and production methods. The remainder of the year is spent in school. Because of the divided nature of the sandwich placement, placement in each category is the responsibility of a senior member of the staff conversant with the necessary practical criteria.

Placement is found either through staff connections or by reconnaissance carried out by the department head. When unemployment in this area is high, a nationwide search must be made for suitable training places.

A member of the staff of the Department of Commerce and Languages carries out the necessary liaison and tutelage responsibilities; but during the fashion and clothing technology period, the head of department personally oversees the students.

ENGINEERING PROGRAM. During the first year, a college course in engineering practice gives the student a knowledge of manufacturing processes. The program includes lectures, films, demonstrations supported by industrial visits, and practical exercises and projects.

The industrial periods have been planned so that the student experiences as wide a range of environments as possible.

Shop floor work during the first period follows the course in engineering practice and provides first-hand experience in an industrial environment, together with an opportunity to observe basic processes of casting and fabrication. The student must acquire sufficient technical background during the first two college periods to enable him to benefit from the work in technical departments during the second industrial period. The third industrial period provides experience in junior management and high-level technical work. During the fourth period, the student is usually placed as a technologist in the department in which he will commence his career upon graduation.

The student's tutor is responsible for ensuring that the experience gained follows as closely as possible the training scheme laid down for the course. The tutor visits the works before the industrial period begins, so that the training scheme can be organized in advance, in agreement with the firm concerned. The student is visited at regular intervals by his tutor during each industrial period; in addition, a responsible official of the firm will follow closely the student's progress in the training program.

During his industrial training, the student is encouraged to develop an engineering attitude toward the processes with which he is concerned. Specifically, the student is given small engineering problems in which he is expected to ascertain why the firm does a job in a particular way and to suggest alternative methods.

Once a student is placed with a firm, he is expected to keep a log book, which must be signed by a member of the firm. In addition, upon returning for his next academic period, he is required to write a report about his training period. These reports are expected to be about 1,500 words long, together with diagrams when appropriate. Reports should include dates and places of work, in index form; description of work done; critical appreciation of the manufacturing processes and industrial organization; and relevant criticism of the value of the training.

Tutors maintain a file for each student, containing a record of all contacts with him, industrial report submitted, and all examination results.

Table 18 shows the schedule for this program.

Students

Students on sandwich courses fall into one of two categories: industry-based and college-based. Industry-based students are employed by firms that make arrangements for them to attend college, normally as student apprentices, and provide the associated periods of training in their own works or offices. College-based students, on the other hand, are not employees of any particular firm but have enrolled directly at the college. The college is their main base and is responsi-

Table 18. ENGINEERING PROGRAM SCHEDULE
Newcastle upon Tyne Polytechnic

Mechanical Engineering Practice (in College)	12 weeks
This section will occupy the third term of the first year. The total number of hours per week will be thirty-five, allocated as follows:	
	Hours
Workshop, laboratory, and project	24
Lecture	4
Drawing office	3
Works visits, films, visiting lecturers	3
Seminar	1
Total	35
First Industrial Period	*Weeks*
Foundry	2
Fabrication	2
Assembly and/or maintenance of machinery or process plant	6
Tool room or inspection	2
Second Industrial Period	
Drawing office	10
Test/development/research	6
Machine shop (as assistant to foreman)	3
Third Industrial Period	
Shop or process plant	10
Planning/costing/design or project	6
Fourth Industrial Period	
Specialist department	13

Individual firms may not possess all the facilities required by the above, in which case alternatives are arranged.

ble for arranging the periods of industrial, commercial, or professional training.

As the course is composed of both academic and industrial periods, a student has two sources of financial assistance. During the academic period, he normally receives a Local Education Authority

Grant, the amount of which is related to parental income. In some cases, a student who is industry-based also receives an honorarium from his firm. While the student is in industry, he receives the normal wage from the firm. Alternately, some industry-based students may at the discretion of the employer be paid the same industrial salary throughout the sandwich course, whether at college or at work. Most firms contribute to the Engineering Industry Training Board fund, in return for which the firm receives from the Training Board a weekly grant for the training of the student.

The matter of the supervision of the student while he is in industry is of prime concern. He must receive the benefit of reasonably wide areas of industrial experience, with various aspects of factory floor, office, and managerial experience being made available to him, both for purposes of observation and participation. Such requires not only careful supervision and tutelage during a period of industrial placement, but close and continual dialogue between the polytechnic or college tutor and his counterpart in the industrial concern in which the student is placed.[1] Each student normally is visited twice during the industrial period. In addition, the coordinator visits the firm prior to the start of the training period in order to discuss the program with company officials.

Practical training, a core criterion of the sandwich plan, must be seen not only as essential to the aims of the course but as part of that more general personal development. Industrial training should provide a real increment to the student's continuing studies, so that when the student receives his degree, he has already taken the first step toward a meaningful career.

Comparison with United States Programs

The basic philosophy of the sandwich plan in England is not markedly different from that of the United States cooperative plan of education, as defined by the National Commission for Cooperative

[1] A useful reference on these aspects is *Training Recommendation No 11* "Industrial Training Associated with Sandwich Courses (Science and Engineering)," published by the Chemical and Allied Products Industry Training Board, Staines House, 158/162 High Street, Staines, Middlesex, England.

Education. There are, however, certain fundamental differences.

First of all, in English practice, placement of a student in industry is an integral part of the total pattern of the course. In some United States institutions such placement may be optional, with only part of the student body participating. In addition, some American institutions exercise a degree of selectivity in choosing those to be placed on jobs; in the sandwich plan no such selectivity exists, since academic performance does not militate against the placement of a student in industry.

Placement procedures also differ, since often in American placement a contractual arrangement exists, putting the employment arrangement on a business basis.

In many American universities and colleges operated on the cooperative plan, a contractual arrangement also exists between the student and the educational institution. According to this arrangement, the student placed in industry holds a regular job under actual business conditions, in competition with other sources of supply. No such industrial-educational contract arrangement exists in the sandwich plan, although the industry-based student can normally expect to be employed by the sponsoring firm at the end of the course.

Furthermore, unlike the American procedure, the sandwich plan does not have procedures in which an employer provides work shared by two students, one of whom is on the job while the other attends college—thereby providing continuous coverage of the job and enabling both students to spend half time in class. The sandwich plan does allow, however, for the training place (industry or job assignment) in an individual firm to alternate between two or even among three students; this is called the "end-on" sandwich scheme.

In the British sandwich plan, a student being placed with a firm is not necessarily interviewed by a representative of the firm, although a number of colleges and polytechnics are finding that there are advantages in having representatives from a training firm on an interview panel. Occasionally a firm will accept the recommendation of the department that the student can ably undertake a period of industrial training.

Finally, in the United States students are usually placed on their cooperative jobs by coordinators, whose function is to deal with industrial contacts. In English practice, contacts with industry are usually established by the head of the department in which a student is reading for a sandwich degree. Depending on the quality of these personal contacts, a firm may simply write to the department head saying that it has places available for trainees from the department and would welcome nominations for placement.

PART THREE

CONDUCT OF PROGRAMS

X

Coordination and Placement

Charles F. Seaverns, Jr., and Roy L. Wooldridge

From the student's point of view, several uses can be made of cooperative education programs. For the student who is vocationally oriented the cooperative periods can be designed to be a series of training assignments leading through progressively more advanced exposures to a specific professional objective. This program occurs most often for students in professional school programs such as engineering, business administration, nursing, pharmacy, and education. An example is an engineering student interested in automotive engineering who is assigned to an automotive firm in the Detroit area and is placed on a training program that gradually leads him toward his objective and possible after-graduation employment. In fields where licensing restrictions do not limit performance, it is not unusual for an able student to be performing the work of a graduate during his junior or senior year.

For the student who does not have a clear vocational objective but who would like assistance in this area, the cooperative program can be used effectively. The students work on a series of assignments, each allowing the testing of his abilities, interests, and aptitudes against job situations. If the student finds a job that fulfills his needs, he may continue with the employer on a training program leading toward a specific professional objective. If not, then he continues to rotate among different employers. For example, a history major may be uncertain as to career goals and want some experience in insurance, banking, social work, or journalism. A series of assignments in these fields is arranged as much as possible. By his graduation, he may still not have found his field. On the other hand, he may have found the journalism experience to be meeting his needs. He then stays in the field of journalism and begins training for an after-graduation career.

Another use of the program can be made by the student who does not have a career goal and is not concerned with such a goal as an educational objective. The student is interested in the broadest possible education. This situation most often occurs with students in liberal arts, although occasionally a student in a professional school program desires this experience. The student is placed on a variety of experiences, preferably in different geographic settings, to give a maximum exposure to off-campus living. For instance, the first assignment may be in San Francisco with a retail firm; the second experience in Dallas with an insurance company; next in Boston with an investment firm; then Chicago with a social agency. An experience or two in Europe or South America may be added to the program. The idea is to offer a new dimension to a liberal education through a variety of experiences in different settings. In many respects, the work experience is not the most critical aspect of the off-campus period; the experience gained by the student in each new geographic area is. Does he become involved in the social and cultural activities of the area? Why do people ask and think the way they do? These represent the concerns of the faculty rather than: What kind of a job does he have? Is it related to his career objective?

Under the latter two plans, the amount of learning during the off-campus period is a function of student initiative. It varies from student to student according to their powers of observation. The student's program is enhanced to the extent that the faculty of the institution recognize the possibilities for learning and capitalize on experiences of the student in their classrooms.

Ideally, the administration and operation of the cooperative education program should be monitored from one central point—the department of cooperative education. Its placement, counseling, and guidance services should be competent, continuous, comprehensive, and convenient to the students. These services are an integral part of the total guidance program of the college and university and should be integrated with the student personnel services already in existence.

In a small cooperative program with a staff of one or two persons, division of labor is not practicable; but in a large department specialization in assignment is necessary. However, regardless of planned specialization, all departments of cooperative education must be versatile. Because of the changing times and the fluctuating labor market, the volume of coordination and placement activities varies considerably over a period of time. Each professional staff member must be able to adapt to various types of assignments, just as the department must be flexible enough to cope with unexpected situations. The total effectiveness of the program depends to an immeasurable degree upon every member of the coordination staff.

Coordination Staff

Staff personnel directly responsible for the placement, counseling, and guidance of cooperative students are called coordinators. A coordinator, usually a full-time faculty member with academic rank, serves in the multifaceted capacity of placement specialist, vocational counselor, salesman, teacher, administrator, educational recruiter, trouble-shooter, mediator, and referral agent.

The size of the coordination staff depends on student enrollment and the extent of the coordination and placement services. Generally the staff consists of a program director, faculty coordinators, and clerical personnel.

A director devotes most of his time to administration and supervision. His responsibilities include making policy decisions; administering the budget; hiring and firing; maintaining liaison with the faculty and administration through committee participation; and handling student and coordinator appeals. He also evaluates the cooperative program—the staff's preparation, training, performance, and morale; administrative and faculty support; effectiveness of the coordination services; and adequacy of physical and personnel facilities.

The coordinator serves as a placement counselor, with direct contact with industry, business, government agencies, and the professions; he also functions as an educator, with direct contact with members of the administration, teaching faculty, and student personnel services. As his main responsibilities, the coordinator supervises and coordinates the placement of students; serves as liaison between the college or university and the employers; assembles individual inventory records of his students for counseling and placement purposes; conducts group orientation meetings for instructional and review purposes; conducts placement follow-up activities by regularly checking job performance through conferences with students and job supervisors; solicits jobs that best suit the needs and qualifications of students; disseminates occupational information to assist students in career planning; counsels students regarding their educational, vocational, and personal development; makes referrals to proper persons when students have special counseling problems; assigns students to one of two divisions to permit alternation of two students holding a single job, thereby ensuring continuity of service to employers; maintains departmental and personal records and reports; represents the viewpoint of the department on various college or university committees; and vigorously promotes the cooperative plan of education among administration, faculty, students, employers, high school guidance counselors, community organizations, and the public.

The appointment of coordinators having the appropriate qualifications is vital to the success of any cooperative program. The attributes of a successful coordinator include maturity and sound judgment, reasonable freedom from biases and prejudices, neatness in personal appearance and possession of good manners, capacity to motivate others, appreciation and understanding of individual differences, ability to relate to people and to communicate effectively with them, ability to accept criticism objectively, a high degree of patience, a great deal of stamina, and a good sense of humor.

Ordinarily, the minimum academic requirement for a coordinator is a bachelor's degree, preferably in the academic field of the students for whose placement he is responsible. If the coordinator does not hold an advanced degree, it is assumed that he will pursue professional graduate study in a field related to his profession. Regardless of the fields in which a coordinator has had experience, he must possess a genuine interest in the field of education. The coordinator should also participate actively in community affairs and be an effective spokesman for his educational institution in the community.

The department of cooperative education at Northeastern University has established the position of administrative assistant (A.A.) to assist coordinators who have a large number of students to place on cooperative work assignments. Primarily, the administrative assistant assists with the interviewing, guidance and counseling, and placement of students; assists the coordinator in contacts with employers; and assists in the preparation of records and reports and other office and clerical functions. The able administrative assistant might also visit students on their off-campus assignments to gain a better understanding and appreciation of the types of jobs available and to establish greater rapport with students and company personnel. The administrative assistant may also substitute for the coordinator during the coordinator's absence. Support personnel also includes secretarial and clerical staff.

Dynamics of Coordination

The coordinator is the primary liaison official between the cooperative institution and the employers. He serves as the middleman, because it is his responsibility to promote harmony and teamwork among all program participants—students, employers, and faculty.

STUDENT RELATIONSHIPS. In order to place students successfully on coop assignments, the coordinator must relate effectively to those students for whom he is responsible. He must correlate placement possibilities and student capabilities, taking into account the career objectives of the students. He must also give students proper guidance so that they can seek opportunities compatible with their interests and consistent with their aptitudes and abilities. In addition, the coordinator must make periodic visits to each student's employer, conduct regularly scheduled conferences with students concerning their progress and adjustment on their cooperative assignments, and maintain records for counseling and administrative purposes.

Most important of all, a coordinator should inspire students to achieve to the fullest extent of their capabilities, to develop the sense of responsibility that goes with personal growth and development. In doing this, the coordinator should consider each student's total personality, handling personal problems sympathetically and on an individual basis.

In guiding the learning processes of his students, the coordinator must help them see things in proper perspective. All experiences have some value, but the coordinator must convey to students the importance of transfer values gained from the integration of classroom learning and off-campus practical experience.

The discussion of relations with students in this chapter is confined to those relationships which pertain to coordinators and placement. A detailed description of relations with students in colleges and universities conducted on the cooperative plan of education can be found in Chapter 11.

EMPLOYER RELATIONSHIPS. Since the cooperative plan is dependent upon the mutual agreement between the educational institution and the employing organization to provide a meaningful educational program for the student, it is essential that the coordinator establish and maintain good rapport with his cooperative employers. He must relate to employers as an interpreter of institutional goals, policies, procedures, and services.

The coordinator should obtain the support of management in the employing organization; that is, he should encourage management to consider the cooperative program as part of its long-range planning pursuant to manpower needs. However, to ensure optimum coordination effectiveness in meeting the needs of the student and the employing organization, the coordinator must also elicit the full support of the personnel responsible for the direct supervision of student employment. These are the people responsible for providing meaningful cooperative employment experience for the students as well as the subsequent supervision, training, guidance, and evaluation of each student's growth and development on the cooperative assignment. In effect, those responsible for the direct supervision of cooperative student employment can make or break the cooperative program. (See also Chapter 12.)

FACULTY RELATIONSHIPS. Communication problems often exist between the coordinator and the teaching faculty—primarily because the coordinator works from a different point of view and with a different methodology. The coordinator is more involved with the student's nonacademic adjustments; the teacher is primarily interested in disseminating subject matter, with emphasis on the intellectual and the scholarly. The coordinator must try to show the teaching faculty that practical experience is an integral and significant part of the total educational process.

Tools of Coordination

The coordinator should develop competencies in interviewing techniques; counseling theory and procedures; the use of psychological tests, records and reports, occupational information, school and community resources; and the application of electronic data processing.

INTERVIEWING TECHNIQUES. Whether a novice or a veteran in the art of interviewing, the coordinator should appreciate the fact that this is a dynamic function. The interview provides the coordinator with an opportunity to obtain information which cannot be obtained through tests, records, observation, or casual contact. The interview further provides the coordinator with an opportunity for supplying the student with specific, personalized information. Finally, the interview provides an excellent opportunity for the interviewer to establish rapport and to stimulate the thinking, feeling, and action of the student.

Interviews may be classified into three types, or methods: The *directed interview* is one in which the coordinator has a specific objective to be achieved. The coordinator directs the progress of an individual interview through the information he wishes to give or receive. The *patterned interview* is highly structured and carefully planned. The questions, on a prepared form, are the same for all students who may be interviewed in a group. The patterned interview assures that certain desired information is obtained by means of identical questions asked of each student. The *nondirected interview* is usually not designed to obtain answers to specific questions, but rather to permit the student to express himself freely on subjects that concern him. This technique is particularly useful in revealing a student's problems or grievances.

In planning his interview schedule, the coordinator should determine the school days most convenient for his students. If necessary, he should project the interview schedule over the total length of the cooperative school period in order to include all of his students. And—most important—he must try to allot sufficient interview time for *all* students, not just those with special problems. Students can be informed of the time and place of their interviews by postcards, class notices, interview schedules on bulletin boards outside the office, or by telephone or telegraph.

COUNSELING THEORY AND PROCEDURES. Counseling is the core of the cooperative education program. Follow-up activities after placement necessitate some type of student counseling by the coordinator. In addition, students need counseling to help them make sound career plans, and to help them generally in their educational, vocational, and personal development.

There are basically two kinds of counseling—directive and nondirective. The difference between the two is primarily one of degree rather than kind. In directive counseling, the counselor assumes a more dominant role in planning, arranging, analyzing, and treating the problem; the nondirective approach is strictly client- or student-centered. The counselor plays a more passive role and does not attempt to solve the student's problem. If a student is merely seeking confirmation for his own solution to a problem, a more direct approach may be used. However, if a student seems confused, upset, or frustrated about a particular problem, then a nondirect approach may be more effective.

Generally speaking, the coordinator should not make the student's decision. Nevertheless, many students come to the coordinator with urgent problems that demand immediate solutions. In such cases, the coordinator cannot spend extensive time helping the student arrive at his own decision. There is as much danger of error in his being too passive as there is in his being domineering or autocratic. The coordinator must be flexible in his approach and adapt his counseling methods in accordance with the particular situation. There is no general procedure that is applicable for all students. The essence of counseling is to do what needs to be done to assist the student.

USE OF PSYCHOLOGICAL TESTS. The coordinator should have some knowledge of the various psychological tests that can be useful in the selection and placement process as well as in career planning. He can then, when appropriate, suggest to a student the need for testing as another diagnostic tool to help him solve a particular personal, vocational, or educational problem.

Most cooperative colleges and universities have as one of their student personnel services a testing and counseling center, which serves primarily as a referral agency for all departments. The coordinator should not refer his students to the center merely as an escape mechanism or cure-all for his placement problems; nor should he consider testing a substitute for other selection and placement procedures. No matter how valuable tests may be, they should never be used as the only method of selection; for they are more meaningful when considered as part of the total framework of pertinent information available for the individual student. Therefore, testing should supplement, not replace, other appraisal techniques.

USE OF RECORDS AND REPORTS. A good system of records is essential to the effective operation of a cooperative program. Accurate and up-to-date records carefully interpreted and evaluated will serve as an important source of information for activity reports, fiscal reports, and student cumulative-data files. Records also serve as valuable instruments for evaluating the present status of the cooperative program, predicting future expansion, and providing useful research material. Coordinators must share the responsibility for accurate office information by keeping their own individual records.

Daily, weekly, monthly, and annual records and reports as well as other pertinent material may be classified as student records, coordinator's records, departmental records and reports, and correspondence.

Cumulative records on students should be clear, up to date, accurate, and readily accessible to facilitate immediate use. The cumulative record about each student should include information about his personal background; standardized test scores, if available; grades; employer's evaluation forms; and teaching faculty and/or coordinator's merit ratings. The coordinator's records should include an active listing of the students in both divisions under his jurisdiction.

In addition, a central file (departmental records) should be maintained on all active cooperative companies. This file should include the name, address, and telephone number of each company; the name and title of the coordinator's contact; the names, year in school, major, and employment dates of the students in both divisions employed with each company; and the job description, hours, and wage rate. Departmental reports include *activity reports* (daily or weekly reports by the coordinator on the number of students interviewed, placed, laid off, or unemployed) and *fiscal reports* (records accounting for funds received and amounts expended for such items as salaries, supplies, equipment, travel, telephone, and postage).

Finally, all correspondence relative to cooperative education should be filed in the cooperative department office. Correspondence from prospective employers regarding job requisitions should be shared by other staff personnel unless a particular coordinator is already handling the company.

USE OF OCCUPATIONAL INFORMATION. As a placement counselor, the coordinator needs a good knowledge of local, regional, and national opportunities for training and employment in the academic fields of his students. He should be familiar with current major sources of published materials on occupational information. In addition, he should have a working knowledge of the related competencies needed in the area of occupational information: the classification of the world of work; the effects of socioeconomic changes; training and placement facilities; collection, evaluation, abstracting, and filing of occupational materials; and use of occupational information with individuals as part of the counseling interview or with groups of students.

USE OF SCHOOL AND COMMUNITY RESOURCES. The effectiveness of the coordinator depends in part upon his knowledge and use of school and community resources to supplement his own counseling. As a *referral agent,* he must be familiar with other departments, in the educational institution and in the community, which serve the needs of the students—vocational, educational, social, health, and other similar needs. He should also be familiar with the functions of such other student personnel services as, the registrar's office, admissions office, financial aid, housing, health services, library, and student activities.

USE OF COMPUTERS. As the size of a cooperative program increases, institutions will find that the computer can provide valuable assistance to the operation of the program. Computer programs used by several schools in their placement processes have greatly enhanced the efficiency and effectiveness of their coordination staffs.

For many years, college and university registrars have used the computer to keep track of enrolled students. Their records identify each student by name and identification number. They show the major course of study each student is pursuing, and they include the student's expected year of graduation. The student's home address, local address, grades and accumulated credits, and grade-point average are also included in the record. More sophisticated programs may include admissions information, such as name and address of parents, high school attended, class rank, and psychological test scores. In a parallel manner, the department of cooperative education can keep track of cooperative placements and student progress on the cooperative program. Useful information would be the name and address of the company at which the student is working, the type of activity in which this company is engaged, the type of job that the student holds, his rate of pay, and starting and ending dates of each assignment. Employer ratings of the student could be included, as well as a grade or rating on the success or failure of the cooperative experience by the student's coordinator.

Information about cooperative employers and students employed should be recorded so that it can be manipulated and retrieved in various forms. Each company at which students are employed should be assigned an identification number so that a list of students working at each company can be printed. Postal zip codes in the company addresses provide geographical distribution of placements. The *Standard Industrial Classification Manual,* published by the U.S. Bureau of the Budget, and *The Directory of Occupational Titles,* published by the Federal Security Agency, provide identifying numbers for company activity and for job titles respectively. Also, cooperative rates of various companies and rates paid all students or designated subgroups of students may be averaged and reported.

Another way in which a computer might be used to assist a cooperative education program is in the maintenance of a job bank. As each cooperative opportunity becomes available, pertinent information regarding the opening can be coded and stored in the computer. Type of job, location, rate of pay, and necessary qualifications of applicants might be included. Periodic review of the recorded openings is essential. A system would have to be devised to keep the bank current, so that openings no longer available can be removed immediately.

A school fortunate enough to have a large number of placement opportunities in a computer with time-sharing capability could have a terminal located in the cooperative education office. This would permit almost instantaneous access to possible openings for coordinators and students. A more practical method, however, would be to ask for a list of the jobs on file to be printed out on a daily or weekly schedule.

Computers can also be very useful when used directly in the placement process. After a series of interviews between companies and students, the desires of each party must be matched, so that both the company and the student are satisfied. Through a series of interviews, employers and students express their choices for each other on a graduated scale. Trying to get the optimum match between students and companies when large numbers of each are involved becomes a difficult task unless it is done by the computer.

Recruiting Employers

In general, employers are favorably disposed toward the utilization of cooperative students. This does not mean that all suitable cooperative jobs for students are easy to obtain or that the coordinator does not have to sell the program vigorously in locating certain specific opportunities. Always the goal is to have the right job for the right student at the right time and in the right location. At times the coordinator of students majoring in a particular field of study may be forced to decline the opportunities presented by some employers in one area while at the same time trying to interest the same types of employers in another location. For example, there may be opportunities for majors in journalism in Boston, but the students majoring in this field may wish to be placed in the Washington area. Similarly, the job openings may be in the wrong vocational field in a particular location.

There may be opportunities for marketing majors in New York, but the available New York students are majoring in electrical engineering.

The receptivity of employers can be encouraged and enhanced by the fair administration of rules and regulations concerning the conduct of the program. Employers will be interested in continuity of service, and the college administration must recognize this fact. Students cannot be left free to come and go on their job assignments. In the final analysis the faculty coordinator must be responsible not only for the assignments of students but also for shifts of employment and for terminations. He must not begin a program with a new employer unless there is a strong likelihood that a continuous supply of students can be maintained over a reasonable period of time. If not, the situation must be made clear to the employer before the first placement is consummated. The good will of employers is essential to the growth and development of a cooperative program.

On the other hand, students cannot be sacrificed to preserve good relations with employers. The coordinator faces the difficult task of treading the thin line between the students, who frequently are impatient for change and advancement, and the employers, who desire stability and continuity. The proper balance will allow the students sufficient flexibility to accomplish their educational objectives while at the same time building friendly and lasting relationships with employers. Interestingly enough, when this is done, the satisfied employers will become the best salesmen for the program in their meetings and discussions with other employers.

There are several advantages to an employer in adopting the cooperative program. The program is an effective recruiting device. As mentioned, employers who utilize the cooperative program for this purpose are very much concerned with continuity and retention of students. To aid and encourage this retention, elaborate training programs are established which can contribute immeasurably to the education of the student. Progressive experience and increasing responsibility are the core of the program. Students are integrated into the company, and an attempt is made to make them part of the company family. Obviously, these training programs are best suited for students who have a clear picture of their vocational goal. Also, these programs are frequently available only to the better students, since the employers are hiring on a long-range basis and show a great concern for quality as exemplified by scholastic achievement. Cooperative relationships based on a recruiting motivation are perhaps the easiest to find, since most large corporations are interested in this approach. Elaborate training programs may be difficult to maintain, however, due to the changeability of students and the high requirements for participation set by the employers.

The coordinator probably will be most successful in finding cooperative assignments if he can interest the employer in utilizing an alternating pair of cooperative students in a regular semiprofessional position, which would have to be filled by full-time employees if cooperative students were not available. Commonly the job involves duties that fall between the capabilities of the high school graduate and the capabilities of the college graduate. If the employer attempts to use college graduates on the work, they soon become disgruntled and unhappy because the work is too routine for their talents. On the other hand, the employer can use high school or technical school graduates after supplying them with some training, but they frequently terminate when they see that a college degree is necessary for future advancement. Cooperative students are an excellent source of manpower to fill these positions. They are eager to succeed, since they are striving for a goal and the job serves as a stepping-stone toward this objective. They bring enthusiasm to the job, since to them it is an opportunity to learn. The employer's turnover problem is solved when the cooperative institution maintains a flow of personnel to ensure continuity. Everyone gains—the employer, the student, and the university.

Coordinators may stimulate an employer to create a new position in his organization for cooperative students. The employer will do this if he believes that the venture would either be more profitable or result in greater efficiency—as it probably would, for instance, if the employer has professional personnel in his organization who spend a great deal of time on subprofessional duties or on "chore work." The employer must be convinced that by hiring a pair of cooperative students to handle this subprofessional work, he can free his high-priced professional personnel to spend their time on more suitable and productive efforts. Drafting, calculating, sorting, checking, and many clerical functions fall into this category of subprofessional work. All are tasks that can be handled with ease and enthusiasm by students.

Finally, a coordinator might be able to motivate some employers by appealing to their professional responsibility. The case is made that successful professional people have always provided training for young aspirants, so that the profession will continue in quality and substance. This logic has its appeal in some special circumstances, such as consulting engineering firms, law offices, libraries, hospitals, and educational institutions.

LOCATION OF SCHOOL. Naturally, the location of the institution has a profound effect upon the recruitment of assignments for students. The institution located in an urban setting and surrounded by a busy economic community will generally have an easier time in locating assignments than the institution situated in a rural setting. Many fine cooperative assignments will be located within commuting distance of the school. This makes control of the program much easier, since coordinators can readily visit employers to handle any troublesome situation that may arise quickly and without warning. Coordinator loads can be larger in the urban setting, since large amounts of time are not consumed by traveling to visit employers; also, travel costs for the coordinator are lower, since few overnight trips are necessary.

Student housing will be affected by the introduction of the cooperative program, and the type of effect depends on the local situation. Many students in urban schools will need housing in university facilities during their work periods as well as during school periods. This is fine if there is a surplus of campus housing and the cooperative program generates more students to fill what would have been empty halls. If housing is in short supply, then the cooperative program is no advantage at all.

In general, when the student must live away from home and the campus during a work period, he is responsible for locating his own housing. Certainly the coordinator may introduce him to other students who live in that area, so that his entrance into the new community is eased. Also, many employers give help in locating suitable living accommodations. Some cooperative schools have set up student housing in distant locations where they have a reasonable concentration of students on assignments. However, this arrangement can be expensive for the institution; and in this day of increasing freedom for students in selecting living accommodations even on campus, it is not looked upon favorably by most students. If such housing is to be economically self-sufficient, the facility must be kept close to full, thus causing the administration to exert some pressure on students to use the facility.

The rural institution may have more problems with parental restrictions than does the urban cooperative institution, particularly if the cooperative program is optional for students. Many times a student finds excitement in the challenge of living in an entirely new environment only to have his parents refuse to allow him to participate in the program if he must live away from home and the campus. This tends to be particularly true for the parents of girls. The urban institution has less of a problem since many positions are close to the school and the student can either commute from home or live in university housing.

In some urban settings, the cooperative program has been used as a community resource in attracting business and industry to locate in the area. In this connection it tends to move bright and able young people into the local employment market, and many are retained on a permanent basis after graduation.

Some institutions are set in a rural area, where there is no short- or long-range possibility for professional employment. Here, the cooperative program opens new horizons for the students by sending them on assignments away from the local area.

For many students the earnings on paid jobs under the cooperative program are a vital source of funds. The location of the school, the cooperative assignment, and the student's home all have an influence on the amount of money that can be saved toward educational costs. The greatest financial advantage for the student is achieved when he is able to commute to an urban institution for his classroom work and commute to his job assignment. In this way his living costs are held to a minimum because his family continues to provide room and board. The least financial advantage is available to the student who attends an institution at a considerable distance from home and who also must live away from home during his work assignment. He must then pay for his room and board for virtually the entire calendar year. Various other combinations yield intermediate results in financial gain, depending on the specific conditions.

JOB PROMOTION. Cooperative job promotion should be planned in relation to the needs and qualifications of the students seeking employment. The coordinator must have a good idea of the personal background and range of ability of the students under his jurisdiction before he can intelligently sell their services to prospective employers. The coordinator obtains his information by conducting preliminary screening interviews with his students prior to their employment.

SOURCES OF JOBS. The coordinator must know the labor market. In conducting a market survey, he might first of all consult the following sources:

United States Census report *invaluable indicator of the industrial and occupational distribution of the gainfully employed and unemployed in given geographic areas as well as a description of population trends.*

Help-wanted advertisements *good source of leads for potential cooperative employment.*

Special news items *information about new organizations being formed, branch offices being opened, and promotions and changes of personnel being made.*

Classified telephone directory *an indication of the number and variety of business activities in the community.*

Trade and association journals *information pertaining to the general situation in a specific vocational area.*

Business and product directories *detailed lists of companies, products, and personnel in different geographic locations.*

The coordinator should consider all sources and facts that may reveal potential cooperative job opportunities. Students will sometimes furnish job leads to the coordinator in his office. Another source of leads is the senior recruiting program conducted in most colleges and universities. Although company representatives are primarily interested in recruiting seniors for postgraduate employment, the coordinator may recommend to a few selected recruiters the institution's cooperative program as an undergraduate recruiting tool.

TYPES OF PLACEMENT. The coordinator must exercise a great deal of judgment in screening the group of employers to be contacted. Large companies are likely to have more potential job openings than small firms, but they may not have the best job assignments. Companies with a high turnover rate usually have more job openings than those where employment is more stable. In general, employers who pay low wages do not warrant intensive solicitation because their jobs are difficult to fill. Although the coordinator should concentrate on year-round jobs, certain seasonal jobs may be helpful as one-term openings. The coordinator should avoid intensive solicitation of the small family-operated type of firms.

Business, industry, and the professions have need for student trainees at all levels of ability and ambition. Since the coordinator must eventually place his students in these jobs, he should solicit a wide variety of jobs, ranging from entry jobs to training programs, to provide the best possible experiences for his students in accordance with their interests, aptitudes, and abilities.

The coordinator's primary task is to find positions that contain educational value for his students rather than high-paying positions. However, students tend to be more attracted by the salary than the educational aspects of the job; and the coordinator must attempt to get them to look at the long-range benefits of a particular experience.

JOB-DEVELOPMENT TECHNIQUES. The personal visit is unquestionably the best method for coordinators to establish rapport and elicit cooperation from the employer. (Only if a personal visit to the company is not possible should the coordinator use a mail campaign or telephone solicitation.) The size of the company and the position of the person to be contacted should be the deciding factors in whether to make an appointment or to call on a hit-or-miss basis. Another determining factor is whether the coordinator is making *saturation visits* (random calls concentrated in a specific location) or making *precision calls* (prearranged, scheduled calls in a specific location).

Usually the coordinator should contact top management first regarding an initial company visit. After he gains support from top management, he will more readily be able to establish the necessary rapport at the personnel department level for an effective working relationship. During the interview the coordinator must sell the employer on the idea of using an alternating pair of students on a regular job assignment within his organization. As mentioned, he can best do so by pointing out the *profitability* and greater *efficiency* of using the student trainees to do more routine assignments, thus releasing high-paid employees for more challenging work; or he might mention the opportunity to recruit potential long-term employees.

It is important for the coordinator to be as knowledgeable as possible about general company facts—type of business, size, credit rating, and location. This information is available in directories. In the initial interview, the coordinator should obtain from the employer specific information about the business, the number of employees by job classification, the existing employment and training practices, and the possibilities of the cooperative institution's helping the employer with his present or future employment needs.

In interviewing the employer regarding salaries, the coordinator should attempt to get him to state a starting figure first, so that it can be compared with the going rate in the particular field in the area. If necessary, the coordinator can then suggest a change to a more competitive figure. If the employer cannot state a rate, the coordinator must be prepared to do so.

The cooperative student should be paid the same rate as a full-time employee with similar background and experience for a particular job. Generally speaking, cooperative salary rates range between the going rate for inexperienced employees in a particular field and the basic starting rate for a recent college graduate entering the same field. The average cooperative salaries of engineering, science, and business administration majors are usually higher than those of students majoring in liberal arts and education.

At the conclusion of the interview, the coordinator should leave his card, a school catalog, a brochure describing the cooperative program, and an operational calendar showing the specific "changeover" dates.

TYPES OF ASSIGNMENTS. Cooperative assignments as paying positions with various type of employers generally fall into one of four categories—formal, semiformal, or informal training programs or just plain jobs.

The objective of a formal training program is after-graduation employment of the participating students. The company is highly selective in its choice of students and usually requests the coordinator to screen potential applicants and to set up a schedule to give the company representative an opportunity to interview eligible students on campus. The program usually consists of scheduled rotational work assignments in competitive, realistic work situations to provide the student trainee with increasing responsibility and progressive job experiences in different departments of the company. The nature of the cooperative assignment depends chiefly on the student's educational background, vocational interests, and career objectives, and on employment needs of the company.

The objective of the semiformal training program is also after-graduation employment. The company again is selective and may request the privilege of recruiting qualified student applicants on campus. The program emphasizes flexibility because the rotational work assignments are only partially laid out in advance. Therefore, the students are not informed in advance what their future cooperative assignments will be with the company. In this case also, the nature of cooperative assignments depends chiefly upon the student's educational background, vocational interest, and career objectives, and on the employment needs of the company.

As with the other training programs, the objective of the informal training program is usually after-graduation employment of the students in the program. The company is selective but will probably never request recruiting privileges on campus. The program is not planned in advance. Diversified on-the-job training for each student is predicated on the company's immediate employment needs and the ability of each individual student. Progress may vary for different students employed with the company.

In providing jobs, rather than a training program, the employer seldom has after-graduation employment as a primary objective. He may try to be selective, but will usually accept direct referrals from the coordinator. The jobs range from entry jobs to semiprofessional assignments. Students perform a specific job function that is necessary to the day-to-day operation of the business. Since advancement opportunities are quite limited, students usually request a job change after one or two work periods.

Basic Elements in Placement

The placement activities of the coordinator include the conduct of some form of group orientation program and individual preliminary or screening interviews with his students, the making of division assignments, and the conduct of follow-up activities with both students and employers.

PREPLACEMENT ACTIVITIES. Practically all cooperative institutions employ some form of group orientation program to inform students about the rationale of cooperative education as well as the specific rules and regulations governing the administration and operation of their programs. These orientation meetings range in length from a minimum of three or four hours to regular sessions extending over a full quarter or semester. A few institutions conduct a formal group guidance class on cooperative education with the emphasis on career-planning information.

Since the extent and methodology of instruction vary considerably, the following four-session orientation program with suggested topics should serve as a basic guideline for the preparation of students to make an effective transition from the academic community to the employing community.

In the *first session,* the coordinator should emphasize the purpose and objectives of the orientation program, including a brief description of the topics to be covered in subsequent sessions. Institutions with a large enrollment may use this session to explain the purpose of the student application form and to have the students fill one out with the supervision of the coordinator. Cooperative education materials—describing the institution's policies, rules and regulations governing student participation in the program—also should be distributed to the students.

The *second session* should include a discussion of the rationale of cooperative education and the importance of career planning. The coordinator should explain the institution's philosophy of cooperative education, with special emphasis on the advantages to students. In explaining the importance of career planning to his students, the coordinator should stress that developing a functional career plan is no small task because the student will have to face himself more realistically than he had ever thought possible. He should further emphasize that career planning becomes a part of the student's total life adjustment.

Topics for the *third session* should include a description of the types of cooperative assignments, tips for job success, and the placement process. The coordinator should describe the nature and scope of the cooperative assignments without attempting to oversell or glamorize the job descriptions. Emphasis should be placed on the educational values of these cooperative assignments, not the monetary gain. In his discussion of job success, the coordinator should explain the role of the student in cooperative education. He should point out ways in which his students can obtain, hold, and succeed on their cooperative assignments. The coordinator should carefully explain the placement process to his students, so that they will be more knowledgeable about the importance and significance of the screening, selection, and placement interviews. Special emphasis should be placed on the need for flexibilty in placement because of the many variables—human as well as mechanical.

The *fourth session* should be devoted to a discussion of the rules and regulations governing student participation in the cooperative program, the employer's evaluation of the student, and the cooperative work report. The coordinator should point out to his students the importance of rules and regulations, including penalties for infractions, by emphasizing that the administration and operation of an effective cooperative program requires an adequate control system to ensure harmony and to protect the vested interests of all the participants in the program. The coordinator should emphasize that the employer's evaluation of the student is a valuable tool in the guidance and counseling process, since these evaluations often concern the personal, educational, and vocational development of students. The coordinator should conclude the orientation session by explaining that the required formal written cooperative work report will give each student a valuable opportunity to gain the maximum experience from his cooperative assignment.

Immediately after the group orientation program, the coordinator should schedule preliminary interviews with his students to review their application forms. Since this is the first formal interview for each student with his coordinator, the coordinator must try to develop a permissive avenue of communication. Information from the student's application form, grade record, and test results (if available) should be used as tools by the coordinator to make an initial appraisal of the student's qualifications for cooperative employment. Since this is a career-probing type of interview, the particular areas of interest to the coordinator are the student's interests, aptitudes, abilities, and personality traits; personal history; previous work experience, including part-time work; extracurricular activities; academic subjects liked and disliked; special skills for employment use; choice of major field; job preferences and aspirations; division preference; ultimate vocational objective; reasons for choosing the cooperative plan; philosophy of life; and attitudes and opinions about self, school, and work.

The coordinator should record the results of each interview as soon as possible after the completion of the interview. He should note particularly how each student conducted himself during the interview, with special emphasis on the following factors: appearance; degree of maturity; personality traits; poise; and peculiarities of speech, manner, and movement. The coordinator should record any other pertinent observations made during the interview, including his opinion regarding the student's "placeability" in the cooperative program.

Depending upon the institution's particular eligibility requirements for student participation in the cooperative program, the coordinator should consider the following factors in making division assignments:

Student's preference *Each student, during his initial interview with his coordinator, should be given an opportunity to express his division preference and the reasons for his choice. The coordinator, however, should inform each student that, although his division choice will be carefully considered, there is no guarantee that it will be granted.*

Imbalance *The coordinator should consider his present balance of upperclassmen before making division assignments for new entrants. Because of attrition among his upper-class students, the coordinator may have to assign additional entrants to a particular division in order to maintain a more even distribution between the two divisions.*

Academic standing *The coordinator should not assign all of his better students and/or all of his marginal students to one particular division. He must make an educated guess about the attrition possibilities of his marginal students and divide these students in the hope that the attrition rate will be about the same in the two divisions.*

Job locations and timing *The coordinator needs to consider the fact that he may have some good jobs which are difficult to fill because of their location. Therefore, he must constantly look for qualified and interested students who live near these specific job locations and assign them to divisions according to the timing of the job openings.*

Geographical locations of students *The coordinator should be careful not to assign all students who live in the same town to the same division. These students often know each other and will try to convince the coordinator that they should be placed in the same division in order to maintain their peer-group friendships during their school years. However, the coordinator must consider the operation of his program and explain to these students the necessity for maintaining two-man teams in all geographic areas to ensure continuity of employment.*

Extracurricular activities *The coordinator should give careful consideration to the division preferences of students who participate in sports and other extracurricular activities. He should make every effort to assign these students to division assignments which most closely coincide with the timing of the particular student activity.*

PLACEMENT ACTIVITIES. The success or failure of the school's cooperative program depends on how well the needs and interests of the students are satisfied and on how well the job needs of the employer are met. Unless good selection is emphasized, employers will lack confidence in the institution's program, and ultimately they may lose faith in the overall system.

The primary purpose of the selection interview is to obtain further information from the student—information that will enable the coordinator and the student to decide on the best cooperative assignment for the student. Although the coordinator has recorded information from the preliminary interview with the student, he should verify the information recorded on the student's application form concerning personal history, education and training, previous work experience, choice of division assignment, choice of major, vocational objective, and type and location of cooperative job assignment; request additional information, if necessary; and determine through further questioning whether the student is qualified for and is interested in a particular cooperative assignment.

Since the selection interview is essentially an exploratory device, the coordinator should appraise the student in the light of what he is and what potential he has for advancement. In addition, the coordinator should attempt to project the student into the working environment by asking himself these questions: Will he perform well on the job? Will he be interested in the work and satisfied with the working environment? Has he growth potential on the job? Does the job fit the abilities and aptitudes of the student and coincide with his interests and career plans?

During the course of the selection interview, the student should not be told too much about a specific job until the coordinator is convinced that the job assignment basically meets the student's needs, qualifications, and future career plans. If the student is given all the information about a particular job first, he might, in his anxiety, make a hasty decision that would not be in his best interests. Therefore, the coordinator should not intentionally or inadvertently compound the problem of selection and placement, creating more troubles for himself and his students.

The placement or referral interview is a discussion of the job description, hours, wage rate, advancement possibilities, fringe benefits (if any), the student's obligations in accepting the cooperative assignment, referral instructions regarding the student's interview with the prospective employer, and subsequent follow-up procedures pertaining to the placement outcome. In addition to supplying the student with the basic referral information, the coordinator should also give the student some helpful suggestions on how to conduct himself in the employment interview to improve his chances of obtaining the job.

Failure of the coordinator to provide his students with dependable information about the employers and employment conditions may result in serious placement problems. Therefore, it is the responsibility of the coordinator to make available to his students up-to-date information regarding working conditions, personnel policies, wage rates, working hours, fringe benefits, and opportunities for advancement.

At the completion of the placement interview, the student is given an *agreement form* to fill out and a *card of introduction* to the employer. The primary purpose of the agreement is to ensure a mutual understanding between the student and the department of cooperative education that the student is to continue on the cooperative assignment until transferred by the coordinator or released by the employer.

The card of introduction, which is a postal card, provides the name and address of the employing organization as well as the name and position of the company representative who is to interview the cooperative student; introduces and identifies the student applicant to the employer; and provides the employer with a form for reporting the results of the interview to the department of cooperative education.

From the coordinator's viewpoint, the number of referrals he makes depends upon his student work load, the time available, and the number and types of job openings to be filled. With the exception of training programs and other similar competitive opportunities, which require multiple referrals, the coordinator should as a general rule consider a *single student referral for a single job opening.* An employment interview should be required for each student on the job site so as to discourage the practice of "blind employment hiring." It is recommended that each student have only one job interview at a time and not be considering a number of cooperative job opportunities at the same time.

FOLLOW-UP ACTIVITIES. Effective follow-up by the coordinator requires contact with both employers and students. This means that the coordinator must make regularly scheduled personal visits to the employers of his students as well as to conduct follow-up interviews with his students after each work period. The purposes for employer visits are to obtain first-hand knowledge of the types of jobs in which his students are engaged; to see that these jobs meet the specific requirements for cooperative work assignments; to obtain progress reports on each student's job performance for counseling purposes; to obtain for record purposes up-to-date information about job descriptions, qualifications needed, working hours, wage rates, and other related company facts; to uncover job openings as well as to suggest expanding the program; to promote good public relations and rapport with employers for the growth and development of cooperative education; to inform employers of any change of status of a student employee regarding his grades, change of major, change of career plans, and to give the employer any feedback information from the student (unless confidential) regarding his feelings about his job, dissatisfaction about his performance report, or after-graduation plans (if applicable); to obtain information from the employer about any pending change in his use of the cooperative plan; and to render such effective service that the employer will wish to maintain student employment at full strength during slow business periods.

The timing of follow-up visits is most important. The coordinator should allow enough time for the employer to evaluate the students and, in turn, for the students to appraise their jobs. For entry jobs, the inquiry may be made approximately two weeks after placement. For training programs, follow-up may be deferred until a month or six weeks after placement. In general, the coordinator should average a minimum of one visit to each local company during a quarter or semester, and at least one visit a year to his out-of-state employers. Although the coordinator must keep in mind the importance of follow-up visits, he must also be careful not to wear out his welcome at the companies he is serving.

To complete successfully the follow-up process of tracing the outcome of each act of placement, the coordinator must conduct post-referral interviews with his students upon their return to campus after each work term. The basic purposes of these interviews are to confirm or reappraise each student's qualifications in light of the employer's evaluation report as well as the coordinator's evaluation based on personal visits to each student's employer, to discuss the student's cooperative work report, and to elicit the student's opinions and comments about his cooperative assignment.

Special Problems in Placement

Certain special placement problems will require the coordinator's sympathetic understanding and best judgment as well as his patience and self-control. The following examples illustrate some of these special problems.

ATHLETES. Since most cooperative institutions operate an elective or optional cooperative program, student athletes can be restricted to the conventional program. However, when athletes do participate in the cooperative program, the coordinator must keep in mind that the athletic department is primarily interested in producing good representative athletic teams rather than a cooperative program. As previously indicated, the coordinator should assign each athlete to a division which enables him to be in school at the same time as the particular sport's activity. The coordinator should place athletes on cooperative assignments where neither the location nor the working hours will conflict with practice sessions. If necessary, athletes can be placed on campus jobs in various academic and administrative departments or in the maintenance department, the library, the cafeteria, or in laboratories.

FOREIGN STUDENTS. Foreign students pose an especially difficult placement problem. Many employers are reluctant to accept them although they offer no specific reason why. Where reasons are given they include: language or accent problems; the fact that the student does not plan to remain for permanent employment, thus reducing the recruiting aspect of cooperative education; security clearance, which bars many foreign students from coop positions with employers having federal contracts; and the fact that federal agencies do not accept foreign coop students, and state and local government agencies tend to follow suit.

The foreign student may have reasons that make his placement difficult as well, including: lack of transportation; fear of being alone in a community; inability to get the food that he believes he requires; religious reasons; lack of social life available in the area of the coop assignment.

MARGINAL STUDENTS. Although some students may be scholastically marginal, they may possess qualities which in large measure compensate for their low grades. It is usually advisable to place them on jobs suited to their capacity. Sometimes these students try to monopolize most of the coordinator's time with their problems. The coordinator should be fair but firm in his counseling approach, because he must help these students realize that their marginal status precludes their being considered for more challenging cooperative assignments.

MARRIED STUDENTS. Since the married student does not always have the same degree of mobility as the single student, the coordinator may be hard-pressed to find suitable cooperative employment reasonably close to the student's place of residence. The coordinator will also find it difficult to control the problem of salary rates for married students. As previously indicated, most employers pay the same going rate for cooperative students as they do for full-time employees with similar qualifications for a particular job. In addition, they do not usually differentiate between married and single students in the matter of salary. Therefore, the coordinator must keep in mind that the employer is primarily interested in whether the student has the necessary qualifications for a particular job, not in his marital status.

WOMEN STUDENTS. Women students enrolled in cooperative education programs need to realize that they are, for a number of reasons, sometimes restricted in job placement. Sometimes lack of transportation, poor housing, poor street lighting, or undesirable hours may make the placement of a woman on the job unwise. Pregnancy sometimes interrupts a woman's academic career; and although day-care centers are on the increase, they are not yet generally available. (The advantages and disadvantages to women in cooperative education are discussed more fully in Chapter 18.)

UNPLACED STUDENTS. For those institutions with mandatory cooperative programs, it is not unusual to have cooperative students who are not placed on cooperative assignments during any one particular work period. There are several reasons for this situation, such as labor-market conditions, health problems, scholastic difficulties, and unwillingness on the part of some students to accept available placement. Since there is no full-time option for students enrolled in a mandatory cooperative program, these problems become more difficult for the coordinator to handle. However, one cooperative institution with a mandatory program has established a Division C classification, which permits these unplaced students to have temporary full-time status until their problems have been solved.

NO VOCATIONAL CHOICE. Since all students are searching for self-realization and direction, most of them understandably have made no definite decisions about their vocational choice. There are also many students who are uncertain about their vocational choice, while others have made an unwise choice. The coordinator should understand that many students with vocational problems really have primarily personal problems (emotional, social, health, or financial) which frequently must be solved before any real progress can be made in the choice of a career. These students, who represent all levels of ability, usually worry a great deal about little things and consequently compound the placement problem by assuming too much or by manufacturing problems that do not exist. Therefore, these students are likely to refuse several cooperative assignments without substantial reason. To help alleviate this situation, the coordinator should attempt to determine what occupations the student has considered and the reasons for each choice; what occupations the student may have rejected and why; the extent of the student's vocational experience and his attitude toward this work experience; the implications and significance of his hobbies, interests, and extracurricular activities in school. The coordinator also should try to help the student understand the reasoning behind the "matching process" in the placement function. Coordinators must not attempt to solve all personal and emotional problems of students.

PHYSICALLY AND EMOTIONALLY HANDICAPPED STUDENTS. The coordinator must exercise sound judgment and discretion in the placement of physically or emotionally handicapped students. He must be sympathetic but, at the same time, realistic about their problems. Some of the more common disabilities the coordinator may encounter are poor vision, poor hearing, loss of limb, speech defect, and paralysis. The coordinator should be especially aware that some of these students have an accompanying emotional problem, which is frequently more difficult to handle than their physical handicap. The coordinator should refer such cases to the health services of the institution. Because of the necessity to qualify by physical examination for company training programs, many handicapped students may be rejected for employment. Speech difficulties may also cause placement problems because the student does not have a chance to make a good impression in the employment interview. Although more employers are beginning to realize the advantages of hiring the handicapped, it is still the responsibility of the coordinator to do an excellent selling job in order to get employers to hire these students. It is suggested that the coordinator approach those cooperative employers with whom he has excellent rapport before contacting new ones.

TRANSFER STUDENTS. Since transfer students have varying types and amounts of advanced-standing credits, integration into the curriculum of their choice with new classmates sometimes becomes a particular problem. While these students may enjoy the status of upperclassmen, they are nevertheless new students to the cooperative institution. Therefore, orientation becomes essential for these students if they are to make a good personal and educational adjustment to the institution's policies, rules, and regulations. It is further important that they understand the rationale of cooperative education as well as the basic administrative and operating requirements governing student participation in the program. From a placement standpoint, these students often become a problem to the coordinator because they have not had initial cooperative employment experience from which they can direct subsequent cooperative experience in accordance with their needs, qualifications, and career plans.

PROBLEMS WITH UNIONS. The coordinator should be as objective as possible about any union influence on employment practices which might affect his cooperative students. Following are illustrations of typical problems which the coordinator might encounter: (1) A student who is working in a production job as part of his cooperative training may be requested by union officials to join the union. (2) A student may be asked to cross the picket line during a strike. (3) A student desires cooperative employment with a union and is first required to join.

It is recommended that the coordinator permit the student to make his own decision in such cases. Since these matters concern the student and the company, the cooperative institution should not intercede except to protect the student if necessary. If the student does not wish to be involved in any union dealings, the coordinator should inform the employer of the student's feelings. If the employer cannot help the student, the coordinator should release the student and place him in another cooperative assignment.

Program Supervision

The coordinator will soon realize that it is not easy to find and to maintain cooperative jobs for his students unless he can make some assurances to employers. Since, as already emphasized, employers will be most interested in continuity of service, those responsible for the administration and operation of the cooperative program should establish and maintain an adequate control system (rules and regulations) to ensure harmony among school officials, employers, and students, and to protect the vested interests of all the participants in the program. These rules and regulations are frequently unilateral in that they impose certain restrictions on students without imposing similar ones on cooperative employers. At the same time, the coordinator should make every effort to ensure that the employer, in looking after his own immediate employment needs, does not sacrifice educational values and does not expect the cooperative institution to sacrifice the student in order to preserve good employment relations.

Generally speaking, the coordinator should not make coop arrangements with a new employer unless there is a reasonable chance of maintaining job coverage for at least a year. In addition, he should keep in mind the employer's need for continuity of service when he is attempting to adjust job assignments for his students, who are frequently seeking change and advancement. Therefore, the cooperative rules and regulations must ensure some reasonable measure of continuity for the employer and still permit adequate flexibility so that the student can be transferred from an entry job to a job situation that provides him with greater responsibilities and educational development.

RULES AND REGULATIONS. Following are some basic rules and regulations that are essential for effective program administration and operation:

Eligibility requirements *Student eligibility for participation in the cooperative program is dependent on the type of program offered by the institution*–mandatory *or* elective. *See Chapter 3.*

Graduation requirement *Although most cooperative institutions do not grant academic credit for cooperative work experience, they do consider successful performance a graduation requirement. Each work period must be completed to the satisfaction of the department of cooperative education. Therefore, the cooperative student must have a satisfactory employment record as well as a satisfactory academic record in order to graduate.*

Cooperative agreement *All cooperative students must sign with the coordinator an agreement to continue on the job assigned* until released *by the coordinator or dismissed by the employer. The agreement should be between the student and the cooperative institution, not with the employer. Contracts with the employers to retain students in their employ are neither necessary nor desirable.*

Adjustment of job assignment *Students must be informed that all co-operative assignments belong to the institution. Therefore, students accepting them are not at liberty to terminate them or dispose of them as they choose. Students must also understand that requests concerning change of cooperative assignment, rate of pay, hours of work, leave of absence from work, participation in student activities while employed, or other related matters must be made through the Department of Cooperative Education rather than directly with the cooperative employer.*

"Own" jobs *Under certain conditions a student may be permitted to obtain his own cooperative employment instead of an assigned job by the coordinator. Before accepting a job on his own, the student should petition his coordinator for approval. Approval of a student's own job must be based on* two *prerequisites: the job must meet the same standards as an assigned cooperative job regarding training potentialities and application to the student's career objectives, and all existing assignments with cooperative employers must be satisfactorily filled. If the job is approved, the student must be informed that it becomes part of the degree requirements. The student is also expected to follow the same rules and regulations governing student participation on regularly assigned cooperative jobs.*

PROCEDURES ON PROBLEMS. The employer's evaluation of the student's job performance as well as the coordinator's personal follow-up visits to employers somtimes reveal evidences of failure by students on their cooperative assignments: one student may have conducted himself badly on the job, so as to bring about his discharge; another has deliberately deserted his job; another is not wanted back for his next work term because of unsatisfactory performance; and still another has failed to inform the department of cooperative education that he has been laid off his cooperative job during the work term. To handle such problems, cooperative institutions should establish a committee composed of representatives from the administration, the teaching faculty, the department of cooperative education, and the student body (usually seniors).

Most conventional institutions usually have three possible ways of dealing with infractions of rules and regulations: suspension, disciplinary probation, and scholastic probation. Cooperative institutions should consider a fourth sanction, called cooperative probation, for those students who fail to perform satisfactorily on their cooperative assignments. For minor infractions, the department of cooperative education may choose simply to send a letter of warning.

COOPERATIVE WORK REPORT. Practically all cooperative institutions require at least one report a year from each student enrolled in the cooperative program. The coordinator is usually the person responsible for the grading of these reports as well as the recording of them on the appropriate student record forms. The primary purpose of the cooperative work report is to enable the student to gain the maximum experience from his cooperative assignment. Experience has shown that the requirement of a formal written report forces the student to develop an inquisitive and investigative attitude toward his job and his work environment.

Other Practical Experience

Certain other forms of off-campus experiences (internships, student or practice teaching, and clinical practice) can be part of the educational process but are not considered strictly placement activities.

Internships usually involve experience that is necessary for licensing, certification, or registration in a particular profession. The character of internships varies considerably according to the requirements of the field. In some areas, such as pharmacy and medical technology, part or all of the internship requirement can be met during cooperative periods on regular paid assignments. Others, like student or practice teaching for certification as a public school teacher, are met before graduation but not normally on paid job assignments; and they are carefully regulated, directed, and monitored by members of the teaching faculty. Furthermore, the student teacher pays a tuition charge for the practice-teaching period and receives a grade for an allotted number of semester or credit hours. The internship in medicine and other fields is undertaken after completion of the formal degree program and involves several years of work at relatively low pay. For many years, various colleges or departments of business administration have placed students for a quarter or a semester in a business organization to obtain practical experience. These programs are administered in a similar manner to the practice teaching in that credit hours and grades are earned by the student and supervision is provided by the teaching faculty.

In some cases, the cooperative program carries the label of internship and under these circumstances does include some or all of the characteristics of an internship, such as academic credit and grades. In general, cooperative programs that are run as intern programs are expensive to operate, since coordinators must carry lighter loads in order to have time for the close supervision. Therefore, an internship experience usually should be separated from a cooperative program, with each clearly labeled and with administrative responsibility for each precisely defined and understood.

Clinical practice occurs in programs such as nursing and pharmacy. Here the experience is quite academic and is normally scheduled along with other classroom and laboratory experiences. One or more teaching faculty members are given the assignment of taking groups of students into clinical settings for observation and some work under closely supervised conditions. There is little relationship to the cooperative program, although institutions that provide the clinical settings may also be related to the university through the use of cooperative students.

Illustration of Cooperative Assignments

As with other educational programs, the cooperative plan becomes a living reality when specific students and their experiences are brought into focus. Therefore, it seemed wise at this point in a chapter devoted to coordination and placement to look at some actual students and their program.

Each spring at Northeastern University several seniors are honored for their performance on the cooperative program. At an appropriate public ceremony, they are given Cooperative Education Awards, which consist of a check for $100 and a framed and inscribed certificate. As each student is presented his award, a brief statement about his accomplishments is read to the audience. Several of these statements are reproduced here as illustrations of the successful operation of the program. The names of the students and other individuals have been deliberately changed to avoid identification, but the actual names of the employing firms have been included.

JOHN C. JONES

College of Engineering—*Majoring in Mechanical Engineering*
Cooperative Assignments: *Singer Company, Elizabeth, New Jersey, four quarters; Singer Company, New York, New York, three quarters.*

At the Elizabeth, New Jersey, facility Mr. Jones revised subassembly procedures for cost-reduction purposes and devised subassembly operations for new product lines. He was involved also with design and installation problems of new plant facilities.

In the New York office he assisted in the development of a Physical Distribution Training Program. His work as a physical distribution consultant took him to Venezuela, Japan, Singapore, and Malaysia. The managing director of the Japan office said, "I would particularly like to express our gratitude for the services of Mr. John Jones, who, aside from being a pleasant presence in our offices, also put his demonstrable analytical skills to use in evolving all of the elements of a practical plan to implement the Inventory Replenishment System. Mr. Jones showed extreme patience in dealing with our local staff in getting them to understand the overall program as well as to make sure that a comprehension of same was sufficient to ensure that it will be properly implemented."

A Distribution Consultant in the New York Office said, "He has proven himself on all occasions to be unusually alert, extremely sensitive to the needs and priorities of the particular situations, most enthusiastic, untiring, highly dependable, and abundantly endowed with the uncommon gift of original thinking."

PETER P. OLIN

College of Engineering—*Majoring in Civil Engineering*
Cooperative Assignment: *Hayes Engineering, Inc., Melrose, Massachusetts, seven quarters.*

Peter Olin started as a rodman in a surveying team and progressed through transitman to chief of party to a management position in which he coordinated the work of three to four survey parties and four draftsmen. As part of his assignment, he has been responsible for dealing with planning boards and municipal organizations on drainage, subdivisions, sewer design, and layout problems.

While maintaining an excellent academic record, he has the unusual distinction of being his own alternate on his cooperative assignment, working full time while attending classes. Additionally, he is a husband and father.

DONALD A. STEEVES

College of Engineering—*Majoring in Mechanical Engineering*
Cooperative Assignment: *Raytheon Company, Bedford, Massachusetts, five quarters.*

Mr. Steeves entered Northeastern in September 1966 as a transfer student from the University of Michigan. He worked in the Aerophysics Department of the Missile Systems Division of Raytheon throughout his career at Northeastern. His assignments ranged from set-up for heat-transfer experiments and data taking, through test design, equipment and instrumentation acquisition, data reduction and reporting, through several projects involving analytical work, design work, and experimental testing. His work on the Sam-D ADM antenna-design effort afforded him valuable exposure to sophisticated thermal-design techniques and reinforced his interest in the heat-transfer field. An outstanding student, he combines high-level coop performance with fine personal qualities and great professional promise.

ANDREW F. OLDER

College of Engineering—*Majoring in Electrical Engineering*
Cooperative Assignments: *Lockheed Missiles and Space Company, Sunnyside, California, seven quarters; Mitre Corporation, Bedford, Massachusetts, one quarter.*

Mr. Older started at Lockheed in the Missile Systems Division as a systems analyst in the Design Requirements and Analysis Department for the Poseidon missile project. He next worked in the Electrical and Environmental Test Lab, testing missile components subjected to adverse environmental conditions. Here he supervised technicians in the performance of various cable tests.

His assignment in the Research and Development Division as a

Systems Analyst led to his selection as Task Leader to conduct a parametric study of the computer program and to propose modifications.

Comments from Lockheed supervisors ranged from "very thorough, shows great concern for accurate, useful data" to "exhibited technical skills and abilities well beyond his contemporaries."

At Mitre Corporation he was responsible for the modification and update of a computer simulation of the hand-wired fast Fourier Transformer. His supervisor wrote: "Mr. Older showed substantial capability to apply and expand upon theory he had learned in school. His potential in the engineering field is very high. He is the best undergraduate coop I have observed to date."

LEWIS R. MARTIN

College of Business Administration—*Majoring in Management*
Cooperative Assignments: *Plymouth Home National Bank, Plymouth, Massachusetts, three quarters; Garland Corporation, Brockton, Massachusetts, four quarters.*

Mr. Martin was given a wide variety of job assignments in production scheduling, inventory control, job description, and purchasing. In all of his activities he showed continued progress and promise. He was the first production-staff member to be exposed to complete job rotation, and he demonstrated to management the advantages of such a program. His performance underscored the distinct advantages to the company in employing individuals schooled in management principles and substantially influenced the company's approach to management training and development.

While completing his final term in school, Lewis is working at Garland with computer personnel on a major project intended to automate inventory-control and production-scheduling procedures. His broad base of experience has uniquely qualified him for this assignment.

RICHARD G. ROBERTS

College of Liberal Arts—*Majoring in Sociology*
Cooperative Assignment: *Roxbury Municipal Court, Boston, Massachusetts, seven quarters.*

Mr. Roberts started his cooperative career in a routine clerical capacity, but early revealed his keen interest in the work of the court. He was given the responsibility of interviewing all males over seventeen years of age before they went to court, recording disposition of each case, and completing the histories of those placed on probation.

He was promoted to Senior Clerk and assisted the probation officers assigned to courtroom duty. Subsequently, he went out into the district with a probation officer to observe and learn, and in his fourth year achieved the title and responsibilities of a probation officer. In all of his assignments he demonstrated maturity, sensitivity, and commitment that has drawn high praise from his supervisors, who have endorsed him as an excellent candidate for social worker or court officer.

EDWARD J. PORTER

College of Liberal Arts—*Majoring in Physics*
Cooperative Assignment: *Massachusetts Institute of Technology, Laboratory for Nuclear Science, Cambridge, Massachusetts, seven quarters.*

Mr. Porter, according to the physics faculty, is one of the finest students in physics to graduate from Northeastern in many years. A cooperative report, which he submitted in June 1968 on a project he had personally undertaken in conjunction with his work at the Cambridge Electron Accelerator, was considered by the physics faculty as approaching a superior master's thesis and the foundation for a fine doctoral dissertation.

Of his work in one particular experiment, his supervisor at the Laboratory for Nuclear Science reported, "His interest, contributions, and perseverance were so far beyond the call of duty that [he was listed] as one of the authors of a paper which was presented at the XIV International Conference on High Energy Physics, Vienna, 1968. No other cooperative student has ever been so honored."

ANNE S. NEWTON

College of Liberal Arts—*Majoring in Biology*
Cooperative Assignment: *Retina Foundation, Boston, Massachusetts, seven quarters.*

Miss Newton's work has involved psychophysical and electrophysical vision research, utilizing both humans and animals as subjects;

the objective of this aspect is to increase the body of knowledge regarding the structure, function, and sensitivity of the normal and abnormal retina. Miss Newton's clinical studies involved testing diabetics and retinal-detachment cases at various stages of treatment.

Miss Newton's major contribution has been the design and evaluation of a Glare Recovery Test, for which new test targets and adequate methods of exposure had to be developed. The system has been incorporated into a commerical Vision Tester.

Miss Newton has been junior author of two papers submitted for publication to the *Journal of the Optical Society of America:* "Dark Adaptation and Light Adaptation with Opposite Time Course: A Comparison of Physiological and Physical Backgrounds" and "Time of Cone Break and Rate of Threshold Changes in Rod Homologous Loci of the Human Retina During Dark Adaptation."

FRANCES M. SMITH

College of Liberal Arts—*Majoring in Modern Languages*
Cooperative Assignments: *Northeastern University, Boston, Massachusetts, three quarters; Office of Education, Washington, D.C., four quarters.*

The Director of the Financial Aid Office wrote: "There are no superlatives strong enough to record our satisfaction with Miss Smith's performance. She takes hold quickly, raises questions, and makes positive criticisms of operating procedures. She is exceptionally effective in handling student requests and inquiries. She puts 150 per cent into every assignment."

As a student assistant with the Task Force on Cooperative Programs in the Office of Education, she was involved in all aspects of the development of the guidelines and application form. She handled correspondence and organized meetings with consultants from institutions of higher education, business and industry, and students. She worked in the National Teaching Fellowship Program, part of Title V-E, Developing Institutions.

The Chairman of the Cooperative Education Task Force wrote, in part, "If the enthusiasm, zeal, productivity, and willingness to assume responsibility that Miss Smith exhibited may be considered to be what an employer might expect from a top cooperative education student, the merits of such a program with respect to benefits to the institution, the employer, and the student are abundantly clear."

SUSAN BARTON

College of Education—*Majoring in English*
Cooperative Assignments: *Y.W.C.A., Cambridge, Massachusetts, three quarters; Danvers Public Schools, Danvers, Massachusetts, two quarters.*

Miss Barton began her cooperative work experience at the Cambridge Y.W.C.A. in the Health Education Department. At the time, Susan was a student at Boston-Bouvé College. Because of her maturity and experience in the field of recreation, she was delegated several responsible assignments, including the teaching of arts and crafts to children, teaching swimming to both children and adults, and supervising "Keep Fit" gym classes for women.

A change in career goals led Susan to transfer to the College of Education as an English major midway through her sophomore year. Although she continued to perform in an exemplary manner at the Cambridge Y.W.C.A. on two subsequent cooperative work assignments, it was at the Holten-Richmond Junior High School in Danvers that Susan displayed those qualities and attributes which gave promise of her becoming an outstanding teacher. In recognition of those qualities, her assignments progressed from such tasks as assisting teachers with paper work and monitoring study halls to substitute teaching in the areas of English and physical education.

JAMES E. McDONALD

College of Education—*Majoring in Social Studies*
Cooperative Assignments: *Paul A. Dever State School, Taunton, Massachusetts, one quarter; Walter E. Fernald State School, Waltham, Massachusetts, five quarters.*

Early in his coop experience as a Junior Vocational Instructor, Mr. McDonald found an area in the field of education to which he has become genuinely dedicated—the education of the mentally retarded child.

The Director of Behavior Research at the Fernald School said, "Jim's work has been consistently of high caliber, and we are honored to have him as the person I consider the outstanding teacher in our Behavior Prosthesis Laboratory. He has continued to demonstrate growing skills in his efforts to determine what training procedures work most effectively with some of our most severely retarded children. His dependability, his ability to work effectively and to persevere in the midst of extraordinarily barren and physically unsuitable conditions for child training, his visionary yet realistic planning for the operation of a unique teaching-evaluation program, and, above all, his commitment to master and adapt existing measurement techniques for development of more precise training procedures have won the admiration of all of us who have first-hand knowledge of his independently conceived work. I believe he has real potential that should be nurtured both in the working situation and in graduate work."

ROBERT F. FOSTER

BOSTON-BOUVÉ COLLEGE—*Majoring in Physical Education*
COOPERATIVE ASSIGNMENT: *Boston State Hospital, Boston, Massachusetts, seven quarters.*

Mr. Foster began his cooperative experience as an attendant nurse working with and developing programs in physical education and recreation for mentally ill, emotionally disturbed, and retarded patients. He developed programs for three severely retarded adolescents and made home visits to work with the parents. He started a public-speaking program for emotionally disturbed high school students and substituted for Boston special-class teachers in reading and science. By working with retarded patients on an individual basis, he was able to introduce them to the Adolescent Unit.

In his final term of coop, Mr. Foster updated the patient case histories, outlining patient achievements and behavior and establishing realistic goals for the patients for the guidance of staff members. To ensure continuity with the patients, Mr. Foster additionally worked fifteen hours per week at the Adolescent Unit while attending classes at Northeastern.

ROBERT S. SALMON

BOSTON-BOUVÉ COLLEGE—*Majoring in Physical Education*
COOPERATIVE ASSIGNMENTS: *Medfield State Hospital, Medfield, Massachusetts, two quarters; Butler Hospital, Providence, Rhode Island, four quarters.*

At Medfield State Hospital Mr. Salmon performed the duties of an attendant nurse—dressing, feeding, escorting, and remotivating mentally ill patients—and was commended for his intelligence and aptitude and for the excellent relationships he developed with personnel and patients.

At Butler (a private psychiatric hospital) he performed the duties of a recreational therapist—maintaining a recreational program for the emotionally disturbed and those with acute mental illness. Among the comments of his supervisors are these: "He has displayed an unusual ability in adapting to the particular work situation at this hospital. He has performed consistently well, his enthusiasm is high, his relationship with staff and patients is excellent, and he is considered a fine asset to our hospital." "He has managed to include certain people who otherwise would not have participated in group activities and to provide them with rewarding experience."

PATRICIA A. LESTER

College of Pharmacy—*Majoring in Pharmacy*
Cooperative Assignments: *Barone Pharmacy, Fitchburg, Massachusetts, two quarters; Emerson Hospital, Concord, Massachusetts, three quarters.*

Miss Lester started her cooperative experience in the field of retail pharmacy; and, although she was only a sophomore, her performance received high praise from her pharmacy preceptor. In her third year she requested an assignment in hospital pharmacy and chose Emerson Hospital.

Excellent progress and performance were evident from all of her evaluation reports; and, following experiences in all aspects of pharmacy, her supervisor at the hospital reported: "I sincerely feel she will be a vital asset in whatever field of pharmacy she will undertake. She has been highly regarded at this institution and I should not hesitate to rehire her if she elects to stay in hospital pharmacy after graduation and registration. Her sincerity, knowledge, and professional conduct have helped elevate the image of hospital pharmacy at Emerson Hospital."

XI

Relations with Students

George H. Miller

"Coop" students, students who enroll in cooperative programs, have certain characteristics in common. They are inclined to be career-oriented, with goals already clearly defined or seeking educational experiences to help them define these goals. They place a high value on education, particularly on education that prepares them for vocational or professional career opportunities. They have a keen appreciation of the educational value of off-campus work experience, travel, research, or independent study related to their major fields of study.

In the past, the coop student was likely to be one whose family had limited resources and who was attracted to cooperative education because of its built-in financial aid. Among such students, the number of minority students is increasing rapidly. These students see cooperative education as a means of getting an education at the college level and introducing themselves into vocations and careers not otherwise open to them. In addition, students who could afford any type of education recently have sought cooperative education because of its relevance, its involvement in contemporary society.

Among today's college students, the coop is indeed fortunate. In addition to relevancy and a head start on a career through on-the-job experience, the coop has a personalized education. The coordinator who places him in his job assignment talks with him frequently as an individual student. He discusses the student's career objectives, educational program, and personal problems. The coordinator has a stake in seeing to it that the coop does well, both in college and on the job. He knows that satisfactory performance in college is essential to placement and that success on the job is essential to holding the job—both for the students now employed and for those who will be seeking employment in the future.

Status of Student

The cooperative education student must be classified as a full-time student by his educational institution during his on-campus and off-campus terms for a variety of reasons. Some educational institutions do not grant financial aid to an individual unless he is enrolled on a full-time basis. Also, during his off-campus terms the student may be denied the right to qualify for honors, to use the library, to participate in recreational and social activities, or to receive health benefits if he is not classified as a full-time student. In addition, unless he is classified as a full-time student, many agencies (Selective Service, the Veterans' Administration, Social Security Administration, and others) will not give the student benefits to which he is entitled.

Coordinator and Student

Crucial to the cooperative plan of education is the coordinator—a person whose responsibility it is to advise, counsel, and place students in off-campus assignments. To function effectively, a coordinator must appreciate his students as individuals; listen to their problems and offer help where possible; encourage them to accept challenging coop assignments to help them to appraise their own progress on the job; and work to find jobs for his students which are both well-paying and of a highly educative nature.

The following is a list of additional considerations.

1. Students should receive adequate orientation into the concept, philosophy, and the mechanics of the cooperative education program.
2. Students should be adequately prepared for participation in the program, through instruction regarding interview techniques, acceptable appearance, appropriate work habits.
3. Students should be interviewed to determine their interests, goals, background, abilities, and personality.
4. Students with special problems should be referred for further assistance in the following areas:
   a. Vocational information
   b. Interest and aptitude testing
   c. Psychological or psychiatric counseling
   d. Financial aid
5. The following problems might affect consideration of specific cooperative assignments:
   a. Economics. If the student is totally dependent on cooperative earnings to continue in school, there will be salary and location restrictions on his placement.
   b. Transportation. Without private means of getting to work, job locations may be restricted to areas with public transportation services.
   c. Married student. A married student finds it extremely difficult to move to a distant work location on a periodic basis. The alternative of long periods of separation is equally unattractive.
   d. Apartment Leases. Students with leases must either sublet or pay extra living expenses if they accept an out-of-town cooperative assignment.
   e. Housing. Adequate housing near job assignment may be limited—particularly true in rural or semirural areas.
   f. Academic work. The necessity for a student to be near education facilities to do make-up work might dictate work locations.
6. The following problems might arise while the student is on a cooperative assignment:
   a. Problems between the student and his employer need the attention of the coordinator for adjustment. Such problems

might involve personality conflicts or misuse of the student's services.

b. Family problems might develop that the student feels have priority over his work assignment. He might, for instance, have to provide full-time nursing care for an ill parent or take over the family business in an emergency.
c. The student on an away-from-home assignment might become seriously ill.
d. The student might have difficulties with the law while working in a strange city.
e. Students in unfamiliar locations could have difficulty meeting friends.
f. In some states, auto registration and drivers' licenses might be considered invalid.

A further discussion of the coordinator's role is found in Chapter 10.

Employer and Student

The employer also has certain responsibilities in his relations with coop students. Employers should be explicit about the type of student wanted, the qualifications expected, the salary that will be paid, and the work to be performed. They should also make prompt decisions on applications for employment, so that students can be satisfactorily placed before the onset of the coop work term.

Employers should make every effort to bring students into their organization through a well-thought-out orientation program and introductions to key people in diverse departments. Supervisors of coop students should be made fully familiar with the purposes and objectives of the coop program, in order that the students' experiences will be meaningful. The employer should make efforts to talk with the student periodically about his job, his progress, his problems, and his accomplishments.

Above and beyond direct on-the-job supervision and encouragement, employers should also consider the extracurricular aspects of a student's life as a company employee. If the student is living away from home and the college campus, efforts should be made to help him become acquainted with various social groups and special-interest clubs within the organization. Sometimes the employer might offer assistance in finding housing or special services such as automobile repair. All such assistance contributes immeasurably to good student-employer relations.

The really dedicated employer may go so far as to provide some form of community orientation program, assist students in taking credit or noncredit courses at local educational institutions, and provide tickets for special events. Some companies offer extensive educational programs, with tuition refund for students who satisfactorily complete accredited college courses at local institutions. Companies also may provide in-plant training programs or outside-reading programs in job-related areas.

In some instances employers have been known to take advantage of coop students and use them to perform menial tasks. In other instances, pressure may be brought to bear upon students to perform tasks that are inappropriate, beyond the student's capabilities, or quite different from those specified at the time of his coop placement. For instance, a student hired as an accountant in a public agency may then be told he is to spend his time campaigning for a superior who is seeking political office. When instances such as this occur, coordinators should take steps to rectify the situation immediately.

Employment by University or College

Many of the points previously discussed also are applicable when the educational institution in which the student is enrolled becomes the cooperative education employer. In some institutions the coop student is considered a full-time employee; in others, he is subject to student wages and hours and denied the fringe benefits that normally accompany full-time employment.

Every institution has many jobs that could, and probably should, be filled by coop students from a variety of disciplines. The institution's physical plant could use engineers; the business office could use accounting and other business majors; the library could use education and liberal-arts majors; and students in many other discipilnes could be employed by the athletic department, laboratories, research projects, and campus security. In every instance, a college or university dedicated to the philosophy of cooperative education should set the pace by treating its own coop employees in an exemplary manner. University-hired coop students should be paid wages in keeping with local business and industrial salaries, and they should have the status and fringe benefits of full-time employees.

Alternatives When Jobs Are Unavailable

Most coordinators have little difficulty in finding engineering, science, and business openings for coop employees. Employers in these fields often seek students; and during periods of a healthy economy, the demand for students in these fields may exceed the supply. In education and liberal arts, however, openings must be found, developed, and constantly maintained; even in good times, suitable jobs are not readily available for education and nonscience liberal-arts majors (although some employers who once accepted only engineering students will now consider students of diverse majors). These groups also are the first to suffer when the economy lags or there is evidence of a recession.

What does the coordinator do when there is no desirable position for an individual student? First of all, the university itself should feel an obligation to hire as many of its own students as possible when off-campus jobs are not available. When this is not feasible or there are not enough jobs to go around, the coordinator might encourage students to spend another term on campus, or to find their own jobs, or to "lay out" for a term, or to take a marginal position for one term in the hope that a more fulfilling position may be available the following work terms.

At colleges and universities where cooperative education is a requirement, it is sometimes against institutional policy to have the student spend the work term in classes. Therefore, the policy may be to have the student "lay out" a term, find a position of his own initiative, or fill a marginal position. At institutions where coop is an elective program, coordinators will probably suggest that the student spend another full-time study term on campus.

Orientation and Policies

In order that all parties concerned fully understand the rules and regulations of a cooperative program, operational guidelines must be published—either in the institution's catalog, or through a specially prepared coop handbook, or through official policy statements issued by the university's administration or governing board. Policy statements should be explicit. Some administrative officials recommend that all such statements be reviewed by the university's legal officer before being released for publication. The question of guaranteed placement affords a good example of the need for a college or university to define its policy clearly. The following statement, quoted from the Northeastern University undergraduate catalog, illustrates how this can be accomplished:

Because of the uncertainties of the employment market as well as other factors beyond its control, the university cannot guarantee to place all students on cooperative assignments. The university also cannot guarantee to place students in any specific geographic location. However, past experience has demonstrated that students who are willing and able to adapt themselves to existing conditions are almost never without employment except in periods of severe economic recession.

Experience indicates that a cooperative education handbook provides the best format for explaining institutional policies on coop programs. A sampling of handbooks reveals many variations in size and content; therefore, those contemplating the design of a handbook would do well to review several samples. Virginia Polytechnic Institute and State University has an outstanding handbook in mimeographed form. The University of South Florida publishes a pocket-sized booklet to serve as its guideline to students. Northeastern University publishes a forty-eight-page printed booklet, complete with photographs and calendars.

Subject headings found in these handbooks include: Historical Background of Cooperative Education; Philosophy of Cooperative Education; Basic Mechanics of Operation of Coop Programs; Policies, Rules, and Regulations; Calendar; Orientation; Initial Placement; Employer Evaluations; Cooperative Education Agreement; Absence from Work; Layoff; Discharge or Desertion; Failure on Job; Insurance; Loans; Emergencies. The excerpts from Northeastern University's *Coop Handbook* in Appendix E indicate the nature of the material included.

If the handbook becomes the official guide for the students, the institution must be sure that each student receives and acknowledges receipt of a copy. Again, the institution's legal officer can indicate what is necessary to make the student responsible for knowledge of the handbook's contents.

Those institutions just beginning a program are advised to start with a mimeographed booklet that can be revised easily after a few trial runs. Where a student advisory committee exists, it may be helpful to have the members review the copy before printing. At many institutions, all copy must be approved by the legal officer and the university editor prior to publication.

RESPONSIBILITY TO COLLEGE AND EMPLOYERS. Some portion of the university's orientation program should be devoted to a discussion of the student's responsibility to his institution and his employer when on a cooperative assignment. In addition to the official rules and regulations cited in the handbook, university officials should be certain that students understand the extent to which they represent the university while on off-campus assignments. If a student commences a job with a critical attitude, is fault-finding of management, is impudent or inconsiderate of other employees, endeavors to politicize other people, takes leave of his job to participate in marches or demonstrations—in other words, fails to perform satisfactorily the task for which he was hired—his shortcomings reflect on his school and may prejudice the employer against hiring other students in the future.

At the same time, the student is *not* asked to relinquish his rights as an individual. Where company policies permit employees time off for political pursuits, for example, coop students should be permitted the same privilege. Many employers have even revised their policies on standards of dress and length of hair, provided the students perform well on the job. The important point is that students should not ask for special considerations not accorded full-time employees.

COLLEGE PLACEMENT VS. STUDENT-FOUND JOBS. While some institutions offering coop programs permit, or even encourage, students to locate their own off-campus assignments, other institutions discourage or forbid this practice. Those who encourage a student to handle his own placement say that he thereby experiences life as it really is, with its many turndowns and disappointments. Those who discourage or forbid this practice argue that students will seek locations offering maximum income and will not consider the educational value of the placements; or that students will look for jobs at places where their friends, male or female, are working. In most instances, the new employers recruited by students know little of cooperative education, its philosophy, or its objectives. According to one coordinator, "more than 90 per cent of the problems" on job assignments "develop with those students and jobs where the student found or developed the job himself. I would highly recommend that all students go through the institution's normal channels of coop placement and rule out other methods of placement, including those positions that the students find themselves."

EXCEPTIONS TO COOP PLACEMENT. A number of institutions are now granting special permission for students to use their cooperative work terms for a wide variety of experiential activities. Students who do not depend on their coop earnings to meet their college expenses are seeking and receiving permission to spend a coop term in full-time political activity, travel at home and abroad, and in volunteer service in such areas as Appalachia or on an Israeli kibbutz. Some elect to spend a term in independent study. Some seek the experience of working on an Indian reservation. For the most part, today's students are highly mobile; and they see in the coop term an opportunity to spend time in a different environment. East Coast students journey to California, and California students gravitate toward New York or Boston.

Needless to say, there must be some perimeters within which the experiential program operates—some requirements for written reports on the student's accomplishments and such other reports as individual institutions deem necessary.

Student Participation in Administrative Affairs

In today's institutions of higher learning, student participation in administrative decisions is becoming universal, and cooperative education is one program where the students' voice can be very important. During the mid-1960s, a number of colleges and universities with cooperative education programs formed student advisory committees or councils. Many of these were patterned on the University of South Florida's Student Coop Advisory Council, a second generation of the

Student Coop Advisory Committee formed in 1961, when the university started its coop program.

Under the South Florida plan, students returning to campus each term from their coop assignments elect council members from their own numbers. In addition, the faculty advisor recommends three members to the coop program director, who then makes the appointments. The council meets once a week, with the faculty advisor and a coop coordinator present. At the first meeting, the council elects a chairman, a vice-chairman, and a secretary. Each term the council makes recommendations—concerning policies, handbook copy, or other administrative matters—to the director. Furthermore, the council receives a budget that permits it a limited amount of social activity plus funds to send delegates to conferences and other places where council members may make appearances.

In addition to the council, which operates as an on-campus organization, the South Florida program looks to student leadership off campus as well. In any location where there are ten or more South Florida coops, the coordinators select one or more students to serve as the student area coordinators. The student coordinators assist the university in any way possible; they may, for instance, locate a student who has changed his address; recommend emergency loans; and host student get-togethers, which are funded by the social program of student government on campus.

Student Activities and Athletics

Coop students can participate in clubs and social activities only when they are recognized as full-time students. One state university permits coops to run for student government office. If elected, however, they are removed from office when they go on a coop assignment, even though they may be employed on campus or in the immediate area. At a number of institutions where the majority of students are coops, student organizations operate with two sets of officers and two sets of planned programs, each related to the coop division presently on campus.

Many student activities, such as student government or work on the campus newspaper, are extremely time-consuming. Therefore, some students who are deeply committed to such activities occasionally will forgo a coop term in order to split their academic work load over a period of two terms.

The student athlete enrolled in a cooperative education program has a number of unique problems with which to contend. It is best when the student-athlete lives at home within commuting distance of the campus. The student who cannot commute has the burden of paying his living expenses year-round. In order to practice and participate in contests, the student must have his coop job near campus, since sports seasons overlap academic and the subsequent coop term. In addition, out-of-season conditioning programs and injury rehabilitation programs require the athlete to be on campus year-round.

More often than not, athletes must forgo top coop jobs in order to make daily practice sessions. Many athletes pass up excellent out-of-state or overseas job opportunities in order to remain in athletics. In addition, many attractive coop positions are not available to the athlete, because employers are unwilling to allow him time off for athletic events out of town. Other opportunities are lost because an employer will not put the student on a daily work schedule with hours that will permit him to be on the practice field within reasonable time. Still another problem arises when the student's coop job is a strenuous one, leaving the student fatigued prior to his athletic workout.

Cooperative Assignments Away from Home

Housing may be a problem for many coop students when they leave their home community or the community where their college or university is located. Some schools permit students to remain in college housing when on a local coop assignment. When this is not possible, assistance may be had from real estate offices handling rental property, the local chamber of commerce, or individual employers.

Where out-of-town coop assignments are concerned, the institution can provide some assistance by arranging a meeting of those traveling to the same location and giving them information on apartments available. Some institutions actually arrange to lease space or forward deposits to landlords so that housing will be available for students. Other institutions ask students to fill out a housing questionnaire (which includes questions on location, cost, and good and bad points about local housing) after a given work term. This information is then made available to other coops planning to work in the same area during the following term. In reality, many apartments become coop apartments, with one group of coop students moving in when another group moves out.

Placement problems also arise when parents object to students' being sent on cooperative assignments away from home. Some find such placements a financial burden; others consider their sons or daughters too young to be living on their own. Whatever their reasons, the facts remain that some students miss excellent job opportunities as a result of their being unwilling or unable to accept out-of-town positions.

The question of engaging in academic studies while on coop is a controversial one. Some institutions encourage it, and others forbid it. Where it is permissible, students are known to enroll in evening courses, sign up for independent study, write reports for credit, and take courses for transfer credit at nearby institutions. Where diligently pursued, this policy can enable a student to shorten the length of his college program, provided the institution's course offerings and calendar are sufficiently flexible.

Financial Aid

Financial aid to the cooperative student may come in many forms. Schools offering full-time first-year programs, followed by upper-class years of alternate work and study periods, often grant financial aid to students during the freshman year only. These institutions look upon cooperative education itself as a financial-aid program in the upper-class years. A growing number of schools view it only as a fringe benefit, however, and make every effort to help students locate part-time jobs during academic terms or "moonlighting" positions during coop terms.

At some institutions, students who enroll in the cooperative education program are immediately barred from receiving all other financial aid, and any scholarships they hold are terminated. In most instances, cooperative earnings will compensate for the financial aid lost; but those in charge of coop programs should see that the coop student has an equal chance with other students to receive the funds necessary to further his education.

From inquiries directed to many institutions with cooperative education programs and other inquiries directed to the National Commission for Cooperative Education, it is evident that many students today select their college or university because of its coop program. Some students select, enroll, and graduate without ever being on a coop program, where such a program is optional. They believe, however, that if financial or other reasons would make use of the cooperative plan desirable, they would be where they could take advantage of it.

LOANS. For most coop students, the critical time for needing a loan is during the first or early terms of school, before they have been out on assignment with an employer. Many times, however, the first need for financial assistance comes when the student leaves his home or college community to establish residence at the location of his cooperative work assignment. Students who leave the campus for such assignments are advised to have sufficient funds to meet their needs for a month or six weeks, or until such time as they will receive their first pay check. Items that must be covered include payments for an apartment or room (sometimes even a lease), food and local transportation, and transportation from the campus to the location of the job. Since these items can amount to several hundred dollars, a number of schools have a "seed loan" plan, whereby the student can obtain $100 to $300 on a short-term basis which he must repay during the coop assignment.

EMERGENCY LOANS. A number of institutions have established the mechanics for handling emergency loans for coop students away from campus. Loans of $25 to $50 can meet an immediate emergency, such as a student's having to buy a new tire or battery for his car while en route to his employer or the loss of a wallet on arrival in the community of his new assignment, leaving him without means for food or housing that night.

The student can secure an emergency loan by telephoning the college coop office and giving the address of the Western Union office nearest to him. The money can then be wired with a guaranteed arrival of within two or three hours. Such loans are made without the student's signature at the time of the loan, although some method of signature may be required before the student leaves campus in order to guarantee that he has such emergency-loan privileges.

FUNDING SPECIAL LOANS. Several institutions, where cooperative education is optional, have found it advisable to permit the coop department to establish and administer its own loan or emergency-loan program for coop students. Such programs can be closer to the needs of the students and can better expedite loans when needed. Cooperative education alumni, coop employers, and even some coop students have given quite generously in support of loan programs designed to serve coop students only.

OTHER SOURCES OF FUNDS. Students on cooperative education assignments with employers should become acquainted with the loan and scholarship programs that are administered by their employers. Employers' credit unions also may be a source for emergency loans or short-term loans.

WORK-STUDY (CWSP) FUNDS. Some colleges and universities use College Work-Study Program funds for paying students on their coop assignments with nonprofit employers, including the college or university. If eligible, the coop student may under the CWSP work part time on campus during his study terms and use the income to supplement his coop-term savings. As noted earlier, however, some colleges consider enrollment on the cooperative plan reason to bar students from CWSP as well as other on-campus financial aid.

Compensation

Rates of pay which cooperative education students receive are governed by a number of variables, including geographic region, nature of business or industry, academic field of study, and fringe benefits included. Coop employers are not under any obligation to provide fringe benefits; however, many companies do offer sick leave, personal leave, health insurance, paid vacations, and other benefits as part of the coop student's compensation. Some companies also count coop employment as part of an employee's length of service when computing fringe benefits. Salaries also vary greatly from institution to institution and to some degree are guided by the philosophy under which the institution operates its program. In general, engineering students have been at the top of the pay scale, closely followed by students in accounting or in the science disciplines. The other business disciplines follow, and education majors fall at the low end of the scale, although they have closed the range in recent years.

At most institutions, students find that they receive the same pay as full-time employees doing similar work for their employer. By the early 1970s, the average rate for student pay reported by a number of institutions was more than $110 a week, with some coop employers reporting starting monthly salaries of more than $650.

The campus coordinator does not enter into pay negotiations between students and employers unless the pay scale is considered unusually low. When such is the case, the coordinator may bring some figures on area or regional averages to the attention of the employer.

Most coordinators, when discussing pay scales with employers, will recommend that there be some rate of increase as the coop student returns to his second, third, and later work periods in order to motivate the student and give him some indication of his progress.

XII

Relations with Private Employers

Donald C. Hunt

Most employers of cooperative students hope that the student trainee who performs well on the job will accept permanent employment with his cooperative employer upon graduation. Usually the coop employee is expected to remain with his cooperative employer for successive work periods, during which he will be exposed to a progressive series of planned work experiences related to his academic field. Or the training program may be less formal, with job rotation dependent upon the company's immediate needs and the coop's abilities. This type of cooperative employment program is particularly valuable for students who have well-defined career objectives, such as students in the fields of nursing, pharmacy, accounting, and engineering.

Other employers find it profitable to employ cooperative students for single work periods. Although positions may be temporary or seasonal, the work may provide valuable training and experience for the cooperative student qualified to fill the position. Positions range from entry jobs to semiprofessional assignments. Such positions do not involve a training program as such; however, they are not necessarily inferior to those held under a formal training program. Positions such as these often appeal to the liberal-arts student who wishes to be exposed to a wide variety of jobs in industry and business, in order to acquire valuable work experience in various fields.

Regardless of the type of employment offered, the prime concern of both the employer and the cooperative college or university must be the provision of on-the-job training which will enhance the cooperative student's on-campus learning experiences.

Advantages to Employer

The following are a few of the more significant advantages of the cooperative program expressed by employers of cooperative students.

Cooperative employers find training programs a very effective recruiting device, as compared to the usual preselection methods used in university placement offices for senior recruiting.

Students can be thoroughly grounded in established employment practices while they are still at the formative level.

The program provides an excellent source of temporary manpower, when used as a planned training experience.

The infusion of bright young people, fresh from an educational environment, can provide an organization with many new ideas and fresh viewpoints.

Most cooperative programs provide continuous job coverage. The employer does not have to be concerned about a lack of job continuity, a problem in other student employment programs.

Upon returning to the campus, the coop student serves as a good-will ambassador for his employer among faculty and other students.

A mutually beneficial employer-college relationship is enhanced through an operational relationship rather than through a public relations program.

Training Programs

In general, those employers who have a formal or informal pattern of training and indoctrination for college graduates follow basically the same pattern when employing cooperative students. The assignments are determined by the skills and abilities of the student and are usually in line with his level of academic achievement.

The following guidelines (CEA, 1970) are suggested for employers wishing to establish cooperative work programs.

(1) A realization on the part of the employer that cooperative education is first and foremost an educational program integrated with practical experience. From an educational viewpoint, the employer should give considerable importance to the meshing of particular academic experiences with practical factors at the working site; a series of coordinated experiences for the student as he returns to the employer in succeeding employment periods; the placing of the student in those areas of employment which will be most conducive to the learning process; and the consideration of the long-range objectives of both *the student and the employer.*

(2) A genuine interest in integrating and developing the cooperative student as a "team member" in the organization.

(3) A top-level management commitment that the cooperative education program will be an important program in the personnel development of the corporation.

(4) The appointment of a well-qualified company coordinator who understands and is in agreement with the objectives of cooperative education. He must have a good knowledge of the colleges and universities with which he will be working and of their academic programs. He should have a recognized position that will enable him to develop the program throughout the corporation.

(5) Close attention to the supervisor of cooperative students, with emphasis on placing the students under supervisors who can see their roles as "educators" as well as supervisors.

(6) Establishment of a separate budget for salaries paid to cooperative students, enabling the student to be placed in any appropriate department. This avoids the imposition on normal operating budgets and tends to be a financial safeguard for the program.

(7) A philosophy within the organization that the program will be sustained to a reasonable degree through normal fluctuations in economic conditions.

(8) A well-planned series of experiences for the student, creating an attractive and viable program which will cause a favorable reaction and contribute to his personal development.

(9) The payment of a salary to the student which is fair and competitive.

(10) While the granting of fringe benefits is not a requirement for participation in a cooperative program, it is desirable to give the student as many advantages as possible. The more he "looks like" a permanent employee, the more likely he is to think in terms of permanent association with the employer.

Recruiting

Since competition is keen for the best candidates, many companies now recruit cooperative students on campus. In order that the campus coordinator may have available a sufficient number of qualified interviewees, recruiting objectives should be planned far in advance of scheduled recruiting visits. College coordinators have only a limited time in which to place their students; therefore, companies which delay the making of recruiting decisions impose a burden on the coordinator, who still must place those students not hired by recruiters. A company's image and ability to attract students may suffer if good recruiting and placement procedures are not followed.

The cost of recruiting college graduates, whether through cooperative programs or senior on-campus recruiting, is a major concern of large employers. Many are convinced that it is less expensive to recruit employees through cooperative education programs. Others question what constitutes "cost of recruiting" and feel that comparisons between the two systems are not reliable or accurate. One company employing a large number of cooperative students feels that the cost of recruiting coops is only 50–60 per cent that of recruiting college graduates. Another large coop employer feels that no savings are realized but that the benefits accruing to the company as the result of its cooperative trainee recruiting program far exceed those of their senior recruiting program.

Interviewing

When cooperative students are invited to a company for interviews, they should be treated in the same manner as college graduate program candidates. This involves the payment of transportation, lodging, and incidental expenses incurred by the cooperative student.

Instructions for Reporting

Instructions for reporting for the initial work period should be as personal as possible. Such data as reporting date and specific directions to reporting location should be included. Such information is particularly important in dealing with out-of-town students. Suggested actions include sending follow-up letters giving information about the specific nature of the initial work assignment; supplying company information, such as newspapers, newsletters, and brochures; and supplying local information about housing.

Orientation

In order that the coop trainee may be made to feel like a full-fledged employee rather than a perpetual visitor to the organization, a thorough orientation program should be planned (Lupton, 1969). During the course of orientation the coop trainee should complete all employment forms, and he should be introduced to all key people, provided with specific information regarding the nature of the business and its organization, familiarized with the firm's physical layout, and introduced to the particular person in the company to whom he may go at any time for counsel and advice.

Development and Appraisal

The initial selection of cooperative students is only the first phase of the college cooperative program. The second step—and the unique feature of the program—is the development and appraisal phase.

Management has the opportunity to test, observe, and counsel program participants during a series of meaningful, challenging work assignments before extending an offer of permanent employment following graduation. Full advantage should be taken of this unique opportunity.

A well-run and well-organized program of student supervision can do more than anything else to assure the success of a training program. Supervisors should receive some training in leading coop students. To be most effective, supervisors should be thoroughly familiar with the objectives of the training program and the student's work plan and progress; otherwise, the student may become "lost" in the organization.

Careful follow-up is especially important. Regularly scheduled review conferences should take place at least once a month, more often when problems arise. Participants generally consist of the supervisor, the student, and, occasionally, the university coordinator. Every effort should be made to determine whether candidates have potential for careers with the employer and whether the student is sincerely interested in a career with the company. From the standpoint of good college relations and good public relations, it is far easier to terminate participants during the first work period than at a later time.

Rotated work assignments are imperative to the success of an effective program. Rotation from one assignment to another gives coop students a sample of the types of work performed in the organization and, in turn, provides supervisors with an indication of the kind of work the participant is best equipped to perform following graduation.

Individual work plans should be prepared for each cooperative student before he begins his initial work assignment. It is not mandatory that the original work plan be followed in detail, but a well-organized plan should outline some specific goals. It is suggested that each new participant be provided with a copy of the work plan or be given an opportunity to review it during his initial work period. The work plan should be directed toward a career objective and should correspond with the maturity, education, experience level, and career aspirations of the program participant.

Evaluation

Every college or university offering a cooperative program requires a written evaluation of performance on every cooperative stu-

Table 19. Employer's Evaluation of Cooperative Student

Name ....

Class .... Course ....

Work Period ....

Assignment ....

Employer ....

Instructions: The immediate supervisor will evaluate the student objectively, comparing him with other students of comparable academic level, with other personnel assigned the same or similarly classified jobs, or with individual standards.

RELATIONS WITH OTHERS
- ☐ Exceptionally well accepted
- ☐ Works well with others
- ☐ Gets along satisfactorily
- ☐ Has some difficulty working with others
- ☐ Works very poorly with others

JUDGMENT
- ☐ Exceptionally mature
- ☐ Above average in making decisions
- ☐ Usually makes the right decision
- ☐ Often uses poor judgment
- ☐ Consistently uses bad judgment

ABILITY TO LEARN
- ☐ Learns very quickly
- ☐ Learns readily
- ☐ Average in learning
- ☐ Rather slow to learn
- ☐ Very slow to learn

ATTENDANCE:
- ☐ Regular
- ☐ Irregular

ATTITUDE—APPLICATION TO WORK
- ☐ Outstanding in enthusiasm
- ☐ Very interested and industrious
- ☐ Average in diligence and interest
- ☐ Somewhat indifferent
- ☐ Definitely not interested

DEPENDABILITY
- ☐ Completely dependable
- ☐ Above average in dependability
- ☐ Usually dependable
- ☐ Sometimes neglectful or careless
- ☐ Unreliable

QUALITY OF WORK
- ☐ Excellent
- ☐ Very good
- ☐ Average
- ☐ Below average
- ☐ Very poor

PUNCTUALITY:
- ☐ Regular
- ☐ Irregular

OVER-ALL PERFORMANCE:

Outstanding	Very Good	+ Average —	Marginal	Unsatisfactory

What traits may help or hinder the student's advancement? (Use other side if necessary)

Types of Work Assignments Completed. (Use other side if necessary)

This report has been discussed with student ☐ Yes ☐ No

(Signed) ....Date ....

(Immediate Supervisor)

dent for each work assignment. Most often these evaluations are the basis for the student's grade at institutions granting credit for cooperative work. For this reason, and for the obvious benefit of the evaluation as a means of improving an employee's performance, the evaluation phase is extremely important.

The cooperative student's immediate supervisor is responsible for preparing an honest evaluation and reviewing it with the student. If a student is not performing satisfactorily, the best time to note this is during the coop work periods, when the student is still learning and his failure can be viewed as part of his educational experience. The student who receives a better rating than he deserves may get the impression that he can continue throughout his career to get away with marginal performance. Such an impression does not help the student or the employer.

Often the student is given an opportunity to read his evaluation sheet and sign it. Actually, if the student has been properly counseled during his work period, the evaluation will not contain any surprises.

The supervisor is responsible for making sure that an evaluation is prepared for each student and is completed on time, that it has been signed by every person who has taken part in the evaluation process (sometimes including the student), and that it is a meaningful tool for assessing and improving performance. Copies of each student's evaluation must be sent to his college coordinator. Table 19 shows a sample evaluation sheet.

Position Offers

The employer has a better opportunity to hire graduating cooperative students if he makes a specific position offer during their last work period, before they return to the campus for graduation. All offers of permanent employment should be made during an interview and confirmed in writing before the student finishes his final work assignment. For best results, the offer should be made six months prior to the student's graduation date. If he has not received an offer by that time, his natural reaction is to interview other companies recruiting on campus.

Graduating cooperative students should be given the same interviewing treatment as that afforded college-graduate applicants, including interviews and luncheon with appropriate managers and supervisors. Generally it is to the company's advantage to invite graduating coop students to the company location during their last school semester for additional follow-up interviews. This practice can give the organization an opportunity to reinforce its interest.

Retention of graduating cooperative students is clearly in the company's interest, inasmuch as these students have been carefully screened before and during their cooperative work assignments and have developed their abilities through a series of well-planned work periods.

Salary

The best evidence of the company's esteem is a substantial salary offer. In recognition of their work experience, most cooperative students will receive offers that are at the maximum or above the current starting salary ranges for noncooperative college graduates.

Salaries paid cooperative students vary greatly depending upon the type of work performed, the business or industry involved, and the geographic location of the business. For instance, students majoring in accounting will find that the highest cooperative salaries are paid in accounting departments of manufacturing plants and professional accounting firms. Lower salaries are paid by financial organizations; the lowest are paid by retail stores and insurance companies. Variations in salary are even greater in other areas. For example, salaries paid liberal-arts students vary from the minimum legal wage paid for positions in the performing arts to a beginning salary of over $700 per month for a position as an industrial-relations trainee in manufacturing. Students in business, while not experiencing as great a variation, will find that management-science majors will receive a greater salary usually than students majoring in finance or marketing. In engineering little variation is found among salaries paid students working in companies engaged in the same business or activity.

Most employers pay the coop student at the same rate paid a full-time employee who has a similar background and is performing a similar job. In businesses and industries regularly employing college graduates, cooperative salaries are generally related to the company's own current rate for college graduates. The starting rate for cooperative students may be set so that an increase in salary is provided during each succeeding cooperative training period up to a maximum amount paid upon graduation. Salaries paid cooperative trainees upon graduation tend to be higher than those paid noncooperative college graduates, since the graduating coop trainee has had more on-the-job experience and is, therefore, better oriented to the job and the employing organization. In some businesses the periodic increase is determined by the student's classification in college rather than by the number of off-campus periods. This step-increase procedure avoids the giving of increases at graduation which are not in line with company policy and also provides the coop trainee with an incentive to plan a career with his cooperative employer.

Table 20 shows the step increases offered to cooperative nursing students working in hospitals during their cooperative work periods in 1971.

Table 20. Salary Increases for Coop Nursing Students

Baccalaureate Degree Program	*Step Increase Per Week*
Second Year	$96
Third Year	$102–108
Fourth Year	$112–116
Senior Year	$125–136
Associate Degree Program	
First Year	$106
Second Year	$104–112
Third Year	$120–130

Students in several coop programs accept voluntary jobs in social agencies, school systems, retail stores, hospitals, and health agencies. These students are primarily interested in receiving field experience related to their programs of on-campus study. In most instances, coop students working on a voluntary basis will receive credit applicable toward the total number of credits required to earn their degrees.

Fringe Benefits

Regarding fringe benefits, a wide range of policies exists among employers. Most employers give cooperative students a regular non-exempt salary classification with restricted benefits. A few use a temporary status, which automatically limits or eliminates all benefits. However, the vast majority do offer coop trainees some fringe benefits. Among the fringe benefits most frequently offered are the opportunity to earn overtime pay, time off with pay, hospitalization coverage, other types of insurance, and longevity. Other benefits offered less often include tuition refunds, reimbursement for travel to and from work to school, cost-of-living adjustments, company discounts, profit sharing, bonuses, and participation in retirement programs. (See Table 21.)

TIME OFF WITH PAY. Usually coop students earn vacations within the company policy on the basis of time worked rather than length of service. Many employers grant the coop trainee one half the vacation allowance due a full-time employee; if, for instance, all full-time employees get two weeks of paid vacation each year, the company might grant one week each to the two coop trainees alternating periods of service on one job.

The coop student who works the day before and the day after a paid holiday is generally entitled to receive pay for the holiday.

Many employers grant coop students paid leaves of absence for such purposes as sick leave and funeral attendance. Again, the amount of paid time off allowed probably will be one half that allowed full-time employees.

INSURANCE. Cooperative students generally participate in medical, life, and disability insurance plans while on the job and are often privileged to continue the benefits at their own expense while at school.

LEAVE WITHOUT PAY. Most employers who give salary status to cooperative students grant them "educational leave" when they return to school. When coops are classified as temporary employees, they are generally terminated at the end of the coop work period and rehired at the beginning of the next period, although this procedure is gradually disappearing.

Table 21. BENEFITS ACCORDED COOPERATIVE EDUCATION STUDENTS BY GEOGRAPHIC REGION[a]

	New England (13)[b]	*Middle Atlantic* (40)	*E. North Central* (50)	*W. North Central* (8)	*S. Atlantic* (15)	*E. South Central* (6)	*W. South Central* (9)	*Mountain* (2)	*Pacific* (6)	*Total* (146)
	PER CENT									
Cost-of-Living Adjustments	30.8	12.5	34.0	37.5	33.3	50.0	22.2	0.0	66.7	29.2
Merit Increases	61.5	40.0	46.0	12.5	33.3	16.7	33.3	0.0	66.7	41.5
Overtime Pay	92.3	92.5	94.0	87.5	80.0	83.3	77.7	100.0	100.0	91.8
Vacation	76.9	22.5	44.0	62.5	53.3	66.7	33.3	0.0	66.7	44.2
Travel to Job	0.0	37.5	20.0	50.0	60.0	0.0	66.6	50.0	83.3	24.0
Travel to School	0.0	32.5	18.0	50.0	46.7	0.0	55.5	50.0	50.0	28.6
Tuition Refund	0.0	10.0	36.0	62.5	33.3	33.3	0.0	50.0	16.7	24.5
Paid Time Off	53.8	70.0	68.0	62.5	80.0	83.3	44.4	100.0	83.3	75.4
Hospitalization	53.8	50.0	66.0	75.0	53.3	83.3	44.4	50.0	100.0	61.9
Insurance	53.8	42.5	58.0	75.0	46.7	83.3	44.4	50.0	100.0	55.8
Other	46.1	20.0	16.0	12.5	6.7	16.7	22.2	50.0	16.7	19.0

[a] Prepared by James W. Wilson, Research Professor of Cooperative Education, Northeastern University, Boston, for the November 1969 issue of the *Journal of Cooperative Education*.

[b] The number of employers responding and the number upon which percentages for this geographic region are based.

LONGEVITY. Many employers grant longevity to cooperative students who become permanent employees after their graduation. Usually the calculation of length of service will date back to the student's starting date as a trainee and includes both school and work periods. This is an important factor in those companies where increased benefits for vacations, savings and stock plans, retirement, and separation allowances are based on length of service.

TRANSPORTATION. Employers generally do not pay transportation expenses to and from school at the completion and start of training periods. A few organizations, situated at considerable distance from the college or university campus, will pay an allowance equal to one-way air fare at the beginning of the first assignment; others pay one round-trip fare during the entire program. In times of shortages of specialized personnel, firms have been known to pay substantial transportation costs, in order to attract coop trainees.

UNEMPLOYMENT BENEFITS. Under Public Law 91-373, employers are not required to pay tax on earnings of coop students under twenty-two years of age; they are required to pay tax on those over twenty-two. Cooperative students over twenty-two are eligible for unemployment compensation under this law if a bona fide unemployment occurs during a cooperative work period, provided the students meet the state eligibility requirements. In order for employers subject to the Federal Unemployment Tax Act to receive federal tax credits, all states must comply with this law.

Extracurricular Services

There are various extracurricular services that an employer might offer to coop trainees. These include community orientation; housing information; the provision of information on offerings at local colleges and universities, cultural activities, volunteer programs; the organization of social activities; tickets to special events; suggestions for outside reading.

Termination

Employers who terminate coop students prior to the students' graduation generally view this action as part of the educational experience and career exploration of the students. Accordingly, personnel records do not contain any notations which might be detrimental to the students' careers or future employment opportunities. Official records often note "termination under mutually satisfactory conditions" or "termination—voluntarily quit under satisfactory conditions."

Unions

As labor unions move into white-collar positions in business, more cooperative students become involved, either as advocates or as antagonists of the movement. Coordinators usually leave all decisions regarding the joining of unions and crossing of picket lines up to the cooperative student. Many coop students hold union cards and perform union jobs. Usually the only benefit accruing to a cooperative student who joins a union is the opportunity to take advantage of pay increases negotiated by the union, since most other union benefits are based upon seniority.

Most employers prefer that cooperative training assignments not be included in the union bargaining unit, in order to give the employer ease in programming training periods. When an assignment falls within the union jurisdiction, arrangements must be made for the rotation of cooperative trainees and variations in assignment, since union regulations regarding movement from one position to another tend to be restrictive.

Often unions do not feel threatened by cooperative students filling jobs usually held by union members as long as the coop trainee does not replace a union employee on the job. This is especially true when the coop student's career objectives clearly diverge from those which fall within the jurisdiction of the union. Many union leaders, for example, feel that there is an advantage in having a coop management trainee work closely with union members, since he may carry with him into management positions after graduation the insight he has gained into the problems and aspirations of union members.

On the other hand, resentments may arise if a coop trainee holds a union job in a field closely related to his major field of study. A civil engineering student, for example, who holds a job as a union crane operator might not be well received by his fellow workers.

Typical Cooperative Positions

Engineering students will find many excellent positions available to them. Typical cooperative positions held by engineering students are field engineer, chief of party, assistant construction superintendent, sanitary engineering trainee, design engineer, process engineer, analytical engineer, quality control engineer, machine designer, technical sales representative, power plant engineer, research technician, development technician, utility engineering trainee, computer programmer, installations engineer, research assistant, development assistant, laboratory technician, industrial engineer, management trainee, production engineer, mechanical testing technician, manufacturing engineer trainee.

In business, as in engineering, students are placed in a great variety of assignments, including the following: general accountant, auditor, cost accountant, salesman, financial analysis assistant, production supervisor, claims adjuster, computer operator, bank examiner, sales promoter, underwriter, security analyst, insurance agent, stock exchange clerk, mortgage specialist, financial analyst, insurance investor, line supervisor, personnel assistant, public relations assistant, marketing statistician, assistant buyer, media study clerk, purchasing clerk, retail manager.

Some of the opportunities for liberal-arts students are newspaper reporter, public relations assistant, copy boy, bank teller, personnel assistant, real estate assistant, editorial assistant, advertising assistant, audio-visual assistant, research assistant, law clerk, retail trainee, financial analysis trainee, legal-research assistant, management trainee, programmer, production manager, television production assistant, library assistant, psychiatric aide, counselor, clerical worker, social worker aide, tour guide, interpreter.

The majority of cooperative nursing students are placed as ward secretary, operating room assistant, laboratory technician, radio therapist, physical therapy aide, medical records processor, escort messenger, nursing assistant.

In pharmacy, cooperative students are placed as hospital extern, retail extern, industrial assistant.

Physics majors will find positions as aerospace research technician, management trainee, pollution control technician, optical technician, expediter, communications technician, research assistant, physics lab technician, mathematics lab assistant, defense research technician.

In education the following opportunities exist: (nonscience

majors) clerical worker, teacher aide, library assistant, office assistant; (mathematics and science education majors) laboratory technician, teacher aide, computer programmer, bank teller; (physical education majors) teacher aide, assistant physical education instructor, swimming and gymnastic instructor, assistant physical director, recreation therapist, athletic field instructor, assistant corrective therapist, recreation therapist.

Relations With Public Employers

Paul E. Dubé and Carole A. Lilley

Public service employment—a career in federal, state, regional, or municipal government—is being sought as never before by college students and recent graduates. Although most of the interest is from students majoring in the liberal arts, it is by no means limited to this group. Students in general are placing less emphasis on income and more on becoming involved with the world around them; therefore, they have shifted from the traditional search for employment in commerce, industry, and finance to areas where they feel they can make a contribution toward a better society.

Fortunately, this movement is gaining momentum just at a time when there is an acute need for new people in public administration and related government services, especially on the state and local levels. Many of those in the highest levels of administration entered public service during the thirties and are now retiring. Although there was an overall growth in public service employment during World War II and the years following, not as many high-caliber people sought this form of employment as during the depression and prewar years. In addition, in the years following World War II there was a rapid growth in the demand for government service due to a shift in life styles. Urban growth, population density, and a heightened living tempo intensified the pressures on those in government responsible for maintaining an orderly society. Government at all levels is seeking more people trained in fields such as law enforcement, medicine and health services, pollution control, mass transportation, urban design, and others. Despite a growth in expertise in these fields, there is still a gap between the need and the available supply of trained workers. Expanding cooperative education programs in government would help close this gap.

Advantages to Public Employers

Employers, public and private, expect to achieve two basic objectives through the implementation of coop programs: in the long term, more efficient recruitment of full-time professionals and, in the short term, employment of productive employees. Hiring full-time employees through the utilization of a coop program can lower the cost of recruiting while simultaneously realizing the value of their work effort.

There is no better means of evaluating an individual's potential for professional employment than observing him in an actual working situation. Such observations are far superior to test scores or references from professors and former employers in determining a worker's potential. His performance is measured over a period of time and under varying conditions. Regardless of the degree of validity and reliability a test may claim, the score is always a measure of a person at a moment in time. At best it is only a hint of his potential. Most references are somewhat favorable exaggerations of the individual's worth.

Through working with coop students in different jobs over a period of time, the employer will come to recognize their strengths and limitations. The employer is thus able to encourage promising students to continue with the agency and to screen out those not so well suited for that particular work.

Moreover, public service employers have found the productivity of most coop students superior to that of other preprofessional government employees. The agency can generally be assured that the young men and women it employs have proven ability, since most coop institutions require the students to successfully complete a portion of their academic program prior to being placed on coop. The students, in anticipation of acquiring meaningful and relevant work experience, look forward to their employment periods with enthusiasm. Viewing the coop work period as an integral part of their education, they report to their jobs with the intent of gaining as much knowledge and experience as the jobs will provide. Because of these qualities—ability, enthusiasm, and motivation—employers can assign responsible work even to young coop students.

Reinforcing the value of coop programs as recruitment vehicles are the economies in training the coops for full-time employment upon graduation. By employing them to perform work that must be accomplished, the agencies can be training their future full-time employees at a minimal cost. Initial observations of coop students can be made while they are employed in lower-level assignments and prior to their receiving the higher salaries and more expensive training given college graduates. When successful in the entry assignment, they can then be moved into more responsible work. The more able students will frequently work side by side with full-time professional employees and perform similar tasks. There is hardly a coop institution with ongoing coop programs in federal agencies that has not received commendations for some of its students, who are performing work normally expected from professional employees two or three pay grades higher.

An important value to some agencies is the opportunity to employ students who are majoring in fields such as engineering and accounting which are short of manpower. Although graduates in these fields are frequently able to command higher salaries in private industry, many—because of an interest developed during their employment with a particular agency—remain with that agency upon graduation. With government salaries now very competitive with those of private industry in the middle-management level, the opportunity to retain these graduates is enhanced.

A significant economy achieved in recruiting coop graduates is the low turnover rate among these employees, as opposed to that experienced with traditional college graduates (U.S. Civil Service Commission, 1970, p. 2). Too frequently, the recent graduates are intrigued by the glamor they attribute to certain agencies, such as the Equal Employment Opportunity Commission and the Office of Education, or by the impressive job titles into which college graduates are hired, such as research assistant or management analyst; yet they know very little about the responsibilities behind these titles. After they have worked awhile, the job is no longer exciting; they become disillusioned and start seeking a change. Frequently they leave shortly after becoming productive, with a resulting loss of money and training time for the agency. Students who have cooped with an agency for a number of periods know before graduation whether they want to accept full-time employment with that agency.

An indirect benefit of any agency's employing coop students is the public relations value with other students on campus. Obviously, this can have a negative return if their coop students are not enthusiastic about the mission of the agency or their employment experience.

Coop programs help agencies establish good relations with college placement officials. Frequently, the placement service and the cooperative education program are in the same department. The public service agency that employs coop students may be granted preferences by college placement officers. In times when certain occupational skills or training are in critical demand, these small advantages may be helpful.

Value to Students and Institutions

Cooperative education programs with public service employers have unique advantages for colleges and universities and for their students. For students in professional areas such as accounting and engineering and those in liberal arts science programs, such as physics, chemistry, biology, and math, the quality of experience is equal and frequently superior to that obtained in the private sector. For those students majoring in the social sciences and humanities, meaningful work experiences are generally more available than in the private sector.

INFORMATION AND CAREER DIRECTION. In addition to providing employment opportunities, coop programs in government agencies provide a great deal of occupational information and career direction for students. Through their employment with agencies, students are exposed to a vast array of occupations. Government agencies cut across such a wide range of activities that students, even though not involved with all divisions of the agency, have an opportunity to observe the necessity of each function and its contribution to the successful operation of the government. By requesting job changes with a single employer or else by arranging with his coop program for different experiences, the student is able to obtain work experience in the specific fields that are important and of interest to him. He could, with a number of coop periods, obtain research experience with a state agency; civil rights enforcement with a federal employer; and urban renewal or community development work with a local authority. This opportunity to test himself in a variety of career fields enables the cooperative student to assess himself and the careers in which his opportunities for success are greatest.

With this knowledge the student may recognize the desirability of preparing for specific careers through altering his curriculum or by selecting the courses that will enhance his chances of entering a chosen field. He may recognize that some careers require graduate professional preparation or that entry into public service may be easier and at a higher level with graduate training. With cooperative experience in fields that have only recently become national concerns—fields such as pollution control and noise abatement—as well as those that are not so new but receiving vast infusions of funds, such as law enforcement, students are exposed to whole new occupational opportunities. Through first-hand observation, the coop student recognizes the increasing demand for those with special training. He is thus able to prepare himself for these new careers both academically and vocationally.

ENRICHMENT OF EDUCATION. Probably as important to the student's development is the exposure to the government process—the politics of give and take by individuals and agencies to obtain the support of others for projects each considers essential. Some students may find their cynicism reinforced by their experiences; many more, however, come away from their coop experience with a new respect for government. They recognize the obstacles that lie in the path of solving society's ills, such as the deferment of valuable projects because of the necessity of protecting the rights of others. These observations may be even more important in the total educational process than the career direction provided by the coop experience.

Nor are these observations limited to those who experience them first hand. Students bring their experiences, observations, and questions back to the classroom. Through this feedback many share in the experiences of a few. Instructors can draw upon the coop experience to make their teaching relevant. What at one time might have been considered dry and unimportant facts begin to have meaning in the lives of the students.

EQUALITY OF OPPORTUNITY. Public service employers, especially federal agencies, tend to provide greater equality of employment opportunity than that found with employers generally. In all areas of the country, however, there is still unnecessary reluctance on the part of local and state employers to employ women in certain positions, while in some sections of the country there exists serious discrimination toward certain minorities. This will unfortunately persist but possibly at diminishing levels. Cooperative institutions, above and beyond their general responsibility to provide an adequate number of meaningful opportunities for all students, must recognize their special responsibility to minority groups and impress on all employers their role in providing equal opportunity for all.

U.S. Civil Service Provisions

The U.S. Civil Service Commission encourages federal agencies to employ cooperative students and has provided guidelines covering the utilization of cooperative programs. Much of the material in this section is related to U.S. Civil Service Bulletin 330-15, dated May 25, 1970, and Letter No. 308–1, June 28, 1971.

HIRING AUTHORITIES. Most cooperative students are hired in excepted appointments, those not made under the regular competitive provisions. The grade and salary of the coop job are determined by the duties assigned to the student, and these duties are usually related to the student's level of academic advancement. Remuneration is the same, and fringe benefits are similar to those provided full-time employees in like assignments. These benefits include one day of vacation and one day of sick leave each month, plus inclusion in the retirement program.

Certain occupations, such as engineering, physical science, and mathematics, may at times be considered shortage occupations. Students majoring in those disciplines are normally hired under an excepted appointing authority known as Schedule B. This authority affords certain provisions not usually afforded students, such as eligibility for a career-conditional appointment (three years of satisfactory service must be provided by the employee before the appointment is permanent) upon completion of the academic and coop work requirements of the student's program. To be employed through this authority, a student must meet certain requirements: (1) He must be majoring in a discipline preparing him for a shortage occupation as identified at the time of his appointment. The list of shortage occupations may be altered; however, the student's appointment is not changed even if his discipline is removed from the shortage occupation category. (2) He must be participating in an organized cooperative education program leading to a bachelor's degree. (3) He must be in a program for which the cooperative work is a structured experience and considered an integral part of the student's education. (4) He must, at the time of his appointment, meet eligibility requirements such as citizenship requirements and suitability as to experience, background, maturity, potential. That he meets these requirements is determined through an investigation by the Civil Service Commission. (5) He must be recommended by his college or university.

The student's appointment may be converted to a career-conditional appointment when he completes the requirements for a bachelor's degree; completes six months' work as a trainee in preprofessional work; meets the eligibility requirements; and is recommended for appointment by his employing agency. He is then eligible for full-time employment with the federal agency without going through the written examination.

Since liberal-arts, general business, and many other students usually do not possess the skills that would place them in shortage occupations, there has not been the same urgency on the part of the federal agencies to establish coop programs for them. In April 1965, the Civil Service Commission revised the temporary appointing authority, known as Schedule A, that had been used for employing student assistants for short periods of time. Prior to that time there was no means of employing students for periods longer than 1,040 hours, or approximately six months; thus, employers were unable to obtain continuity in job coverage. The revision permitted college students participating in established cooperative programs to be employed by federal agencies without limitation on hours worked or income earned in any fiscal or calendar year. Schedule A was a hiring authority for temporary employment; the appointment had to be renewed each year. It did not provide for conversion to a career-conditional appointment as did Schedule B. Upon graduation, the former coop student still had to take the written competitive Federal Service Entrance Examination and achieve a score high enough on the Civil Service register to be within reach. The uncertainty of being able to employ its coop students upon graduation made many federal agencies reluctant to undertake this kind of program. The lack of conversion provisions was doubly unfortunate in that many liberal-arts coop students found federal employment meaningful; yet they were not always able to score high enough on the Federal Service Entrance Examination to be employed full time upon graduation. Because so many of these students were able to perform well on their coop jobs in the federal agencies that did employ through Schedule A, there was growing pressure to find a means for them to be hired upon graduation without taking the competitive written examination. Another major source of pressure was the federal government's desire to employ more minority college graduates. The minority college graduates were having less success than college graduates generally in obtaining sufficienctly high scores to be employed through the FSEE.

On May 25, 1970, the United States Civil Service Commission issued Cooperative Work Student Bulletin No. 330-15, outlining the provisions which enabled coop students employed by federal agencies under Schedule A to be eligible for competitive appointments under Federal Service Entrance Examination requirements without taking the written test, provided they could meet certain requirements: (1) They must have completed all academic requirements for a bachelor's degree. (2) They must have completed two or more work periods,

Table 22. PAY RATES OF THE GENERAL SCHEDULE (5 U.S.C. 5332), AS ADJUSTED BY EXECUTIVE ORDER, JANUARY 8, 1971

Grade	ANNUAL RATES AND STEPS									
	1	*2*	*3*	*4*	*5*	*6*	*7*	*8*	*9*	*10*
GS- 1	$ 4,326	$ 4,470	$ 4,614	$ 4,758	$ 4,902	$ 5,046	$ 5,190	$ 5,334	$ 5,478	$ 5,622
GS- 2	4,897	5,060	5,223	5,386	5,549	5,712	5,875	6,038	6,201	6,364
GS- 3	5,524	5,708	5,892	6,076	6,260	6,444	6,628	7,651	6,996	7,180
GS- 4	6,202	6,409	6,616	6,823	7,030	7,237	7,444	6,812	7,858	8,065
GS- 5	6,938	7,169	7,400	7,631	7,862	8,093	8,324	8,555	8,786	9,017
GS- 6	7,727	7,985	8,243	8,501	8,759	9,017	9,275	9,533	9,791	10,049
GS- 7	8,582	8,868	9,154	9,440	9,726	10,012	10,298	10,584	10,870	11,156
GS- 8	9,493	9,809	10,125	10,441	10,757	11,073	11,389	11,705	12,021	12,337
GS- 9	10,470	10,819	11,168	11,517	11,866	12,215	12,564	12,913	13,262	13,611
GS-10	11,517	11,901	12,285	12,669	13,053	13,437	13,821	14,205	14,589	14,973
GS-11	12,615	13,036	13,457	13,878	14,299	14,720	15,141	15,562	15,983	16,404
GS-12	15,040	15,541	16,042	16,543	17,044	17,545	18,046	18,547	19,048	19,549
GS-13	17,761	18,353	18,945	19,537	20,129	20,721	21,313	21,905	22,497	23,089
GS-14	20,815	21,509	22,202	22,897	23,591	24,285	24,979	25,673	26,367	27,061
GS-15	24,251	25,059	25,867	26,675	27,483	28,291	29,099	29,907	30,715	31,523
GS-16	28,129	29,067	30,005	30,943	31,881	32,819	33,757	34,695	35,633	
GS-17	32,546	33,631	34,716	35,801	36,886[a]					
GS-18	37,624[a]									

[a] The rate of basic pay for employees at these rates is limited by section 5308 of title 5 of the United States Code, as added by the Federal Pay Comparability Act of 1970, to the rate for level V of the Executive Schedule (as of the effective date of this salary adjustment, $36,000).

of no fewer than thirty-six weeks, of career-related work in progressively responsible assignments and according to the cooperative agreement. (3) They must have demonstrated an aptitude and ability for federal employment through satisfactory coop work performance. (4) They must show evidence of being a student with above-average ability or potential.

CLASSIFICATION AND COMPENSATION. Cooperative students employed by federal agencies are hired at a level consistent with the number of years of college completed. Generally, students do not start their coop employment prior to completing one year of college. Academic standards governing grade eligibility are GS-2, completion of high school and prior to completing freshman year; GS-3, completion of one full academic year; GS-4, completion of two academic years; GS-5, completion of three fourths of the requirements for the degree and one period of employment as a GS-4, or completion of two and one-half academic years and six months of employment as a GS-4. A full academic year is a period of study equivalent to two semesters or three quarters.

Table 22 shows the federal-service salary schedule that became effective January 1, 1971.

AGREEMENTS BETWEEN FEDERAL AGENCIES AND COOPERATIVE INSTITUTIONS. With the inauguration of conversion for both Schedule B and Schedule A, the United States Civil Service Commission requested each agency employing coop students to implement a written agreement between the agency and the college to cover the conditions under which the students are employed. These conditions include the number of positions; criteria for hiring, rehiring, and promoting; and the benefits comprising the total package. The agreements outline the contributions expected of the cooperative institution. In addition to the student requirements, there is need to exchange information concerning the progress of the students and their attitudes toward the employing agency.

State and Local Civil Service Requirements

Most state and local agencies have not recognized cooperative education as either recruitment vehicles or education media. Although not exhaustive, a survey of cooperative education institutions in thirteen states, accounting for more than two thirds of the nation's coop students, disclosed that only three states have made provisions for the employment of cooperative students by the state's agencies. These are Florida, in which provisions were spelled out in detail; and Massachusetts and Michigan, where the provisions, although permissive, nevertheless do little to encourage the utilization of coop programs.

Florida's provisions for employing coops seem quite clear, with the exception of the means by which a student is converted to a career appointment. The terms of employment are not as favorable as those of the federal program. There is an allowance for paying coop students less than the regular rate at every level of employment, although this gap decreases as the student progresses academically. Coop students are not eligible for sick leave, holiday, or vacation pay.

Chapter 7 of the Civil Service Laws of Massachusetts for 1970 and Chapter 203 of the Laws of 1968 provide for employment of coop students by state agencies in excepted positions. In an effort to assure that a financially competitive position would be available to the student upon graduation, the state personnel department required that a professional position be utilized. This requirement has almost totally prevented the legislation from being used to employ coop students, since few state agencies are willing to set aside professional positions for the employment of students. Rather, students are employed in temporary and middle-level clerical positions, even when the assigned work is actually on a professional level. The cooperative institutions in Michigan have been able to structure an arrangement with the state personnel division permitting the employment of cooperative students. These students are in engineering, for the most part; and the arrangement is really a permissive arrangement (one that is not formally encouraged but is permitted).

Even though there may be no enabling legislation encouraging or even mentioning the employment of coop students, agencies in most states can usually employ coop students, if there is a position open and money available, through the use of temporary hiring provisions. In other circumstances, students may be employed as consultants. In most states there are also agencies with a number of positions established outside the civil service code. It would seem that a great deal has yet to be accomplished in the form of designing a uniform policy if meaningful legislation is to be passed on the state level.

Regulations covering the employment of coop students by municipalities are generally controlled by the state civil service laws. There is no known legislation encouraging municipalities to utilize coop programs. As with state agencies, however, there usually are provisions in the civil service codes permitting the employment of these students if there is an open position and available money. Municipal agencies, such as urban renewal and model cities, are usually exempt from the civil service structure.

Organization of Program

In structuring the coop program the employer and the institution should understand and agree upon the objectives sought. From the employer's standpoint, these usually include work output, recruiting, communication with higher education, reduction of turnover, and keeping the agency staff abreast of academic developments in the field. The cooperative institution is concerned with obtaining good supervision and well-structured and meaningful work experiences. These will promote personal growth and development, an enriched educational experience, and career advancement. (The organization of a coop program is developed in detail in Chapter 10.)

Types of Programs

Almost all local, state, and federal agencies can offer employment opportunities to cooperative work students in diverse fields of study. An urban renewal agency, for example, may employ engineering students to work in traffic planning, business students to do budget work, and liberal-arts students to assist in relocating families and businesses that must move because of renewal projects. However, the nature of any particular agency's mission usually does dictate a greater need for students with a specific type of background. The following outline of employment programs with government agencies is therefore divided into programs available to students in specialized fields such as engineering, the sciences, mathematics, science education, business, criminal justice, nursing, and pharmacy, and programs available to students in general courses of study—that is, liberal arts and nonscience education. The information presented here is by no means all-inclusive; the programs discussed serve merely as representative examples of the types of cooperative employment opportunities available with government agencies.

FEDERAL EMPLOYMENT FOR SPECIALISTS AND PROFESSIONALS. On the federal level, the Department of Defense ranks as one of the major employers of cooperative work students in the fields of engineering, the sciences, and mathematics. Students are employed by the Air Force, Army, and Navy at research and engineering centers throughout the country. Job duties generally include assisting in the design, testing, building, field testing, and evaluation of equipment and materials. The Armed Services and the Defense Contract Administration also employ business students to work in personnel, where they are familiarized with techniques of interviewing, data gathering, and applying job standards. In addition to personnel, the Defense Contract Administration provides employment for both business and engineering students in quality control and contract administration.

Examples of federal employment for science majors are found in the programs offered by the Interior Department's Bureau of Commercial Fisheries, the Environmental Protection Agency, and the Environmental Science Services Administration of the Commerce Department. Biology and chemistry majors work with fisheries technicians; do quantitative analysis of water samples; collect and record data; and help initiate, maintain, and complete experiments.

Business students are employed by many federal agencies to do personnel or budget work. Also of interest to many business students is employment as assistant bank examiners or research assistants with the Federal Deposit Insurance Corporation, the National Bank Administration, the Federal Reserve Banks, and the Federal Reserve Board of Governors. The Internal Revenue Service also employs business majors, particularly accounting students, as assistant tax examiners.

Employment possibilities with the federal government also exist for students in specialized fields other than engineering, the sciences, and business. Pharmacy and nursing students, for example, are employed as assistants in Veterans' Administration hospitals. Criminal justice students work as customs enforcement officers for the U.S. Customs Service, and they are employed by the National Park Service as assistant Park Rangers, working in visitor protection and security.

STATE AND LOCAL EMPLOYMENT FOR SPECIALISTS AND PROFESSIONALS. In state governments, public health departments provide a variety of cooperative work experiences for engineering and science majors. Students are employed in environmental control, air use management, water pollution control, and virus diagnosis. Duties include reviewing and checking plans for sewers and treatment plants; inspecting, servicing, and maintaining air pollution monitoring sites; analyzing samples; conducting river studies; and evaluating and investigating sources of water pollution. Chemistry majors obtain similar experience with the occupational hygiene divisions of state labor and industries departments, performing analytical analysis of air samples from factory areas in which hazardous chemicals and solvents are used. Engineering students also do basic research, testing, and evaluation of road-building materials for state public works departments.

As with federal agencies, state agencies employ business students to do personnel and budget work. Rate-setting commissions, such as the insurance commission that sets automobile insurance rates or the Workmen's Compensation Rates Commission, also provide employment for business majors. Students conduct surveys and compile information that is used to determine premiums and classifications.

Criminal justice students are employed by state public safety departments to assist in the enforcement of public safety codes, as social service assistants in state correctional institutions, as investigative clerks in state attorney generals' offices, and as assistants in state police crime laboratories.

Local public works departments and health departments provide much the same type of cooperative work experience for science and engineering majors as is found as the state level. Civil engineering majors are also employed by planning boards and urban renewal agencies to work in planning and structure rehabilitation.

Science education majors gain experience working as teachers' aides in public school systems. Local police departments employ criminal justice students as police interns.

FEDERAL EMPLOYMENT FOR GENERALISTS. The Department of

Health, Education and Welfare, because of the broad scope of its activities and its general support of the concept of cooperative education, is one of the major employers of liberal-arts and nonscience education students. Most positions are in Washington, D.C., although some may be located in regional offices. The major areas of employment are the Office of the Secretary, the Office of Education, and the Social Security Administration. In general, students are given work assignments in specific areas of their own preference. Work responsibility includes doing research for professional reports, helping conduct surveys, preparing answers to public and congressional inquiries, and assisting in the writing of internal newsletters and agency publications. When possible, the Social Security Administration allows cooperative work students to participate in a three-month training program preparing them to work as Social Security Claims Representatives.

Students interested in history and teaching are employed by the National Park Service, which provides a number of cooperative work opportunities, primarily for history, political science, English, and education majors. Students employed as assistant historians at National Historical Parks and Sites are responsible for interpreting the history and significance of the park areas to visitors. Since large numbers of school groups visit the National Parks annually, prospective teachers gain valuable related experience. A limited number of students are employed as history research assistants.

Other federal agencies providing cooperative work opportunities include the Defense Contract Administration, the Department of Labor, the Department of Justice, the Equal Employment Opportunity Commission, National Aeronautic and Space Administration, National Security Agency, and the General Services Administration. The Defense Contract Administration employs liberal-arts students in the same areas in which business students are employed; personnel, quality control, and contract administration. Employment opportunities with the Department of Labor are in the Equal Employment Opportunity Division and the Public Service Careers Division of the Manpower Administration. Duties include drafting reports of congressional hearings, writing reports, answering memos and inquiries for information, and assisting with budget analysis.

Within the Department of Justice, the Civil Rights Division and Community Relations Service employ cooperative education students. Working as special clerk-analysts in the Civil Rights Division, students gather and analyze information which is used by the division's lawyers. As interns with the Community Relations Service, students have an opportunity to familiarize themselves with the overall mission of the agency through work on special projects. Work in the Washington office is followed by an assignment to a field office when possible. Students employed by the Equal Employment Opportunity Commission do research on projects related to the administration of grants to state human-rights agencies. Although interesting to all, students interested in law careers find these work experiences most beneficial.

The General Services Administration provides liberal-arts students with work experiences at federal records centers and presidential libraries.

STATE AND LOCAL EMPLOYMENT FOR GENERALISTS. On the state level, liberal-arts and education students are employed by legislatures, governors' offices, attorney generals' offices, state departments of corrections, education, child guardianship and youth services, and state divisons of immigration.

Students employed as interns in state legislatures are assigned to various committees or House or Senate majority and minority leaders. Their assignments involve doing research on legislative proposals, keeping track of bills as they go through the legislative process, obtaining information to answer public inquiries, and doing research on special topics of interest to the legislature.

State governors' offices employ liberal-arts students in secretarial-receptionist positions, as legislative aides, and as research assistants gathering information on various topics and answering inquiries to the governor's office.

Students planning careers in law find excellent employment opportunities in state attorney generals' offices and departments of correction. As investigative clerks in an attorney general's office, students assist in locating, compiling, and disseminating intelligence information. In state correction departments, students aid in structuring research designs, gathering data, and producing research reports in the field of corrections.

State departments of education, child guardianship, and youth services provide employment for students interested in education careers or social service. Assisting professional staff members in the department of education and participating in staff meetings and seminars increases a student's knowledge of his chosen field. Employment in the youth services and child guardianship divisions gives students first-hand exposure to many of the social problems which confront society and provides experience in dealing with these problems.

Language majors are employed in state divisions of immigration to translate documents and assist non-English-speaking clients.

In local government, political science and government majors are employed by mayors' offices, town and city managers, and executive secretaries. Work generally involves special projects such as assisting with summer youth programs or helping to compile annual reports.

Liberal-arts and education majors employed in libraries gain experience in all phases of library work. Local school systems employ education majors as teachers' aides, library assistants, and clerks. Agencies responsible for planning, housing, and urban renewal are of particular interest to many liberal-arts students. These agencies provide meaningful employment in planning, property management, and relocation and are in fields that concern today's student.

PART FOUR

ADMINISTRATION

XIV

General Administration

Asa S. Knowles

The offering of cooperative education by any college or university gives rise to certain unique administrative and financial considerations which do not apply to institutions operating traditional programs.

Basic Concepts

Officers of general administration should understand that the following basic concepts are fundamental to the success of any cooperative plan of higher education:

SUPPORT OF ADMINISTRATION. The president, deans of colleges, and heads of departments offering cooperative education programs must give full support to these programs if they are to be successful.

SUPPORT OF FACULTY. The understanding and enthusiastic endorsement of cooperative education by the faculty of a college or uni-

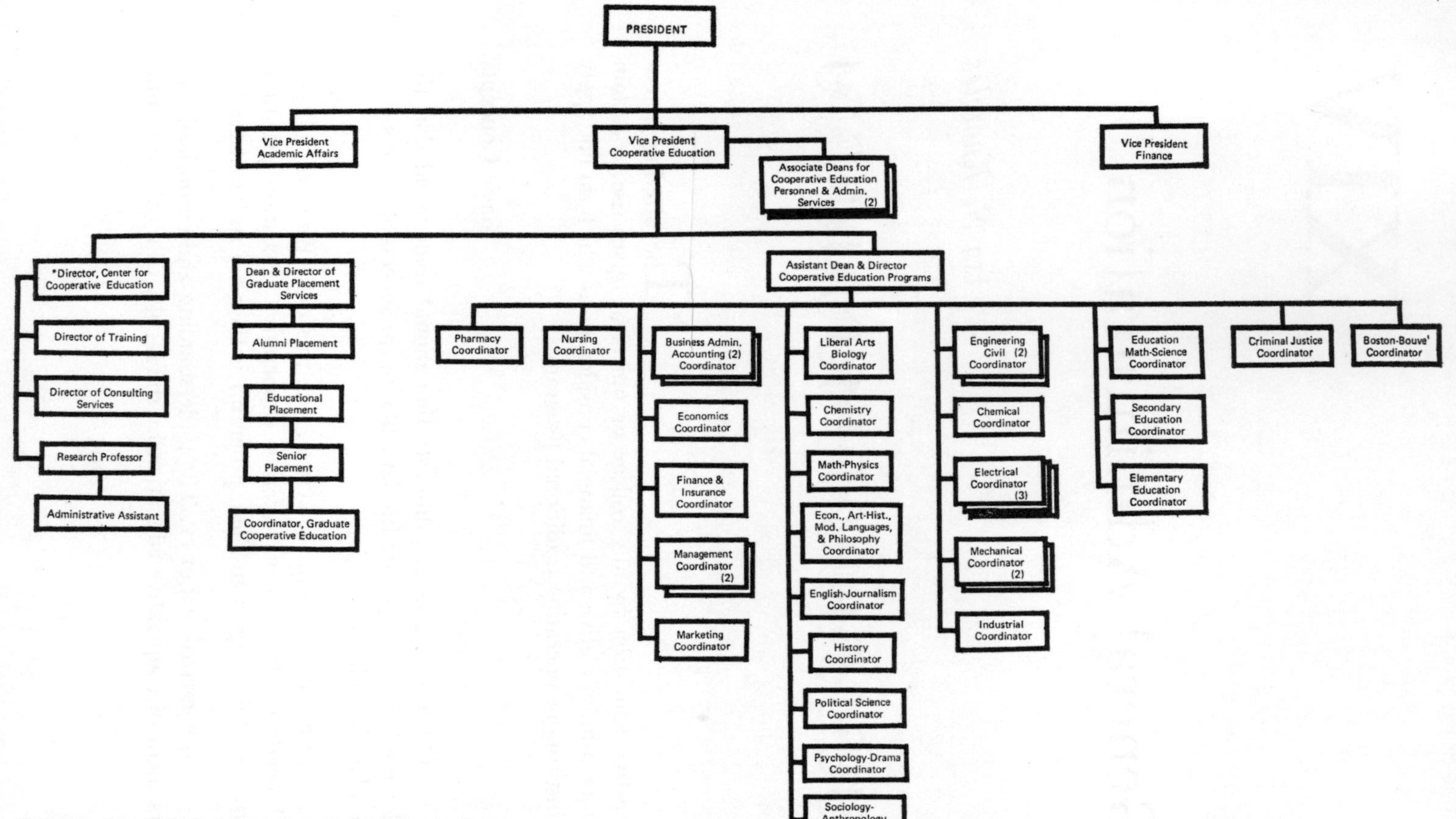

FIGURE 2. Independent organization of a Department of Cooperative Education with a vice-president for cooperative education, who is responsible for the program and who reports directly to the president.

versity, and particularly by those involved in the program, is essential to the success of cooperative education programs.

AVAILABILITY OF JOBS AND ASSIGNMENTS. Work opportunities and other assignments for the placement of students enrolled in cooperative education programs must be assured before any cooperative education program is undertaken.

REQUIREMENT FOR DEGREE. Paid cooperative work or other off-campus experience should be required for whatever degree is awarded.

PUBLIC RELATIONS. An internal and external public relations program, directed toward an understanding of the role of cooperative education in the college or university and in the community at large, is essential to the success of a program, particularly if it is just being established.

Administrative Organization and Program Size

The persons in charge of the operation of cooperative education programs must be accorded a specific place, which is commensurate with the size of the program and the responsibilities involved, in a college or university organization.

Figure 2 shows a suggested organization for a large program where the whole institution is committed to the conduct of all programs on the cooperative plan of higher education.

Figure 3 shows a suggested organization for an institution with two or more colleges committed to cooperative education.

Figure 4 shows a possible type of organization for institutions with very small programs, such as a departmental program offered on a selective or optional basis.

Placement of Cooperative Students vs. Graduates

In many institutions, senior and alumni placement and cooperative education are administered by the same office, since the firms that recruit seniors and employ alumni are potentially employers of cooperative students. Likewise, as coordinators are visiting employers of cooperative students, they will pick up opportunities for full-time employment for alumni.

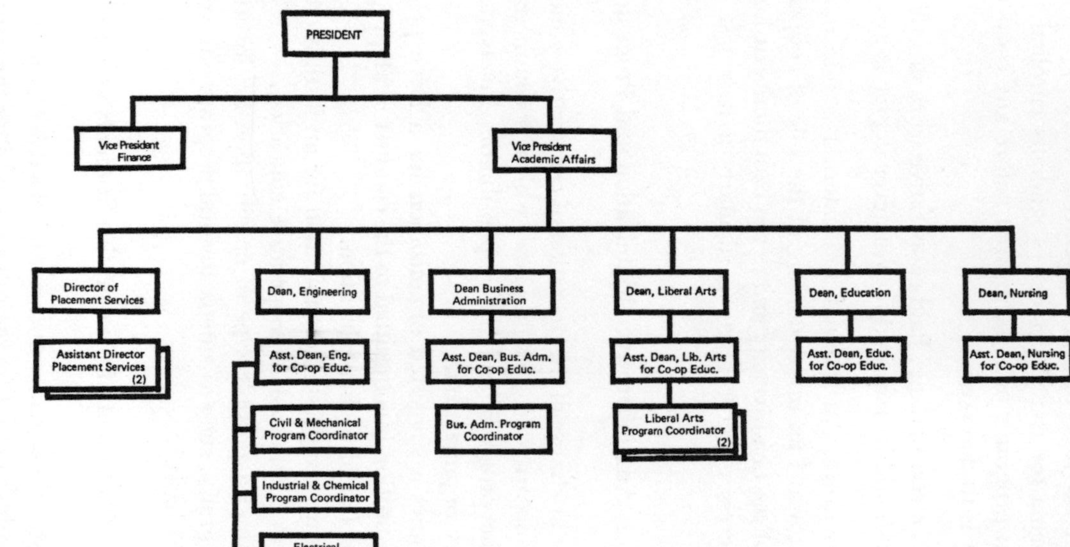

FIGURE 3. Full-time coordinators responsible for the Cooperative Education Program, reporting to the deans of the colleges, who, in turn, report to the academic vice-president.

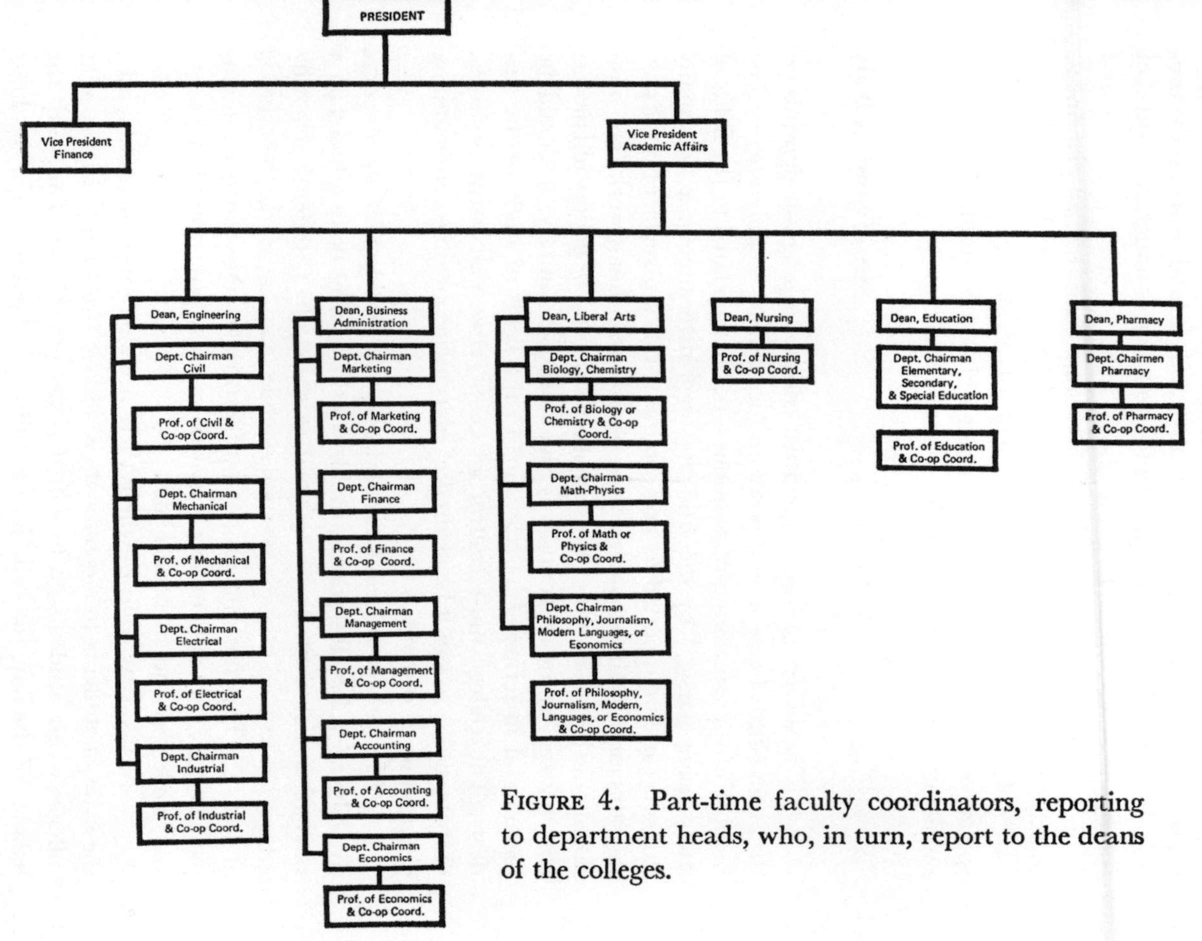

FIGURE 4. Part-time faculty coordinators, reporting to department heads, who, in turn, report to the deans of the colleges.

With the current complex of financial assistance, consisting of various combinations of grants, loans, and federal work-study programs, it seems best to leave part-time employment under the control of the financial-aid office. In some small schools, career planning and financial aid are housed together in one office; and then all placement, including the cooperative program, may be centralized.

Ideally, a separate department of cooperative education, a special office, or a particular officer should be responsible for the administration and operation of the cooperative program.

Size of Student Body

The success of any cooperative education program depends on the availability of meaningful positions for off-campus assignments. The number of these meaningful positions—positions related to the fields of study being pursued by the students—will determine just how many students can be supported by any program. When placement is for pay, the rates must be those paid to others performing similar work. The position should also last for the duration of one off-campus period and preferably for two or more periods. If the work is voluntary, it should be meaningful in terms of its relevance to the fields of study of the students. The college must control all cooperative placement positions. Only by doing so can it be assured of placement openings for oncoming generations of students.

In a college offering a mandatory alternating plan of cooperative education for all students, the size of the student body is based on a ratio of two students to be assigned to each job. (Students generally are paired to hold a single position—while one is at work, the other is at school.) This formula cannot be followed exactly, since some employers want only one student and will cover the position in some other way while the student is at school.

In two-year colleges where there are alternating plans of study, the ratio of students to assignments would be two to one. In two-year colleges where students go to school a few hours a day and work the balance of the day, the ratio is one student to a position. For graduate students, the ratio is most likely to be one to one, since the types of positions held by graduate students are usually specialized and do not always lend themselves to an alternating basis. In some graduate programs, however, students do hold positions on an alternating basis; and in these programs the ratio would be two students to one position.

Spreading Risks

In periods of recession or adverse business conditions, college students employed by business or industry, or by public employers, may find job preference being given to full-time employees and to persons with family responsibilities. Even in periods of general prosperity, a single business can come upon hard times and have to reduce its staff. It is desirable, therefore, to limit the number of students employed in any location or by any single employer—even though coordinators in general are naturally hesitant to reject placement opportunities, particularly when loyal and long-standing employers want or need the students. The establishment of a policy of spreading the risks is the responsibility of general administration. Here are some suggested guidelines: (1) Not more than 10 per cent of the students in any single or total program should be assigned to any single employer. (2) Not more than 75 per cent of the students in any single or total program should be given off-campus assignments in a single metropolitan area (population of 500,000 or over) or 50 per cent in a medium-sized locality (250,000 or over), or 25 per cent in a small locality (less than 250,000 in population). (3) At least 20 per cent of the students should be placed outside of the immediate locality of the college or university, preferably in a region comprising several states. (4) Ten per cent of those enrolled in cooperative education programs should be placed nationwide or abroad.

Reports on Placement

The cooperative college or university which cannot place in off-campus assignments a relatively high percentage of its students is heading for disaster or, at best, a difficult public relations situation. There are always some students who are ill, repeating course work, changing programs or jobs, or not employable for a variety of reasons. This number of students may range from 2 to 5 per cent of all students enrolled in the cooperative plan.

The presidents of all colleges and universities operated on the cooperative plan of education (whether the program is optional, selective, or mandatory) must review periodically the placement of students and the success of the constant ongoing search for employers of students. For this purpose, they will require periodic reports from coordinators. Such reports may be weekly, monthly, by the term, or annually. The larger the program, the more frequently reports seem to be required, no doubt as a means of assisting the coordination of the institution's entire cooperative education program. Such reports serve as a productivity report for the coordinator as well as being a view of the total placement of students.

Table 23 illustrates a weekly report form on the placement of college students.

Financial Aid

The granting of financial aid for students enrolled in cooperative programs of education is discussed briefly in Chapter 11. Mention is made that some cooperative students in some colleges are not eligible for financial aid and that students must be registered as enrollees during off-campus assignments or lose their eligibility for financial aid during these periods. There are, in addition, some broad policy considerations of concern to the general administrator.

In most colleges offering the cooperative plan of education, the freshman year is the same as that of the traditional or "noncoop" college. Many students will hold paid jobs as off-campus assignments in their upper-class years. It is desirable, therefore, to have a published policy stating clearly that financial aid offered to freshmen and other new students is for the first year only and is not automatically renewable. A suggested catalog statement follows: "In most instances, you will earn enough money to defray the cost of your tuition, books, and incidentals during upper-class years as a coop student." This statement perhaps more than any other is a major inducement for students with limited financial means to enroll in a cooperative plan of education. The potential freshman and his family look upon the coop system as a vital resource for pursuing his degree objectives.

As the concept of cooperative education is broadened to include other types of off-campus experience, such as independent study and volunteer service without pay, financial aid must be made available for the students involved. If his off-campus experience is located at some distance from the main campus of the college or university, the student with limited financial resources may require substantial amounts of financial aid. In colleges and universities where the off-campus assignments involve traditional work assignments and where such assignments may be in any part of the United States or abroad, financial aid is often needed by these students to pay travel costs and living expenses as well as tuition and fees.

Students who live at home and have paid jobs within commuting distance of their homes can usually earn and save a sufficient amount to meet college expenses, but this is not the situation for students who attend college at some distance from their homes and hold paid jobs which require expenses away from home.

UPPER-CLASS STUDENTS. In the upper-class years, the student seeking financial aid should file an application for financial aid term by term, supplying the office of financial aid with the usual family-income information and also the relevant information regarding income and expense during his cooperative work period.

At this point, the first philosophical disagreement may occur within the institution. The coordinator views the off-campus assignment as an educational experience; the financial-aid officer looks upon the assignment as a major resource in financing the student's education. With proper planning and cooperation between the cooperative education department and the financial aid department, this seeming disadvantage can be used to strengthen both areas. The financial-aid officer should reserve funds to be used for job incentive in those areas having traditionally low salaries, such as social work or teaching, but having tremendous educational value and opportunity for learning experiences. Students should be assured that even though they have an off-campus job assignment away from home at a relatively low salary rate, this factor will be taken into consideration and may even enhance their financial aid. The coordinator should work closely with the aid officer in those situations where the student feels that the income from the cooperative job will deter his progress toward his degree objective. The student can receive an aid commitment in some cases prior to his coop work period. For example:

Student A and Student B come from similar economic backgrounds.

Table 23. REPORT FORM ON PLACEMENT OF COOPERATIVE STUDENTS
Northeastern University

REPORT FOR WEEK ENDING—MAY 29—DIVISION A AT WORK

Program	*Students Working*	*Students Not Working*		*Total Coop Enrollment*	*Percent of Students Working*	*Conferences with Students*	*Visits with Employers*
		Avail.	*Not Avail.*				
ENGINEERING							
Chemical	106	2	1	109	97	65	5
Civil	198	1	3	202	98	76	8
Electrical	317	25	4	346	92	96	13
Industrial	104	2	3	109	95	51	12
Mechanical	200	13	3	216	92	99	3
Total	925	43	14	982	94	387	41
BUSINESS ADMINISTRATION							
Accounting	185	8	2	195	95	76	2
Economics	2	0	0	2	100	0	0
Finance & Insurance	109	2	0	111	98	65	3
Industrial Relations	29	0	0	29	100	56	3
Management	238	0	1	239	99	26	0
Marketing	120	0	1	121	99	0	4
Total	683	10	4	697	98	223	12

LIBERAL ARTS							
Soc Sci & Humanities	475	15	7	497	96	—	—
Science & Math	240	1	1	242	99	—	—
Total	715	16	8	739	97	216	9
EDUCATION							
Elementary Level	168	0	1	169	99	—	—
Secondary Level	109	4	3	116	94	—	—
Speech and Hearing	44	1	1	46	96	—	—
Total	321	5	5	331	97	94	10
BOSTON-BOUVÉ							
Physical Educ.—Men	47	0	0	47	100	—	—
Physical Educ.—Women	18	0	0	18	100	—	—
Recreation Education	23	0	0	23	100	—	—
Physical Therapy	25	0	0	25	100	—	—
Total	113	0	0	113	100	93	4
NURSING							
Associate Program	27	0	0	27	100	—	—
Baccalaureate Prog.	133	0	1	134	99	—	—
Total	160	0	1	161	99	58	1
PHARMACY	79	0	0	79	100	35	0
CRIMINAL JUSTICE	126	8	0	134	94	72	0
GRAND TOTALS	3,122	82	32	3,236	97	1,178	77

Total Active Employers: 1,957

Remarks: 3% of students available for employment are currently unemployed.

The expected parental contribution, as per the College Scholarship Service of Princeton, New Jersey, is the same. Student A is an engineer who lives at home while on his coop job assignment and commutes to work each day on public transportation. His net salary is $120 per week. Student B is a political science major who has a job assignment away from home in Washington, D.C. His net salary is $85 per week.

Student A will earn a net salary of $1,560 during a thirteen-week work term. Given the fact that he is living at home and incurring modest expenses, he would be expected to return to school with about $1,100 to be used as a resource toward his educational costs.

Student B will earn a net salary of $1,105 during a thirteen-week work term. Because he is working away from home on an educationally rewarding work assignment, he will incur expenses above the ordinary in transportation and in room and board. When the costs of transportation and a modest amount of personal needs are added to Student B's budget, it would be unreasonable to expect that he could return to school with much more than $200 as a resource toward his educational costs.

FULL-TIME AND GRADUATE STUDENTS. Some colleges operating mandatory cooperative plans of education for all students will have a number of so-called "full-time students" enrolled at any given time. These are students who are changing programs, repeating work, and in some instances attempting to speed up their educational programs prior to entering graduate or professional schools.

Generally, college priorities will determine the aid amount available to these full-time students as compared to cooperative students. If there is not a distinct recognition of this problem early in the program, the full-time students could conceivably receive the bulk of the financial aid available each year. A policy should be established that financial aid for students *voluntarily* following a full-time program will be considered for only two quarters' assistance in any one academic year, and the student will be expected to provide from his own savings the equivalent to two quarters' savings from cooperative work earnings.

Students who, because of the economy or job market, are involuntarily on a full-time status should be assisted on a quarter-by-quarter basis, with recognition that they are available for cooperative work.

GRADUATE STUDENTS. The majority of graduate cooperative

plan students are sufficiently able to assist themselves financially because of their maturity and resourcefulness in seeking part-time jobs when they need them. The aid that is generally tendered to the graduate cooperative student is in the form of National Defense Loans, guaranteed loans through their local banks or short-term tuition loans through the institution.

FINANCIAL-AID OFFICE STAFFING. The aid officer in the conventional institution generally has only one award period each year. At a cooperative institution, depending on the calendar used (semester, trimester, or quarter), the aid officer may have two or three award periods for an applicant in any one academic year. Also, because of the complexity of "packaged aid" plans, governmental forms, recomputation-of-the-need analysis, the paper work seems to be overwhelming. The aid counselor must be someone who believes deeply in self-help and the cooperative plan, in order to treat each individual applicant as fairly as possible. He must view cooperative work as paid employment that can help considerably in meeting college costs.

Foreign Students

Some of the problems involved in the enrollment and placement of foreign students in programs of cooperative education are discussed in Chapters 10 and 11. Colleges offering cooperative education programs should have a general policy statement setting forth the regulations for enrollment of foreign students, such as the following:

Academic requirement *Required completion of secondary education equivalent to U.S. secondary education and such examinations or tests as may be required.*

English proficiency *Recommended minimum TOEFL score of 450 for all applicants whose native language is not English.*

Financial resources *Required signed statement indicating that the student has sufficient financial resources to meet payment of all fees and other expenses while a student. Foreign students cannot depend on paid cooperative work assignments to meet expenses. If a student's financial status should change, so that he cannot meet tuition and/or living expenses, the college or university cannot assume any obligation of the student, and he must be prepared in these circumstances for loss of his student visa and for return to his country. It is advisable, therefore, that he have an emergency fund to cover return passage and subsistence.*

Housing *In recent years the housing problem has become critical. If university housing is unavailable, foreign students should expect to have to find their own off-campus housing.*

Student visa *A Certificate of Eligibility (I-20) is issued only to full-time students already qualified and accepted for a degree-granting program. Part-time and special students are not qualified. A committee made up of the foreign student adviser and staff members of the admissions and financial-aid departments who work with foreign students will certify that a satisfactory assurance of financial responsibility has been obtained before an I-20 form is issued to any undergraduate student.*

Use of Physical Plant

Any college or university whose entire student body is enrolled in a cooperative program, alternating regularly periods of work and study, will achieve a more efficient use of its physical plant.

The physical plant may be in operation throughout the entire calendar year, but it will not be fully occupied during the summer term. Since the alternating plan of work and study requires the placement of students in the fall following their freshman year, the freshmen returning for the sophomore year are not on campus during the summer months. Similarly, seniors on the cooperative plan have graduated. Therefore, the operation during the summer months may be one of only partial use of the capacity of the physical plant. There is a growing tendency to begin off-campus placement following the completion of the freshman academic year. If this can be accomplished, and at the same time other students are encouraged to attend during the summer months, the plant will be used more fully. There is, however, some advantage to having a smaller enrollment during the summer months, since maintenance and repair of buildings may be carried out then.

One of the greatest advantages of total commitment to cooperative education on the part of a college or university is the accommodation of a larger number of students in an existing plant. Many assume that a traditional college converting to the cooperative plan of education can automatically double its upper-class enrollment using the same classroom and housing facilities. This is a false assumption, because the freshman class has to be increased substantially in size to provide an enrollment large enough to provide full occupancy of the plant in each of the two upper-class alternating divisions. Dormitory space, therefore, would limit the size of the upper-class enrollment in a residential college, whereas a commuting college might possibly double its enrollment provided it has the necessary classroom facilities to conduct its educational program.

One might assume that the number of spaces in upper-class residence halls need be only half the total enrollment of upper-class students for those colleges that have students equally divided between alternating periods of work and classroom experience. Actually, this is not the case. Many students live in the dormitories and hold jobs near the college and, therefore, occupy the rooms throughout the academic year and often during the summer months. On the other hand, some students taking jobs that require moving to another community may need to relinquish their rooms during the college year, thereby causing dormitory vacancies.

There will be a sizable vacancy in dormitories during the summer months, since the freshmen have finished their academic year and are on vacation and the seniors have graduated. Budgeting for dormitory operations must take this into account, and rates should be scaled so as to provide the annual income essential to cover the operating costs of dormitories, knowing that there will be a lower occupancy for part of the calendar year.

The cost of operating the dormitory remains essentially the same whether or not there is a 10–15 per cent vacancy. Hence, a coop college which can make rooms available to students placed in off-campus assignments near the university, as well as those students who are attending classes, has a financial advantage. The additional income is, in reality, extra income which would not otherwise be available, since the planned operation of the dormitories does not involve full occupancy.

Statistical Projections

Statistical projections of enrollments usually performed by the college registrar or by the comptroller, are basic to the calculation of income for budgeting purposes. The projection of enrollments in a cooperative college involves calculation of the numbers expected to be enrolled on campus and the numbers to be placed on off-campus assignments. In a cooperative plan generally, the freshman year is on a continuous basis, and the summer following the freshman year is the last summer that is a student's own. The registrar is called upon to estimate the number of sophomores expected in the fall of the year. The department of cooperative education begins placing half of these sophomores in off-campus assignments during the summer. The other half begin classes in the fall. If the registrar estimated that one thousand sophomores would enroll in the fall, then the cooperative education department would place five hundred. The other five hundred would enroll for class attendance. If the registrar is wrong in his projection, so that only a total of eight hundred sophomores return to college or accept cooperative assignments, then five hundred students would be placed in off-campus assignments and only three hundred enrolled as on-campus students. The resulting imbalance of classes would mean a discrepancy in off-campus assignments and an imbalance in teaching loads.

Students enrolled in cooperative plans of higher education are subject to lower attrition rates than those enrolled in traditional programs. In large part this is due to the motivation provided by off-campus experience and to cooperative placement earnings—a built-in financial-aid feature. One cooperative university reports the following retention rates: freshmen, 85 per cent; sophomores, 87 per cent; middlers (third year), 92 per cent; juniors, 96 per cent. The loss of students in the upper-class years at the end of each quarter is approximately 3 per cent for second- and third-year students and 2 per cent for fourth- and fifth-year students.

Statistical patterns of attrition should be based on the past experience of the particular institution. Alertness should be maintained for any shifts that may be developing. These changes will often be dictated by events external to the institution—for instance, by changes in draft laws or by unemployment in areas of the economy. Failure to detect modifying influences in attrition patterns can result in poor resource predictions, leading to management difficulty.

The development of incoming-freshman patterns should also be observed carefully. Number quotas are a necessity for facility, staffing, and financial-management planning. The progress toward quotas should be observed continually, with an eye for shifts in curriculum selection. Changes in curriculum choices will affect not only the freshman year but also, if they are substantial, the distribution of students in future upper-class years. In addition, shifts in academic interests of students may have an impact upon the cooperative work phases of the program, in terms of type of work experiences desired. Broad examples of these shifts in recent years are the drift away from the science-oriented programs to the nonscience and, in a more general sense, from undergraduate professional programs to more general or nonscience fields of study.

Budgeting

The sources of revenues of colleges and universities having cooperative plans of education are the same as for other types of institutions—endowment income or taxpayers' support, grants by foundations and government agencies, gifts, tuition and fees.

In those private colleges whose cooperative plan is one of alternating periods of work and study during four or five years, tuition charges must be sufficient to pay all instructional costs and general overhead as well as the costs of placement and supervision of students during their off-campus experience. Colleges and universities operating optional and selective programs may charge special fees to meet the costs of coordination and placement. Some selective programs impose a charge on employers for the privilege of having coop students.

Budgeting for the conduct of cooperative programs has these special features:

First, the budgets for the cooperative plan programs which require alternating periods of study and off-campus assignment must be for a full calendar year of operation.

Second, conversion to the cooperative plan does not mean that upper-class enrollments are doubled, because half the student body is on off-campus assignments. Thus, to make full use of the physical plant, the traditional college that adopts a cooperative plan must substantially increase its freshman class to provide for two groups of upper-class students, each of which when combined with freshman enrollment will make complete use of the physical plant. A doubling of the size of upper classes can be planned if the physical plant can accommodate the on-campus instruction and requirements for living accommodations.

Third, the overhead expense applicable to cooperative colleges or programs can be spread over a larger number of students, including both those on campus and those having off-campus assignments. Since much overhead expense has the tendency to be fixed, the cooperative program minimizes the per-student overhead cost.

Fourth, the budgeting of the physical plant's operation on a twelve-month basis must take into account the curtailment of activities during the summer months. Because those completing the freshman year are on vacation and the senior class has graduated, dormitory space and classrooms will not be used to capacity.

Fifth, budgeting for a sizable in-house maintenance staff to do alterations and repair work may be undesirable. It may be necessary to contract for such work, since the plant is occupied throughout the calendar year, thereby allowing only a short period of time when repair work and alterations can be undertaken.

Sixth, the financing of payrolls and operations during the summer months minimizes the potential need to borrow funds. In a large operation, the need may even be eliminated. The cash flow continues because of the summer operations.

Seventh, the optional and selective programs of cooperative education may increase the total costs of operation. Additional (trailer) courses may have to be offered in order to allow the students in these programs to complete their degree requirements. Moreover, the cost of a coordination and placement office may be an added expense not covered by existing tuition costs.

Eighth, dormitory financial planning must take into account the accommodation of upper-class students living on campus while on off-campus assignments in the community where the college or university is located. Therefore, it cannot be assumed that dormitory space is needed for only half of the number of upper-class enrollment.

Ninth, reserves to stabilize dormitory and food-service income should be established in recognition of the unpredictability of placements in off-campus assignments. In one term a larger number of students may be living on campus because their off-campus assignments are located in a community adjacent to the college; in another term, placements may require students to live either at home or where their off-campus assignments are situated.

Tenth, in planning income based upon enrollments, a college can offset attrition of upper-class students by accepting transfer students in each of the terms when the cooperative plan is in operation. This not only increases income from students but also helps to balance the numbers enrolled in two divisions. At times the attrition in one division will be larger than in another.

Eleventh, cooperative education operated on a two-division basis in the upper-class years lends itself to the admission of a second or late-fall freshman class, thereby enhancing the income from tuition and fees. This class may be scheduled into courses regularly offered, thereby saving costs of tuition; or courses may be offered for the group on a separate basis, using faculty who do not have full teaching loads. In the fall term following the freshman year, this second group can be combined with the regular freshman class.

Twelfth, in times of declining enrollments (such as in a war period or a period of business recession), colleges that have all students alternating periods of on-campus studies and off-campus assignments can make economies by placing each of the upper classes (second, third, fourth, and fifth years) in a single division. For example, second-year students might be in one division and third-year students in another. Course programs can then be offered once instead of being repeated for the two divisions. A similar arrangement can be made in offering the fourth- and fifth-year courses. Colleges on the cooperative plan can also effect economies by allowing credit for coop experience, thereby reducing the number of courses required for the degree which must be taught by on-campus faculty. Moreover, students can be encouraged to undertake off-campus projects for credit, such as studying the organization of businesses, industries, and health agencies where they are undertaking their off-campus assignments. Moreover, students can be given sizable blocks of credit for independent study conducted in the evenings when they are located off campus. To the extent that the granting of these credits reduces on-campus class hours, economies in the cost of instruction can result.

Thirteenth, the cash income of a college or university committed to the cooperative plan of education simplifies the financial management. Similarly, the cash income of an optional or selective program of a college or university will provide a continuing flow of cash for a twelve-month period. In the college operated on the quarter plan, cash is received every three months, thereby making allocation and use of these funds less difficult than when income is received once or twice a year or possibly three times a year.

Public Relations

Colleges and universities offering cooperative programs of study, particularly those that are totally committed as an institution or in one or more colleges, must include in their public relations programs a continuing emphasis on developing an understanding and appreciation of cooperative education. It is essential that there be an ongoing internal public relations program to give administrators and faculty information about the cooperative plan and to keep them abreast of new developments. Neglect of this may result in apathetic or adverse attitudes toward the program. The principal means of keeping administrators and faculty informed are orientation programs for all new faculty and newsletters to keep them informed about ongoing and new programs.

Guidance officers in secondary schools and employment managers in industries and in health and government agencies change frequently. There is, therefore, a need to educate each new appointee to these positions on the value of cooperative education. Some may have little or no understanding of it. Therefore, frequent publicity must be aimed at the schools and employers, not only reporting news and events but also indirectly selling the program and its advantages.

The following media can be used to promote cooperative education: (1) the public press, to present studies about cooperative education and the development of new programs; (2) weekly and hometown newspapers, to describe the unique positions held by students, featuring their coop assignments; (3) magazines, newspapers, and publications of employers, to describe the coop program and the students involved; (4) fund-raising literature stressing the advantages of cooperative education; (5) campus literature, such as flyers welcoming persons to the campus, making a feature of cooperative education; and (6) newsletters or bulletins to be sent by the college or university regularly to secondary school principals and guidance officers and presidents and employment managers and coop placement directors of employers.

The use of recognition awards promotes an appreciation of the cooperative program among employers, students, faculty, and the general public. This involves the giving of certificates and possibly cash awards to students who have been outstanding in the completion of their coop assignments. Coordinators and employers are invited to submit lists of names of students who have been outstanding in the performance of their coop assignments for consideration as award recipients. Once the nominations for these awards have been made, it is desirable that a committee be appointed to assure the impartial selection of those who are to be recipients.

Representatives of the companies or organizations where the recipients of the awards have completed their cooperative work assignments, representatives of the university, and, of course, the immediate supervisors and coordinators of the recipients may be hosted at a luncheon or convocation. Photographs of the award presentations can then be taken and sent to the hometown newspapers of the recipients, publications of the organizations where the recipients were assigned, and the general press.

The basis for selection of students is the regular reports by employers describing the effectiveness of students in completing their coop assignments, the individual appraisal of the supervisor, and the judgment of the coordinator who has been working with the student.

Alumni Relations and Development

Most of the students who enroll in cooperative education programs become loyal alumni. Many have found cooperative education to be a path to a college degree, as well as to a superior kind of education. The value they place on cooperative education is demonstrated by the large numbers of graduates who want their own sons and daughters to profit from this kind of education. Moreover, many graduates of cooperative programs become employers of cooperative students and particularly of those students enrolled at their alma maters.

Officers in charge of alumni relations at cooperative colleges and universities report that the recent graduate of a cooperative education school is usually more mature and independent than his counterpart at a noncooperative education school. Alumni functions such as reunions, homecoming, luncheon and alumni club meetings must therefore be planned with this in mind. Because their campus life was interrupted by cooperative education work terms, and because classes had two divisions, these students do not always display enthusiastic class allegiance and are often reluctant to attend alumni functions. These difficulties tend to diminish with the length of time an individual has been an alumnus.

From the standpoint of development, specific fund-raising advantages stem from cooperative education. A cooperative education graduate employed by the company where he worked as a student usually has a head start over other new employees. Since the retention of coop students by many employers averages 50 per cent or more of the cooperative education students employed, there are large numbers of alumni in the employ of many businesses and industries. When this fact is combined with the numbers of cooperative education students employed at businesses and industries, a very strong case can be built for corporate financial support of the cooperative education colleges or universities. In some large businesses and industries in the United States, the largest group of graduates of any single college is composed of those graduated from colleges having cooperative education programs.

A further plus factor is that an increasing number of businesses and industries are tending to rely on cooperative education as a major source of new employees. They recognize the value of employing cooperative education trainees, retaining those who are best qualified and who have developed loyalty to the firms employing them. They also recognize that the employee is already oriented toward the company and that this form of recruitment is far superior to the interview and plant visit, far less expensive, with fewer turnovers. This, of course, also facilitates alumni placement at the college or university.

It must be recognized, however, that some employers of cooperative students feel that they are making a contribution to the college or university when they employ students. These employers are not good gift prospects until they become aware that the institution and the corporation mutually share the many advantages of cooperative education. In addition, many of the employers of cooperative education students include governmental, health, and social agencies. These are not sources of financial support, but they are vital to the placement and education of students.

In light of the foregoing, it is not surprising that many colleges having cooperative education programs, and particularly those wholly committed to cooperative education, have the most meaningful case when seeking corporate gifts. The case also has a tremendous positive influence when dealing with foundations and individuals, particularly due to its unique and superior type of education and its attractiveness to disadvantaged and minority groups. This attractiveness could explain the necessity for increased efforts to obtain and sustain a high percentage of individual giving. Since many alumni of cooperative education schools are the first family generation to obtain a college education, they have not been exposed to, nor in the habit of charitable giving.

XV

Academic Administration

Asa S. Knowles

Faculty personnel policies in cooperative colleges and universities regarding such areas as tenure, academic freedom, appointment procedures, and contractual agreements are generally the same as those in most traditional institutions. Special salary policies must be established, however, for faculty who teach extra summer courses in the year-round cooperative program (see Chapter 20).

One of the difficulties encountered in cooperative education programs over the years has been the lack of support, and at times outright hostility, toward the system itself on the part of some faculty members, particularly those accustomed to the shorter programs of traditional colleges. They dislike the repetition of course materials, the shorter holiday and summer vacation periods, and the fact that they have to teach during the summer at all.

Some faculty who are very critical of the cooperative system at the outset of their careers may in time become among the most enthusiastic. Among other things, they recognize the maturity of their students, and the value of the off-campus experience as a supplement to their classroom teaching.

The administration of any cooperative institution should establish comprehensive orientation periods for new faculty each year in order to explain thoroughly the details of operation and the benefits of the system as a whole. As is true with students and administrators, faculty must be wholly committed to the cooperative plan in order to ensure its continuing success.

Faculty who are not wholly committed to the philosophy of cooperative education have been known to cause morale problems, not only among their colleagues but among their students. When the cooperative plan is optional at an institution, some have tried to persuade students to study on a full-time basis and disregard the off-campus-experience aspect of the program. These faculty could profitably be referred to the Epiloque of this book—especially the recommendations made by three recent national studies on higher education.

Many faculty members realize that cooperative students who gain work experience in the field may establish higher standards for them than would normally be the case at more traditional institutions. Cooperative students can be critical evaluators, their evaluations often resulting in the retention of the more competent instructor and the one who is interested in each individual student in his course.

Influence of Cooperative Education on Curricula

In spite of the negative attitude on the part of some faculty toward the cooperative system, studies show that most faculties (particularly those in professional curricula such as engineering, business administration, pharmacy, and nursing, where the validity of the cooperative concept in career preparation is most evident) appreciate the values of cooperative education and support it. Faculty in liberal-arts curricula—philosophy, history, literature, and language arts, for example—may be less receptive, because their students cannot always be placed in work situations directly related to their fields of study.

With the current variety in forms of cooperative off-campus experience, however, this problem is rapidly becoming minimized—particularly since direct connections between the work and study aspects of the educational program are being deemphasized, especially in the humanities and social sciences. In nontechnical areas, emphasis often is on the human development of the student as an individual, for the role he sees for himself in society in the years ahead.

As mentioned, the relevance of the cooperative experience is particularly evident in business administration, engineering, and such health professions as pharmacy and nursing. In business administration, the cooperative program has little if any influence on the sequence of courses, but a definite impact on their content. It must be up to date. Students return to the classroom from many different areas of the business world, many times with numerous questions stimulated by their experiences. The faculty member must have the answers, thereby bringing even greater relevance not only to his teachings but to his own learning process.

It is much the same in engineering. In traditional engineering colleges, laboratories have been necessary to illustrate practical applications of complex theories. Their purpose, to an extent, has been to simulate the real world or industrial environment. The on-campus laboratory, unfortunately, is too often an artificial, unthinking, and mechanical set of procedures and not a meaningful educational experience. In a cooperative program, where many of the students are exposed to a real industrial environment, complete with associated tools, equipment, and machinery, the on-campus laboratory experience can be minimized.

The advantages of internship or apprenticeship cooperative periods to pharmacy and nursing students are obvious. They are working in hospitals, clinics, pharmacies, and health agencies of all types, acquiring knowledge invaluable to them—not only in their academic and laboratory work on the campus but in preparation for their future careers as members of vitally needed medical teams.

Faculty Involvement in Placement

Faculties of cooperative colleges, which are generally larger than those of more traditional institutions due to the very nature of the educational system, should have a voice in the placement of their students in off-campus experiences. The correlation between the job and the teaching in many instances is of vital importance. Although some faculty will never be persuaded that they should not have *full* control over the student's off-campus experience, it has been proven that a systematic effort on the part of the institution's coordination staff to keep faculty informed on the student's progress results in a positive working relationship between the two groups. Most cooperative coordinators have faculty status and are thus able to relate on an effective professional level with most teaching faculty.

Academic Credit for Off-Campus Experience

In 1968 the Cooperative Education Association and the Cooperative Education Division of the American Society for Engineering Education appointed joint committees to study certain matters particularly relevant to the cooperative education movement in the United States and Canada. One of these committees was the Committee on Academic Credit.

In its report to CEA-CED in January 1971, the committees stated that "a climate of opinion favorable for granting academic credit now exists." This conclusion was based on information received from a series of questionnaires sent to cooperative students and to academic and employer coordinators.

CEA and CED approved the following recommendations "as a general guideline":

Institutions providing cooperative educational experiences to their students should grant academic credit for these off-campus assignments under the following circumstances: (1) The student completes all required off-campus cooperative educational assignments in his specific program. (2) The student submits a final written report to the educational institution after the conclusion of the final work period for consideration for academic credit. (3) Evaluation will be on a pass-fail basis.

These recommendations were subsequently supported "in principle" by ASEE's executive board.

The questionnaires used by the joint CEA-CED committee revealed the following information:

Thirty-two per cent of the schools do not require a specific number of work assignments; 26 per cent do not register students on work assignments; work assignments themselves vary in length from five or fewer weeks to six months.

By a large majority, students favor academic credit, even if additional work is required on their part. When students were asked how many hours they would work for the credit, answers ranged up to forty hours. The students also indicated a preference to be graded by their industrial supervisor, and on a pass-fail basis.

A large majority of government and industry coordinators feel that their students perform on the job at a level of difficulty worthy of academic credit. On the other hand, favorable attitudes toward granting credit were reflected by slightly less than half the employers if extra work were required of the company.

The CEA-CED report listed three necessary steps to be taken: (1) A concerted effort should be made to have all schools register their students when they are on an off-campus assignment. (2) A certain minimum number of off-campus assignments for participation in the cooperative program should be adopted. (3) The question of whether work experience is "academic" should be resolved. Step 3 represents one of the major problems for any institution considering the awarding of academic credit for work experience. In the words of the CEA-CED committee:

It is recognized that certain off-campus experiences may be of a lesser quality than others. Also, a certain student may accomplish more than some other student on the job, and, therefore, the range of individual student experiences will vary. For this reason, it seems that academic credit should be granted for the total educational experience off campus, rather than for individual off-campus periods in industry. The final report submitted by the student to the faculty after completion of all off-campus experiences could consist of a comprehensive report covering all phases of the student's work, or individual reports which would be examined for their total content. In either case, the faculty would be required to make a judgment on how much, if any, academic credit could be granted for the total off-campus experiences.

The CEA-CED committee also feels that any academic credit awarded for work experience should not be of the "add-on" variety, since the original objective is to allow a student to use the off-campus experience as a partial fulfillment of his degree requirements.

A more recent survey on academic credit, conducted in the spring of 1971 by the author, revealed additional information on the subject of academic credit. In this survey, answered by 78 per cent of the 210 cooperative institutions contacted, 58 per cent said that they awarded some type of academic credit for off-campus work experience. Many did so in a limited manner, depending usually upon the field of study involved.

Most of the institutions granted the credit for paid employment or for independent study and research, although some did so for activities such as volunteer services, work in the Peace Corps or Vista, and foreign travel.

More than half of the institutions required that the off-campus experience correspond very closely to academic work, while only a few indicated that any type of relation between them was unimportant. The remainder required correspondence between work and study "to some extent."

In addition to the actual off-campus experience, many institutions require a related report, paper, collateral reading, or participation in seminars in order for students to earn academic credit.

Responsibility for the granting of academic credit, plus determining what off-campus experiences are acceptable for credit, rests in slightly more than half of the institutions with the teaching faculty. At the remainder of the institutions, the coordination staff and variously composed special committees (most often the former) have the responsibility.

The number of academic credits a student can earn through off-campus experience varies considerably from school to school, generally ranging from two to fifteen semester hours, depending upon the nature and scope of the project.

Most of the institutions specify that the credits earned through off-campus experience take the place of regular on-campus courses (usually electives), although a few use the "add-on" system, thus requiring a greater number of credits for graduation than would normally be the case. As mentioned earlier, the CEA-CED committee strongly opposes any type of "add-on" system, since the off-campus experience is supposedly of enough value to replace an on-campus credit course.

Many institutions whose coordination departments cannot provide off-campus experiences worthy of academic credit provide substitute methods. Among them are extra classroom experiences, additional course loads, on-campus employment, and various independent-study programs.

More than half of the institutions surveyed permit or encourage their students to take courses for academic credit while on their off-campus experience, either on their own campus or at other institutions. Some indicate that the courses *must* be taken on the student's own campus, while others require exactly the opposite. A few do not allow the taking of courses during the off-campus period. Those who do allow the taking of extra courses usually require students to obtain permission of the faculty advisor, coordinator, or in some cases the cooperative employer.

For information regarding student fees for the off-campus experience, as well as faculty compensation for teaching summer courses in the year-round cooperative school, see Chapter 20.

Accreditation

Agencies that accredit colleges and universities (those that accredit professional programs within an institution, and those that accredit the institution as a whole) have not been consistent in their policies with respect to recognition of academic credit for off-campus experiences. Several of the agencies accrediting professional programs of study are willing to recognize the satisfactory completion of an off-campus cooperative experience as a requirement toward the degree. They have always stipulated, however, that the experience be of the "add-on" variety and not part of (or taking the place of) the traditional credits earned in an on-campus academic program. Accrediting agencies concerned with the institution as a whole (Higher Education Commissions of the Regional Associations of Colleges and Schools) have been willing to accept academic credit for off-campus experience as equal in value to those earned in the classroom.

A shift in attitude is now developing, however; and recognition of off-campus experiences for academic credit by professional accrediting agencies may require professional licensing boards to modify their standards. With increasing emphasis on relevance of education through off-campus experience, and the growing trend in many colleges toward awarding credit for paid work, volunteer services, and other types of experience, a continuation of this shift seems virtually assured.

Reserve Officers' Training Corps Administration

Traditionally, students enrolled in the senior Reserve Officers' Training Corps (ROTC) have undergone a four-year training program which consists of two years of a basic course and two of an advanced program. The number of hours or courses required will vary according to the service program (Army, Navy, or Air Force) and will also vary from institution to institution.

Institutions hosting ROTC units and operating on other than the standard four-year curriculum, such as colleges operating on the cooperative plan of education, face a number of problems because of the "four-year orientation" of the national ROTC program. These schools must "tailor" their programs according to the needs of their coop students. While many of the special arrangements can be completed between the ROTC commander and the institution, some of the special tailoring requires the approval of the Department of the Army, Navy, or Air Force before it can be implemented.

Certain of the colleges in such institutions as Drexel University, University of Cincinnati, University of Detroit, and Northeastern University include all, or a large number, of their students in the cooperative program. This creates one set of unique administrative problems for the staff of the ROTC department. For example, enrollment and processing procedures have to be repeated each time a group of students returns to school. This nearly doubles the administrative workload of the ROTC administrative staff, and is a determining factor in the assignment of ROTC personnel to a coop institution. In addition, because of the nature of the cooperative calendar, it is not feasible to send the ROTC cadet to summer training until after graduation. Consequently, while the student may be well versed in military theory, his adaptability and qualifications under field conditions remain questionable until after he has completed the academic portion of the cur-

Table 24. ROTC Scheduling at Northeastern University (where coop is the major educational plan)

	Fall	*Winter*	*Spring*	*Summer*
First	Freshman 1 ROTC 1	Freshman 2 ROTC 2	Freshman 3 ROTC 3	Vacation
Second	Sophomore 1 ROTC 4	Work	Sophomore 2 ROTC 5	Work
Third	Work	Middler 1 ROTC 6	Work	Middler 2 ROTC 7
Fourth	Junior 1 ROTC 8	Work	Junior 2 ROTC 9	Work
Fifth	Work	Senior 1 ROTC 10	Senior 2 ROTC 11	

Table 25. ROTC Scheduling at Virginia Polytechnic Institute (where coop is an optional educational plan)

	Fall	*Winter*	*Spring*	*Summer*
First	Freshman 1 ROTC 1	Freshman 2 ROTC 2	Work 1	Freshman 3 ROTC 3
Second	Work	Sophomore 1 ROTC 5	Work 3	Sophomore 2 ROTC 4 or 6
Third	Work 4	Sophomore 3 ROTC 4 or 6	Work 5	Junior 1 ROTC 7 or 9
Fourth	Work 6	Junior 2 ROTC 8	Work 7	Junior 3 ROTC 7 or 9
Fifth	Senior 1 ROTC 10	Senior 2 ROTC 11	Senior 3 ROTC 12	

riculum. The Northeastern University calendar, shown in Table 24, indicates the ROTC scheduling for an institution which is almost exclusively cooperative in nature.

Under the cooperative plan, a faultless system of communications must be established between the ROTC department and the student. Since many ROTC administrative changes are ongoing throughout the five-year period, the ROTC department must maintain contact with all members of the cadet corps while they are on their cooperative assignments. This separation of student and institution is also responsible for causing ROTC officials some anxious moments when they are attempting to meet deadlines levied by higher headquarters.

At such schools as Georgia Institute of Technology, University of Tennessee, Illinois Institute of Technology, and Northwestern University, the administrative problems of ROTC are compounded because of the optional feature of coop. When cooperative students are enrolled in ROTC at these schools, the appropriate military department must adjust the curriculum to ensure that they complete their ROTC courses prior to graduation. Although each particular situation cannot be discussed here, sufficient flexibility must be maintained to incorporate these students in a viable ROTC program that permits them to complete their ROTC subjects prior to or in conjunction with their degree completion. This can be done by adjusting the student's ROTC schedule to meet his individual needs, by tutoring the student, or possibly by having him take double sessions in ROTC subjects during certain school quarters. In addition, it may be possible to offer ROTC courses out of sequence with the normal academic calendar. An example of this alternative is presented in Table 25, the academic calendar of Virginia Polytechnic Institute, which shows how VPI alternates its Army ROTC program.

Registration, Record Keeping, and Projections

In the college operated on the traditional plan of education, the academic calendar usually involves two semesters or possibly three quarters and a separate summer session, most of the time under a different administrative unit. In the college operated on the cooperative plan of education, however, the operation of the registrar's office involves certain unique administrative procedures. These procedures are associated with areas of operation, interpretation, and communication.

OPERATION. First of all, a cooperative college registrar has double registrations. If the cooperative plan consists of four equal quarters in a calendar year, there will be four registrations. In the traditional college, it would be two. If the cooperative plan were a 10-10-5, such as existed at Northeastern University for a long time, the registrar would have six registrations in a calendar year. Because of the extra registrations, which must be handled in a shorter period so as not to interfere with the classroom schedule, reduced periods demand increased efficiency.

One of the cardinal princlples of cooperative systems is that the divisions be as nearly equal as possible—so that students can be paired on a job and so that teaching loads can be equalized as they are between divisions.

Other operational procedures include double grade recording (which means that those difficulties sometimes associated with obtaining grades from faculty become even more numerous), double examination scheduling, and double issuance of grades (since more terms of classroom attendance under the cooperative plan are required for a degree, more grades need to be recorded on the permanent records).

INTERPRETATION. The cooperative plan is sometimes very difficult to interpret, and students and faculty do not understand its operation or its consequences. A student may, for example, petition for a change in division, not appreciating that a shift from a division that attends classes in the fall to a division that attends school in the winter would merely place him back in a class for a curriculum he has already had. It is difficult to explain to students and parents that under a cooperative plan one division must not have an advantage over another. A student who begins a fall term and fails courses knows that they will be offered in the winter term for the returning division. He sees no reason why he cannot forgo a term of cooperative work and repeat the courses. This opportunity is not available to the division that comes second at any time. This is particularly critical on the part of seniors who finish their last term earlier than students who were out on cooperative work, and need to come back to take their last term. It is difficult to explain the system to people who cannot understand how a student can be out on coop and still be a duly registered student meeting his degree requirements. It is the registrar usually who is called upon to explain this. When a transcript is sent to another institution, the transcript shows regular gaps in the chronology of the student's record, usually requiring detailed explanation.

COMMUNICATION. The problem of alternate periods between school and work means that the registrar needs to communicate with the student about matters pertaining to his next registration or to those pertaining to his last grading period. He must try to reach the student at his place of employment. This means that any validity to an address for a student who is on cooperative work is very suspect. All matters such as academic action following a term, or advice with respect to next term's registration, must be done by mail. This is usually a very unsatisfactory procedure.

A cooperative college registrar finds it very difficult to set vacation periods for his staff, since his office is operating almost with a full student body all year-round. He must also constantly be looking forward to the next succeeding term. As the modern trend toward freer course election takes place in cooperative colleges, the job of preregistration will become very difficult. For instance, preregistration for a spring term must take place during the fall and for the fall term during the spring. This means that class schedules and offerings must be pinned down well in advance of the registration involving these courses.

Finally, the cooperative college registrar must be more involved in the general administration of the college than in a traditional college, since he is the one who must caution his colleagues on the consequences of any administrative changes having to be gone through twice.

XVI

Legal Aspects

Thomas J. O'Toole

Nothing can more surely destroy an administrator's capacity to perform his task well than an excessive preoccupation with the legal consequences of his actions. Like a surgeon who is beset by a fear of being sued for malpractice, the university administrator may impose upon himself a kind of paralysis if at each turn he worries about the legal liabilities that might follow from his work. Nevertheless, we are in a litigious age, and increasingly the courts are being called upon to reexamine the policies and practices of university officials. In the interest of ordinary prudence, therefore, the responsible administrator should have some general idea of the legal rules that principally affect this area of activity.

The information contained in this chapter is not intended as an invitation for every man to serve as his own lawyer. In important matters, there is no substitute for sound legal advice given by a competent lawyer who has had an opportunity to examine the specific situation. The main function of this chapter is to assist in alerting the administrator to recognize the situations in which legal advice should be sought.

Legal Obligations to Students

The legal relationship between a matriculated student and a university is usually viewed as being governed in basic matters by principles of contract law. The student enrolls in the university to accept the offer which the university makes through its catalogs and other literature. The basic offer is that of courses of instruction, usually leading to a degree upon satisfactory completion. In a cooperative university, there is also an undertaking to assist the students in obtaining cooperative jobs. The university should take care that it does not promise more than it is willing to be required to deliver. If it represents that a cooperative job will be obtained for each student, it is making a promise to which it could be held, with liability for loss of earnings should a student not be placed in a job. Care should therefore be taken that the literature expresses the university's undertaking as one of making a good-faith and intelligent effort to obtain job opportunities.

In the administration of cooperative education plans, the university is legally obligated to inform a student of such safety risks on the job as are not likely to be appreciated by the student and are either known to the university or, in the exercise of ordinary prudence, should have been discovered by the university.

The university's intrusion into the terms and conditions of employment should not be so pervasive as to put the university in control of these terms and conditions. These matters should be left to adjustment between the student and his employer, so that the university is not subjected to any of the potential legal liabilities that properly fall upon an employer.

In this connection, it should be noted that the ordinary operation of a program of cooperative education has the university serving as a job broker. Insofar as the university's activities are limited to the placement of students as part of a bona fide plan of cooperative education, the university does not subject itself to regulation of statutes designed to control employment agencies. In order to perpetuate this freedom from a regulatory scheme which was designed to combat evil practices in commercial employment agencies, the university must not allow its placement activities to be operated for a placement fee or in favor of persons not connected with the university's educational program.

Legal Obligations to Employers

The usual arrangement between a university conducting a cooperative plan of education and the employers who hire students does not involve any fixed or continuing obligation on the part of the university to supply students to fill any given number of positions. The university should avoid making any such commitment, because the failure to meet such an undertaking could result in legal liability. The university should, however, have definite and written arrangements with the employer for supplying those reports on student job performance which are essential for completion of the student's record and which are useful in appraising the educational value of the job.

When a cooperative education coordinator presents a student to fill a particular kind of job, he thereby makes representations on behalf of the university that he has no reason to know that the student is incompetent for the position. Where the student's record indicates that his working at a particular job would pose a particular threat to the property, materials, or personnel of the employer, there is an obligation to make this known. In the event of nondisclosure, the university could be held liable.

Too often it is supposed in academic circles (and elsewhere) that a corporate organization can control its liabilities by having resolutions of the Board of Trustees (or Board of Directors) limiting to a few designated persons the power to bind the university in contract. The designation of official contracting officers has important utility, especially in dealing with banks and other financial institutions. It does not, however, overcome the common-law principle that one who deals with a person who holds an office is entitled to assume that that person has full authority to carry out those matters which reasonably appear to relate to his office and, in connection therewith, to make commitments binding upon the university. Unless one is specifically informed of a limitation upon his authority, one is legally protected in dealing with him on the basis of appearances. It must therefore be understood that a person in the position of a cooperative education coordinator has a capacity to obligate the university beyond its expectations if he does not conduct himself prudently. By developing a set of standard policies, and inventing printed forms to be used in dealings with employers, the university can reduce the risk of an unintended liability.

Status of Student during Working Periods

Because the basic theory of cooperative education is that the work experience is part of the educational process, the student is still viewed as a student even during working periods. This position has been taken under the Military Manpower Act, and whenever the student's status carries with it his draft exemption, the exemption persists throughout the working period. On the other hand, benefits such as those offered by the Veterans' Administration, which are contingent upon a student's taking a stated minimum number of class hours per week, do not continue but are interrupted. As a corollary, cooperative work periods are not counted in determining whether a veteran's eligibility time for educational benefits has been consumed. It is, of course, understood that statutory date limits for the use of veterans' benefits, based upon lapse of time since discharge from the armed services, are not suspended by working periods.

TAXATION OF EARNINGS. Whether earnings obtained on a cooperative education job are taxable has been the subject of lively debate. The usual practice is to treat them as wages earned, subject to withholding tax and reportable as earned income. A theoretical case can be made for their exemption because of the underlying educational purpose of cooperative education. However, the Internal Revenue Service takes the tax collector's view.

UNION MEMBERSHIP. Once the student is on a cooperative job, his status for purposes of union membership, collective-bargaining agreements, and related matters can in no way be controlled by the university. Questions of this type usually hinge upon definitions of the word "employee." No categorical answer can be given as to whether a cooperative education student who is working on a job is an "employee"; for the answer may vary, even for the same job, depending upon the specific context in which the question arises. Much of importance may hinge upon the answer which is given, especially as it affects students' rights to fringe benefits. University personnel should not attempt to advise students on these matters but should refer the question to the employer.

RIGHTS TO INVENTION. Elsewhere in this book (Chapter 6) there is an indication of how the problem of rights to inventions might be handled. In employment situations where there is a foreseeable possibility of invention, the employer is almost certain to have a policy concerning ownership. The university can assist in the prevention of misunderstandings and disagreements by inquiring into the question and making sure that the appropriate forms are executed by the student.

Foreign Students

Aliens admitted to this country on student visas are restricted in their right to accept gainful employment. This restriction obviously affects their eligibility for cooperative education experiences. In its literature, the university should make clear that there are these limitations and, in any event, should specifically notify any foreign students it is accepting for matriculation that there are these restrictions. The present regulations are set forth in Volume 8 of the Code of Federal Regulations, Part 214.2(3). Aliens on student visas may be employed for no more than eighteen months, in time increments not to exceed six months. The work must be certified as necessary practical training in connection with the educational program. Current information concerning this matter can be obtained from the District Director of Immigration and Naturalization in whose district the university is located.

Laws against Discrimination

Under Title VI of the Civil Rights Act, and under similar state legislation, discrimination in employment and education is prohibited. While state laws vary in their scope, we are clearly reaching a point in history where discrimination by reason of race, color, creed, sex, or age will be outlawed. In conducting a cooperative education program, the university of course must comply with these norms and should see that they are extended not simply to its admission process but also to its cooperative job-placement activity. The problem can become particularly delicate when the university confronts a cooperative employer who chooses not to obey the law. Obviously, the obligation of the university is to refrain from lending assistance to those employers whose practices are illegal. It is not the function of the university to become a policeman to enforce the law or to make moral or legal judgments based upon mere suspicion; but when it is clear that the employer persists in following legally proscribed policies, the university should terminate its relationship with this employer.

Legal Obligations of Student to University

Under the contractual arrangement made between the university and the students, the student is free to withdraw at any time, subject to such loss of credit as may be provided under the university's academic regulations and subject to meeting the financial obligations he has already incurred. Unauthorized withdrawals obviously interfere with the operation of a cooperative plan of education. It is customary for the university to obtain from a student a written agreement that he has accepted the cooperative job offered to him and that he will continue to work until released or transferred with the approval of the cooperative education offices. These agreements run between the student and the university and should be carefully drafted to avoid any appearance that they are contracts of employment. The sanctions for breach of such agreement must be limited to academic penalties. Despite the importance to the university that the student commit himself to the job, these agreements are inappropriate for legal enforcement.

Placement activities in connection with cooperative education cannot be administered effectively unless the university is in a position to supply to prospective employers relevant information concerning a student's background and achievement. In recent years there has been a growing sense of the right to privacy, and in some universities the release of information in student files has become a controversial issue. The university therefore should ask the student to sign an appropriate form authorizing the disclosure of such information from the student's file as appears appropriate for job-placement purposes. These consent forms should be kept in the student's file.

Legal Aspects from Employer's Perspective

The foregoing discussion should make it clear that under a plan of cooperative education the employer cannot expect the university to make a contractually enforceable undertaking to supply students for the positions they may offer. It should also be clear that the contract of employment runs directly between the employer and the student, and the university is in no sense a party to that contract. Terms and conditions of employment must be arranged by the employer and accepted by the student. The university's role in these matters is to reject those positions which do not offer decent and competitive terms.

It is important for the employer to resolve the question discussed concerning the status of the cooperative student while on the job. For all purposes of public law, the student will be an employee, but whether he falls within the collective-bargaining agreement would require scrutiny of the individual agreement involved. An employer who regularly hires cooperative students might well consider negotiating into a collective-bargaining agreement an explicit provision defining the extent to which cooperative students are covered by the labor agreement.

XVII

Admissions and Relations with Secondary Schools

Gilbert C. Garland

The admission requirements of a cooperative institution are little different from those of any other type of institution. All are subject to similar academic standards and regulations. Where cooperative programs are available, however, a number of unique factors govern admissions policies and procedures.

Those who staff admissions offices in colleges which operate cooperative plans should be professionally qualified in career guidance and educational guidance as well. In addition, they must be sound in their evaluation of young talent, alert to employment trends, and convinced that cooperative education is quality education which affords maturing and challenging experiences for their prospective students.

Influence of Program

There are many different plans of cooperative education. Some programs are mandatory, some are optional, and some are selective. Moreover, there are differences in the length of these programs. Some have cooperative work for two years out of a four-year program, and some have coop for six to eight weeks during each of the four years. Among the four-year schools, some programs lead to a degree in four years, but some require five.

Whether the cooperative plan is mandatory or optional will govern the size of the pool of candidates from which an entering class is selected. If the program is available only to selected students of high academic potential, such a plan will obviously attract applicants who represent only a fraction of the total pool of high school graduates. In this type of plan, applicants should be advised that their involvement in coop will not be automatic but will be governed by their academic achievement.

When educational travel at the student's expense is encouraged, or when no income is realized from cooperative employment, the pool of candidates for admission will be different from the pool of candidates who regard cooperative job income as indispensable to meeting their tuition and other college expenses. In the one instance, applicants tend to come from affluent communities which are willing to support high-quality public education. In the other instance, applicants tend to come from communities in the middle- or lower-middle-income range, with fewer tax dollars invested in teacher salaries and school facilities. In either case the quality of secondary school preparation will be affected.

When cooperative work programs are required of all students, those who apply for admission tend to be more career conscious than those who seek entrance to noncooperative schools. If their career choices have not been defined, students see in cooperative education an opportunity to explore a number of career fields and eventually to focus in upon those areas that may have appeal. Admissions counselors are strongly advised to stress the career-guidance benefits of cooperative education as they interview students. Work experience is, indeed, the unique facet of schools which offer coop programs; through it the young adult can grow in motivation and in total human development. Many students cite a change from the usual routine of class work, library research, and examinations as a principal reason for applying for admission to cooperative education programs. Increasingly, also, both students and parents recognize the maturing values of the work experience. Today, in a national period of economic and social unrest, applicants for admission speak of involvement and relevancy as qualities which they demand in their education. They find these qualities as they gain experience in a ghetto social agency, a rehabilitation center, a school system, or an industrial unit concerned with such issues as waste disposal and conservation. Cooperative education is, indeed, a strong promotional tool for the admissions counselor.

Students enrolled in cooperative programs at publicly supported institutions have the advantage of low tuition and coop earnings. This combination enables them to meet their living expenses and, in many instances, to afford educational travel. Those who attend privately supported institutions where the coop plan is mandatory also profit from their weekly salaries to the extent that, even if employed away from home, they may be able to reduce their total expenses by as much as one half. These financial advantages have great student appeal, and they serve to lessen the possibility that in a given year the supply of candidates for admission will drop sharply.

Complete frankness on the part of the admissions counselor is imperative, however, when he discusses the financial advantages of cooperative education. Special student fees may be required when the work experience is regarded as a privilege rather than a requirement. Such fees also exist for educational travel or for other variations in the cooperative program that require special supervisory or administrative costs. Job assignments may not be as lucrative as the student might wish, and the economic market at any given time may directly affect wages. Volunteer work or independent research will likely be at the student's own expense. Such matters as these should be treated fairly when the student asks to what extent his cooperative earnings will reduce the costs of college attendance.

At a time when tuition and other college costs continue to mount, cooperative education is becoming increasingly attractive to students and their parents. Candidates for admission weigh total costs against anticipated earnings from cooperative employment and discover that to attend a state-supported school is not the only option available to them. At times a coop school can be less expensive than a state school if the student can live at home and save his earnings for tuition and other direct college costs.

Since many cooperative programs require a freshman year of full-time study before students are involved in the alternation of work and study, financial-aid programs tend to invest a sizable amount of their total student-aid package in the first year. Thereafter, financial aid necessarily takes into account the student's cooperative earning capacity and the location of his job (that is, whether he is employed within commuting distance of his home community). The institution's total financial-aid commitment to students is obviously smaller than might be expected, since many upper-class students, as a result of their earning capaciites, are self-sustaining for at least half of a school year. Other students may well exceed that financial achievement.

Informing High School Counselors

College placement officers at the secondary school level are in a most strategic position to advise their students in the matter of college selection. Therefore, college admissions personnel should help secondary school counselors become as familiar as possible with those colleges to which they refer students. This must be a process of continual education; for curriculum change, the addition of new teaching facilities, and the strengthening of student service programs are among developments of extreme importance to future students.

Those who control the admissions operations of cooperative colleges must explain the objectives and operations of these programs as they exist at their own institutions. Their ability to do this through a variety of communications media will directly affect an admissions department's recruiting efforts. In some instances, erroneous conceptions of cooperative education must be corrected. In other instances, due to the frequent turnover of school guidance personnel, counselors may be ignorant of cooperative education and the many benefits it affords enrolled students. For example, although the cooperative plan is as effective in the education of young women as it is in the education of young men, school guidance counselors tend to discourage girls from considering career fields which may traditionally be considered male strongholds. Therefore, girls may avoid such courses as mathematics and the physical sciences. In their visits to secondary schools, admissions counselors should stress that cooperative education can open doors to many employment situations that historically have been dominated by males—such fields as actuarial science, computer programming, law enforcement, environmental science, animal husbandry, and a variety of opportunities within the broad field of engineering. Admissions counselors should point out to school counselors that cooperative education can be especially helpful to girls, since through their coop assignments a great broadening of career opportunities can result. Recent national enrollment trends show an increase of 4.4 per cent for women as opposed to 3.2 per cent for men over the previous year. The pool of women's applications deserves the close attention of admissions counselors in coop schools, which can offer unique employment opportunities for such students.

Effective instruments for the education of school counselors include the following: (1) On-campus programs can be arranged for counselors to meet with those who are responsible for coop placement of students. A series of small-group workshops may prove to be especially fruitful. (2) Conferences can be scheduled at the secondary school whereby admissions personnel may discuss cooperative education with an entire guidance staff. (3) Special literature and visual aids, which feature actual case studies of coop students and their jobs, can be developed. The literature should emphasize the way in which those jobs contributed to the personal development of the students. (4) Coop students themselves can visit the secondary schools from which they graduated. Few colleges make effective use of the talents of their own students as spokesmen for cooperative education; and where this approach has been used, the results are invariably excellent. (5) An attractive and informative catalog can be developed for pre-freshmen only. Such a publication can contain information on entrance requirements, programs of study, and financial aid; but it can also serve a career-guidance function as well. Specifically, it should contain a complete description of the cooperative plan. As such, it will become a welcome addition to the school counselor's library of resource material. It can also be sent to prospective student applicants.

Presentation in National Educational Services

Commercially or professionally sponsored publications and questionnaires which devote themselves to college profiles, and which have a student and school library distribution, frequently give minor attention to coop programs, or make no reference to them at all. The admissions officer, as well as those in the college's publications or public relations office, must constantly review such publications to verify reference or lack of reference to cooperative education. It may be necessary to write to the editors of these publications, or to the sponsors of institutional questionnaires, if inadequate copy is devoted to the program.

In recent years computer programs have developed on the national scene. These programs are intended to help the student match his own profile with the profiles of colleges that meet his requirements. One such program, now referred to as the College Locater Service, is currently being developed by the College Entrance Examination Board. These efforts are to be commended; and admissions personnel should study them closely to make certain that the concept of cooperative education is fully and fairly presented.

Presentation to Potential Students

In general, when an institution is fully committed in all its programs to cooperative education, applicants for admission should be informed that an additional year may be required in order to complete the degree program; that they will be studying or working during an entire calendar year, so that the usual long summer vacations will not be available to them as cooperative work students; that requirements for the baccalaureate degree demand not only satisfactory academic achievement but also satisfactory performance on cooperative work assignments; that not all students will realize the financial benefits of those who are employed near their homes or those who profit from employer subsidies; and that students in the social sciences and humanities will probably have lower earnings than those whose interests lie in science and technology.

Questions will still arise, however; more often than not, they concern the additional year required to meet degree requirements (where such is the case) and the nature of cooperative work assignments.

ADDITIONAL YEAR. It is not uncommon for a cooperative plan's calendar to require an additional year before degree requirements are met; and often this is the single most objectionable feature in the minds of some students. When this objection is voiced, the admissions counselor should point in a positive way to the fact that wages earned will enable the student to gain a good measure of financial independence—a feature that has strong appeal to most young adults. The counselor also can point out that the student will make valuable employment contacts prior to graduation, that he can escape the frustrations of a search for summer jobs when such jobs tend to be scarce, that his career goals will be defined more clearly, and that he will gain the maturity and personal enrichment which other college students may not experience until after graduation.

WORK ASSIGNMENTS. Regarding work assignments, the admissions counselor should stress mainly their flexibility. However, if students are expected to find their own jobs, if they are discouraged from doing so, if they are able to enroll for part-time study during work periods, these are points that should be discussed prior to enrollment.

Also, frequently raised in the admissions interview are questions about geographical placement on the coop job. Some who seek admission may make this a major issue, and it should be discussed honestly and realistically. The student is advised that a variety of factors—particularly the economy of different areas—control placement and that therefore no assurance of a particular job location can be given. Once students understand that their employment should, if at all possible, be related to their field of study, wherever the opportunity may exist, they also understand why the geography of placement cannot be predetermined.

Students then may seek assurance that their coop assignments will in fact be directly related to the academic programs in which they wish to enroll. Admissions counselors are advised to suggest to such students that every effort is made to relate the job to the academic field but that such assurance cannot be guaranteed. There are maturing values in all job experiences, but this position may not be readily appreciated by the young adult.

When questions about the nature of employment are raised in the admissions conference, a portrayal of case studies showing actual coop students on their jobs is a very effective response. Case studies have a telling effect upon student decisions to enroll. Prospective students are also impressed by the variety of jobs held by coop students and the progressively more significant jobs they hold as they advance in their educational programs.

The trends in career interests of young adults who enter college, as reported annually in *School and Society* (published by the Society for the Advancement of Education, 1860 Broadway, New York, New York), have a direct impact upon the recruiting efforts of admissions personnel. At this writing there is a national shortage of high school graduates entering colleges of engineering. This is in large part due to the temporary lack of job opportunities for certain types of engineers. A high school student may assume, therefore, that there are no coop jobs available in certain engineering fields. Actually, the opposite may be true because companies may not have jobs for senior engineers but may still want to bring in a substantial number of trainees. To correct this false impression requires career guidance on the part of the admissions counselor. Historically, there tends to be a rise and fall in most fields of study. Career trends are in a constant state of flux. For this reason, since a freshman class may be composed of several quotas in a number of different areas of study, it is important that such quotas have a degree of flexibility to permit adjustment in size as circumstances may warrant.

Nontraditional Students

A primary responsibility of the admissions counselor is to evaluate the academic potential of an applicant. Future employability is usually not considered to be one of the admissions criteria. Cooperative employment may be discussed, however, and probably should be discussed, with increasing numbers of applicants who can best be described as *nontraditional*—that is, a candidate for admission who does not come directly from secondary school. He may be an older student who seeks to enroll following a period of military duty which interrupted his high school education. The applicant may be one who has been employed for some time and earned a high school equivalency diploma through independent study. Or again, the applicant may have had valuable experience as a licensed practical nurse and now seeks to enter a degree program in nursing. Such students as these bring maturity to an entering freshman class; at the same time, that very maturity may be a source of future coop placement difficulties.

Each of these older, more experienced applicants must be treated on an individual basis and with sensitivity. Ultimate college entrance for these students need not be confined to part-time evening programs; and certainly, age alone cannot be considered a barrier to admission or cooperative employment. The matter of future placement, however, should be discussed with the older student in order that he may fully appreciate the role of the employer as a member of the cooperating team.

The College Level Examination Program, a testing service provided by the College Entrance Examination Board, provides an excellent vehicle for assessing the level of achievement of nontraditional students. Testing results also may be used for placement and for granting college credit upon entrance. CLEP, as it is commonly called, provides a measurement of general competencies and acquired knowledge in more than thirty subject-matter fields.

Physically Handicapped Students

The physically disabled applicant deserves special consideration. His disability may not adversely affect ultimate job placement; but, as the admissions counselor should tell him, it may limit the kinds of jobs to which he can be assigned. In the case of a severe disability, full health clearance should be required. In less severe cases, the admissions counselor may wish to refer the student to a counselor in the Department of Cooperative Education. Admissions personnel should not place themselves in the position of making medical judgments. In such programs as nursing, physical therapy, and physical education, applicants for admission may be required to receive full health clearance prior to the fact of entrance.

Married Students

Most colleges report a continuing growth in the number of enrolled married students, although only a few may be married at the time of entrance. In those few instances, admissions counselors should point out that, for a variety of personal reasons, marital status may create very serious obstacles to future efforts. For example, married students who have rented an apartment near the college may not be able to afford to accept an off-campus assignment which requires living in another community. Despite this restriction, married students should not be denied admission on this basis alone. Some coop students find marriage advantageous when both are students and can arrange for one to be at school and the other at work during their upper-class years. This provides a steady flow of income.

Disadvantaged Youth

Institutions which offer cooperative education programs tend to be attractive to minority and low-income students, who see these programs as a means of developing job skills, thereby improving future placement opportunities and gaining entrance to employment and career doors which otherwise might be closed to them or about which they possess little or no knowledge.

The following resolution was approved by the College Entrance Examination Board membership at the annual meeting of October, 1970: "Be it resolved that the institutional members here present urge that colleges and universities in the selection of their minority-group/low-income students use the Scholastic Aptitude Test and Achievements Tests with sensitivity in the admissions process and that they also use them for diagnostic and placement purposes. . . ." The institution that commits itself to enrolling a given number of disadvantaged students must not only use the results of entrance tests "with sensitivity"; it must also recognize that many of these students will be the products of large urban high schools that lack the educational resources of schools in economically favored suburban communities. For lack of statistical evidence as a predictive tool of measurement, admissions personnel must attempt to identify those human qualities which are important to successful study. Frequently, the advice of counselors in community social agencies must be sought, for they often have closer relationships with these young adults than their counterparts in public schools. Such qualities as determination, courage in the face of adversity, and recognized leadership potential become important in the evaluation process since many minority group students have only a vague idea at best of the demands of certain career fields. It is to the student's credit if he has not avoided demanding college preparatory subjects during his secondary school career.

At Northeastern University a student-faculty admissions committee, with black and white members, has been very successful in recruiting and identifying minority-group students who deserve an opportunity to succeed. Once these students have been admitted, they deserve the institution's commitment to provide such learning resources as tutorial assistance, programmed learning, and extraordinary counseling services. In addition, summer school opportunities prior to enrollment are strongly recommended as a means of strengthening subject-matter preparation, reading skills, and study habits. To lower standards in seeking minority-group freshmen is to invite further damage to human morale and to aggravate those frustrations which students have already experienced. To use other standards, different standards, in the evaluation process is the single key to the highly difficult task of predicting success.

Foreign Students

Apart from such important matters as proficiency in English and the student's finances, there are problems of future placement of foreign students on cooperative work jobs. In some instances, federal security regulations prohibit the employment of such students in certain science and technology areas. In other instances, employers may lack interest in employing such students, who may be required to return to their native countries after they have completed their studies.

As real as these problems may be to those responsible for coop placement, foreign students do not really look upon the problems as serious and are convinced that they can readily be solved. For this reason, admissions officers should develop special informational literature for students from foreign countries, so that they can better understand and appreciate the realities of placement for noncitizens. Such literature should be cooperatively developed by admissions personnel, the foreign student advisor, and those responsible for placement. When a substantial number of foreign students are involved, the development of a committee on foreign students may be necessary. This committee should be involved in the welfare of students both before and after the fact of admission.

Transfer Students

A special category of "new" students consists of those who enter as transfer students from other institutions. In all likelihood, such students will have spent a year or more in a college that operates under a conventional full-time calendar. It is important, therefore, that they be fully informed about cooperative education, its basic objectives, its operational schedule, and how and when they will be introduced to the work periods of the calendar.

The amount of allowable transfer credit will, of course, determine at what level the transfer student enters. Special orientation programs for these students are strongly recommended, for they will be more immediately involved in the cooperative plan than entering freshmen. The orientation program for transfer students should acquaint them with the university campus and its regulations, the philosophy of cooperative education, the responsibilities of the students to their employers, and the specific requirements of the college or university with respect to the satisfactory completion of off-campus assignments as a requisite for graduation. The special needs of transfer students are all too often unrecognized, and when cooperative work placement is added to the concerns of these new students, their need for guidance is further emphasized.

Sponsored Students

Certain business and industrial firms, regarding entering freshmen as a source of future manpower, may offer attractive scholarship opportunities to selected students who agree to work as coop students for that firm. The identification and selection of such students may be jointly shared by admissions and by the sponsoring company. Once the student has completed his degree program, and his coop experience with the sponsoring company has been fully satisfactory, the hope is that he will remain with the company for full-time employment. Under such a program, the student will receive full tuition benefits or more, while the college may receive a comparable grant to cover administrative and supervisory costs. Although such an arrangement is not of a legal nature, it does bind the student in an ethical way to follow through with his employment commitment. He should therefore completely understand the commitment which he will be asked to make.

Industry-sponsored programs of this kind tend to flourish or disintegrate depending upon the specific terms of the scholarship program and upon the student's satisfaction with his employment situation.

If these programs draw upon student talent from a restricted geographical area, or if they make it difficult for students to change their major fields of study as career interests become more clearly defined, they tend to be less attractive to students of high intellectual promise. Yet, from a financial standpoint, that student whose career goal is definite and who is challenged by the employment opportunity stands to profit greatly from a program of this nature. Since at best the prediction of academic success is an elusive quality, there is much to be said in favor of company-sponsored programs which select students after the freshman year, when success has been demonstrated and career goals are more firmly established.

PART FIVE

RELEVANCY TO SPECIAL GROUPS

XVII

Professional Development of Women

Harriet P. Van Sickle

In the fourth century B.C., the battle was raging over the proper place of women. Aristotle contended, "The male is by nature superior, and the female inferior; and the one rules, and the other is ruled; this principle, of necessity, extends to all mankind." In contrast, Plato—through the words of the Athenian Stranger—declared, "Nothing can be more absurd than the practice which prevails in our own country, of men and women not following the same pursuits with all their strength and with one mind, for thus the state, instead of being a whole, is reduced to a half, but has the same imposts to pay and the same toils to undergo; and what can be a greater mistake for any legislator to make than this?" Has the debate come full circle, or is it a never ending one?

Although the controversies of the Old World extended into

the New World, in America the prevailing opinion was that "a woman's place is in the home." It was more than a philosophy; it was a fact, for where else could a woman go and what else could she do? In nineteenth-century America, however, changes began to occur. While the winds were blowing gently across the pioneer settlements of the Great Plains and the Far West, women in the East were filtering by the thousands into wage-earning occupations. They found employment primarily in the factories and the needlework trades. By the onset of the twentieth century, women made up 18 per cent of the work force; and a few women, often against great odds, began to enter professions such as medicine, engineering, and law, formerly considered the exclusive province of men.

The nation's shift from an agriculture-based economy to an economy based on goods-producing activities and services resulted in more urban than rural living. Widespread use of labor-saving devices in the home, plus rising aspirations toward a higher standard of living and more education, impelled the exodus of women from the home. In addition, when American involvement in World War II created manpower shortages, women entered a variety of new labor fields.

Working Women

The reasons for women's seeking employment today are diverse. Some women work because they must, while others work for social reasons. Some work because they want to acquire luxuries not otherwise obtainable, and others work for personal or psychological satisfaction. Many debutantes, who formerly were content to live entirely within the whirl of their social set, now work because "that's where the action is."

Career patterns tend to differ as the result of these various reasons. Some women work full time year around, others work part time by the day or part time during the year. Still others follow an in-and-out pattern. These intermittent careerists are generally women who work after completing their education or stay at home while the children are small and enter the labor market once their family is in school. In any event, today's women feel that preparation for a career is a necessity, even if it serves only as a private insurance policy against the exigencies of life.

As one looks more closely at the employment picture, other differences soon become apparent. Although the number of women is gradually easing up toward the 42 per cent mark of the total number employed, their work in various occupations is distributed quite differently from that of men. In 1968, fully two thirds of the women were employed in clerical work and as operatives and service workers. Only slightly over 14 per cent were active in the professional and technical fields (U.S. Department of Labor, 1971, p. 92).

If the small proportion of women in the professional and technical fields was due to lack of education and training, the figures would not be significant. However, statistics compiled in March 1969 showed that the educational backgrounds of a great many women were not being utilized on their jobs. A startling 7 per cent of employed women who had completed five or more years of college were working as service workers, including some in private households, and also as operatives, saleswomen, or clerical workers. Nearly 20 per cent of the women with four years of college and 62 per cent of those who had completed one to three years of college were also employed in these occupations.

Why are many women with college backgrounds underutilized? The Women's Bureau of the Department of Labor states, "There are still barriers which deny women the freedom to prepare for and enter employment suited to their individual interests and abilities, and to advance and achieve recognition (monetary or otherwise) to the full extent of which they are capable" (U.S. Department of Labor, 1971, p. 111). It is felt that barriers are still high against employing women in professions other than those traditionally associated with women, and many myths still prevail regarding women's ability to hold administrative and managerial positions.

Two acts indicative of an effort to eradicate discrimination are of particular interest to women, the Equal Pay Act of 1963 and the Civil Rights Act of 1964. These acts carry provisions prohibiting discriminatory employment in regard to sex and wages. Although these acts cover only government agencies and businesses engaged in interstate commerce, they serve as torch bearers of the coming era. As an indication of this, many employees not covered under the federal acts have since been enveloped in others passed by the majority of state legislatures. Many private enterprises are also adopting nondiscriminatory provisions.

In spite of the surprising numbers of college-trained women working in clerical and related fields, most young women in college are preparing themselves for professional or managerial positions. And there has been tremendous growth in these fields. In the two decades since 1950, over two million more women were engaged in professional and technical work than ever before.

The health and teaching fields claim by far the highest representation in professional and technical careers. Teaching continues to be the most popular one. Although women have traditionally made up the largest part of the teacher corps, in recent years a large proportion of men have entered teaching on all academic levels—particularly in institutions of higher learning, where women made up 28 per cent of the faculty in 1940 but only 22 per cent in 1969 (U.S. Department of Labor, 1971, p. 11). Roughly one fourth of all women professionals serve as nurses, medical technologists, dental technicians, nutritionists, therapists, and physicians and surgeons.

Outside of these two major fields, relatively large numbers of women serve as accountants and auditors, social workers, librarians, editors and reporters, industrial engineers, mathematicians, aeronautical engineers, labor and personnel-relations workers, public relations experts, and publicity writers.

Women are quite well represented in the professions in total numbers, but in some specialties their proportion compared to men is very low. For example, women physicians account for only 7 per cent of all physicians; women scientists, 9 per cent; lawyers, 3 per cent; and engineers, 1 per cent.

In the management classification, about one out of six managers is a woman. Many are small-business proprietors; those who are not often serve as salaried managers in small retail stores or as buyers and department heads in larger stores. A few women hold public administration or management positions in banking, insurance, real estate, finance, and business services.

Key to Opportunity

But the outlook for women in the professions is changing, and the horizon is bright with promise. Through cooperative education college-educated women are gaining entrance into the professions, including those in what may be termed nontraditional fields of feminine endeavor.

As young high school students, many girls are preconditioned by parents and teachers to avoid individual courses or fields of study which have traditionally been considered "inappropriate" for members of their sex. Furthermore, many high school guidance counselors still raise their eyebrows at the suggestion that girls should enroll in, much less enjoy, hard-core subjects in science, mathematics, or technology: "All the smartest boys take those courses; you'd never be able to hold your own; English or perhaps a modern language would be more appropriate." Colleges and universities offering cooperative programs need to reach secondary school guidance personnel with evidence that times are changing. New career fields are opening up to women, and preparation for these fields must begin at the high school level. The girl who avoids courses in the sciences and mathematics, for example, may find herself with insufficient preparatory courses for many of the new college curricula now open to her.

In addition to offering young girls a wide variety of career fields from which to choose, cooperative education also enables many young women to attend college who otherwise might not be able to afford it. In large families or families of limited means, parents often feel obligated to educate their sons ahead of their daughters, with the result that funds for the daughter's education are not available. Cooperative education, with its paid work experience, enables such girls to gain a college education by helping them to meet college expenses through coop earnings.

Cooperative earnings also give young women the financial independence that many are seeking, even in homes of ample monetary means. Out-of-town coop assignments also contribute to these students' sense of independence, particularly if they are living at home during their academic terms.

The art of combining marriage and a career also is aided by enrollment in a cooperative institution. Alternating periods of work and study enable women to meet both the boys on campus and the young professionals employed in their individual cooperative work areas. Cooperative education also opens up a variety of fields which are compatible with the desire to combine career and marriage. Law, for example, may be practiced on a part-time basis in the confines of one's home. Interestingly enough, reports indicate that female applications to law schools are on the increase, particularly at Northeastern University, where a cooperative law school offers women the opportunity to gain employment in such traditionally male-dominated bastions as law offices, the courts, and offices of attorneys general.

New Career Fields

Until recent years, cooperative education was confined primarily to programs in business and engineering, neither of which enrolls a large number of women. Cooperative colleges now are offering many new professions to women which have previously been denied them —in actuarial science, animal husbandry, biomedical engineering, chemistry, chemical engineering, civil engineering, criminal justice, environmental science, forestry, industrial management, mathematics, mechanical engineering, physics, and statistics, to name but a few. Cooperative work assignments enable students, some of them women, to gain employment in these fields and thereby enter traditional male strongholds. For example, a public works department might not be willing to hire a woman civil engineer on a full-time basis but will agree to "temporarily" employing a woman coop engineering student. Once in the door, the woman has the opportunity to prove her worth, and the employer may find to his surprise that her presence is a definite asset to his staff.

Cooperative work assignments also enable women to enter training programs as students which might be denied them as college graduates. If, for example, a woman student performs well on a coop assignment in business, she is placed in a managerial training program and thereby enters the executive training ground. In addition, coop assignments expose young women to many career field specializations which they might not otherwise have an opportunity to consider.

Cooperative work assignments also give women employment experience, which marriage immediately after graduation may deny them until their family responsibilities are over. If they should want to enter the labor market at a later stage in life, this experience enables them to list some period of employment on their résumé, proving that they are not "untested" in the labor market.

By and large, cooperative education helps to break down two

major barriers to the entrance of women into the professions—the opportunity to enter new career fields and the opportunity to gain equal pay for equal work. Coop students are paid in accordance with their year in school, not their sex, thereby establishing women students on an equal footing with their male contemporaries. As a result, a large number of women are now enjoying professional status with equal pay in a variety of career fields. In addition, some women are beginning to break down the barriers against women's serving in positions of managerial responsibility.

Problems in Placement

The placement of women students is not without its problems, however. Coop coordinators do at times engage in intentional or unintentional discrimination when they fail to suggest certain job opportunities to women if they foresee difficulties. And some jobs do present problems for women: late hours, bad neighborhoods, poor transportation, improper street lighting, inadequate housing, and the lack of adequate washroom facilities in a male-dominated environment such as a construction job or in engineering field work. Sometimes, of course, these problems exist even on jobs that are clearly within the realm of the traditional woman's world—for instance, on nursing assignments in hospitals located in potentially unsafe neighborhoods.

Other problems are created by the women themselves. Many coordinators report that some women students insist on having high-paying jobs rather than those offering valuable long-range contributions to one's career. This is true of some, but most can be persuaded to view a coop assignment in terms of a forty-year-career objective. In addition, some coordinators state that women are more inclined to refuse a job or leave a job for no other reason than the fact that they "were not happy there" because of a grouchy boss or uninteresting colleagues, or for some other reason totally unrelated to the job itself.

At times the employers are to blame. Some employers hesitate to hire women coop students because they find it difficult to correct them when their work is unsatisfactory. For many men, the dual standard still exists; they are quite willing to chastise a man for poor work, but they feel uncomfortable calling a woman on the carpet for the improper execution of her duties.

Finally, although many new career fields are now available to women, some of these fields are not well suited to every woman's life style. For this reason, care must be taken not to give girls the impression that they can always return to their profession after an absence of several years and pick up where they left off before marriage and family responsibilities. In those fields in which rapid technological change is taking place, reentry is virtually impossible. Girls should consider this in determining their career objectives.

Minority Students

Lena M. McKinney

Cooperative education represents one of the most significant types of education for economically and socially disadvantaged students. The problems faced by this segment of the population are many and varied; moreover, they are in excess of the usual problems faced by students merely as students or, more specifically, by the average student of the majority group. The minorities of low income are the victims of numerous social ills, many of which are beyond their control: poor housing, inadequate health care, a high rate of unemployment and the attendant consequences thereof.

Among the solutions to the limitations is an education designed to attract, hold, motivate, and prepare minority youth for creative involvement and constructive activity in their own communities or wherever else they may find places to serve. In other words, what is needed among low-income minorities is a type of educational opportunity that is wholly feasible for them as well as functionally significant.

Such an opportunity has often been lacking among American blacks, Indians, and Puerto Ricans. Public education has indeed been provided at various levels, but in too many instances the stimulus and proper motivation have been lacking, largely because members of minority groups often have met frustrations in their attempts to find satisfying and self-fulfilling employment.

The new emphasis upon equal employment opportunities has resulted in a much larger variety of occupations open to minorities than ever before. Since this development, the demand for minority personnel in certain highly skilled and administrative posts has often exceeded the supply. This excess of demand presents a real challenge and opportunity to the colleges comprised primarily of low-income minority groups. To meet this challenge, these colleges must adjust their curricula. For many of them, the cooperative education plan represents the most viable program through which they may be able to prepare their students to meet the new demands for their services in industry, government, and other agencies.

Basic Needs

The education of any people should be closely related to their basic needs. It is true that, ultimately, the basic needs of disadvantaged minority students are the same as those of the majority: freedom to develop talents and abilities fully, freedom to pursue satisfying careers, recognition of oneself as a real person by one's peers and by the general society of which he is a part. Nevertheless, some specific needs of disadvantaged minority students are identifiable and distinctive.

FINANCIAL SUPPORT. Few black students can make it through college if they must depend exclusively upon family support. The large majority require financial assistance from the college in the form of work-study grants, loans, or scholarships. Many find jobs in the community. Some carry a full class load while working as many as forty hours a week. Indeed, there are hardy and ambitious students who work at night while going to college full time during the day. In view of the limited financial resources available to the average black student, it is remarkable that as many aspire to and complete a college education as statistics indicate. The estimated enrollment of the forty-five predominantly black colleges responding to a questionnaire study (to be discussed later in this chapter) was 91,607 students. Of this number, it is safe to say that a large percentage are from families in which no one has attended college before. As late as 1965, United States Census figures show that the average black adult over twenty-five years of age had an education of approximately nine grades (U.S. Department of Commerce, 1965, p. 2). The consequences of this limited educational background are reflected in a variety of ways, especially financial. Since the cooperative educational program makes it possible for the student to earn his college expenses while engaging in a career type of employment, it represents a most important solution to the financial problems of the low-income minority student who desires a college education.

EXPOSURE TO WORLD. Another of the specific needs of the low-income minority student is exposure to the larger world—the world beyond the community, often a ghetto, in which he lives. Thousands of black youth grow up without ever having a constructive contact with a white person. In several instances black students have remarked to one cooperative education director that the interview arranged by him with a recruiter from industry was the very first opportunity they had ever had for this type of contact with a white person. Moreover, since *de facto* segregation exists in most communities in the United States, the opportunities for black youth to have first-hand contact with what is going on in the larger society are very limited. Often these youth, lacking acquaintance with role models of persons of their own sociological group who have achieved in the larger society, have no conception of their own possibilities in that society. Here again, cooperative education can be the means of broadening contacts and enlarging visions of disadvantaged youth.

SOCIAL ADJUSTMENT. In those situations where the home or community environment does not provide the bases for the establishment of rapport and cooperation with persons outside of one's normal area of operation, the need for social adjustment can become acute. Many minority students have little or no knowledge about the business world—its customs, traditions, and the personal relationships which must exist in any work environment.

WIDER VOCATIONAL SELECTION. For generations, college-trained black youth were restricted to such occupations as teaching, law, religious vocations, medicine, and social work. Although this situation has changed rapidly during the last ten years, many of these youth are still not sufficiently acquainted with the opportunities available in other types of employment to aspire toward them. Cooperative education opens up these wider horizons to them.

VOCATIONAL GUIDANCE. Counselors in some high schools across the country have systematically directed black students away from certain occupations, either on the ground that these occupations were traditionally closed to blacks or because the counselors did not recognize the full potential of the disadvantaged student. Since the coordinator of the cooperative program is aware of a variety of employment opportunities and the varying demands and requirements associated with them, he is able—after interviewing the student and examining his academic and other pertinent data—to provide the student with the kind of counseling best suited to his personality, aptitudes, and needs.

EXPERIENCE IN BUSINESS WORLD. Most black businesses are run on a small scale. In most communities, practically all of the principal establishments providing goods and services to blacks are owned and operated by others. Capital and experience in establishing and successfully managing business enterprises have been limited. High-level experience in the large industries and corporations of this country has been denied to all but very few black individuals. Certainly, no program in higher education can better fill the need for widening experience in the business world than that of cooperative education.

Objectives in the Minority College

The ultimate aims of the cooperative education program in the low-income minority colleges will differ little if at all from such aims in all other institutions. Stated in general terms, these objectives include (1) provision of guidance and experiences leading to the optimum personal development of the student; (2) orientation of the student to meaningful work experiences as well as to a knowledge of a broad variety of occupational choices open to him; and (3) training of the student to develop skills for earning a living while maintaining effective relations with his fellows both on the job and in the community.

PERSONAL DEVELOPMENT. The low-income minority college

student starts out having to rise above the limitations of his home and community environment. The program of cooperative education leads to personal development because it provides an opportunity for the student to discover himself, his talents, his personal resources, and his real strengths and weaknesses.

The cooperative work experience should result in the development of personal discipline as well as a sense of responsibility and independence. This is especially significant for the low-income minority student. Just to be in college is a privilege for him. To have the experience of engaging in a career type of employment normally results in a sense of achievement. Those students who come from families of the lowest poverty level, requiring public assistance, probably have never had the experience of holding a steady job. Thus, the conditions are established for the development of a new sense of responsibility.

Moreover, in the cooperative work experience, personal development is enhanced by exposure to new points of view and new value systems, which cause one to examine or reevaluate his own. The resulting assessment may strengthen the student's positive self-image or cause him to broaden constructively his scale of values. Again, the opportunity to travel, occasioned by some work assignments, should be a broadening experience. For some students the coop assignment represents the first opportunity for an extended stay away from home. Few experiences are more satisfying to those directing coop programs than to observe participating students develop occupational skills, social and emotional maturity, a sense of responsibility, and independence.

MEANINGFUL WORK EXPERIENCE. Most of the low-income minority students who have had employment prior to the coop program have not had the type of job that is generally satisfying and self-fulfilling. Placement in a responsible career type of situation may give the minority student his first realization and appreciation of what it means to be a significant part of a meaningful enterprise rather than merely a nontitled functionary. The student is introduced to the world of work. He is able to see the relationship of his newly assigned task to other sectors of the economy. He is also enabled to envision his own possibilities for growth, promotion, and the assumption of steadily increasing responsibilities. At the same time, the conditions are established whereby he can more clearly see the relationship between his academic studies and their practical application.

The cooperative job may have added meaning to the low-income minority student if it represents the breaking of new ground for his particular sociological group. In such instances he may feel an added sense of responsibility to be as efficient as he can so that similar opportunities may come to other members of his group.

SKILL IN EARNING A LIVING. Although the coop education plan is directed primarily toward educational goals rather than financial ends, its objectives must reflect a recognition of what has been referred to as the "bread and butter" side of education. In other words, a significant purpose of the coop program is preparation for making a living. But the low-income minority student cannot think of securing a college education without recognizing the need for substantial financial assistance during the process.

Low-income students often go into teaching—not because they are deeply committed to this profession but because they can secure a college degree only through a teacher grant; and if they enter some other field prior to teaching the minimum number of terms, they are obligated to repay the state. The coop education program not only provides students with a knowledge of a variety of opportunities in the business world but also ensures that they have the financial means to prepare for these careers.

Status among Black Americans

Prior to 1971, under the federal Department of Health, Education, and Welfare, between forty and fifty colleges composed primarily of low-income minority students were awarded grants to assist them in developing cooperative education programs. Other federal agencies, notably Civil Service, are cooperating with these colleges in providing opportunities for students to participate in work-study projects. Some colleges are grouped in consortia to facilitate planning and implementing, as well as in working out the details and problems incidental to effective cooperative education programs.

Early in 1971, seventy questionnaires were sent by the writer to the leading black colleges; forty-five, or 63 per cent, of the colleges responded. Of this number, twenty-one (46 per cent) were tax-supported and twenty-four (54 per cent) were private. Twenty-five, or 55 per cent, of the forty-five colleges responding to the questionnaire reported that they had a cooperative education program. The remaining twenty reported that serious consideration had been given to establishing one. In this latter group, three colleges indicated that they already had a planning grant, two had applied for such assistance, and two indicated simply that they were in a planning stage but presumably without a grant.

Most of these institutions are only in the early stages of conducting this kind of program. Eight reported having had a program in operation from three to seven years. The others had had a program going for ten and thirteen years respectively. For those twenty-two colleges with programs in operation a year or more, the average length of time was 3.8 years. Seven of the twenty-five colleges indicated that their coop programs were only in the exploratory stage, nine were in the implementary stage, and nine others were in the expansion stage.

The total enrollment of the twenty-five colleges with a cooperative education program was 64,041. The ten private colleges accounted for 13,330 students (21 per cent of the total) while the fifteen public institutions reported 50,711 (79 per cent).

The total number of students enrolled in cooperative education programs is the true index to their present impact. Twenty-four of the twenty-five colleges reported a total of 870 students participating in the cooperative education plan. Of this number fourteen of fifteen public colleges showed 541 students, for an average of 38.6 students per college. Of the ten private colleges with a coop program, nine reported a total of 329 students involved, for an average of 36.4 per institution. The range for the colleges as a whole was from 2 to 140 students. The total enrollment for twenty-four of these schools was 62,841. The 870 students participating in the coop programs of these twenty-four schools, then, represent only .01 per cent of the total enrollment.

One private college, Wilberforce University in Ohio, was not included in these figures because its entire curriculum was restructured six years ago along the lines of the cooperative education plan. This institution reports an enrollment of 1,200 students, all on the cooperative education plan involving two hundred employers. As for the other twenty-four colleges, a total of 458 employers were involved in connection with the 870 students enrolled. Apparently, during normal employment times there has been little difficulty in securing the cooperation of employers in the cooperative education programs in the predominantly black colleges.

Most of the nineteen colleges with a cooperative education program divide the work periods by semesters. One college uses a six-month division; three use a division by quarters, and one divides by half days. Since most colleges operate on the semester plan, the division between periods of work and study on this plan is naturally the most feasible arrangement for them.

The disciplines of the students participating in the cooperative education program is another index to its outreach. Nineteen of the colleges report that an average of 45.73 per cent of their students were from the business department. Eleven reported an average of 25 per cent from the natural sciences; ten, an average of 34.5 per cent from the social sciences; four, an average of 30.75 per cent from the humanities; three, an average of 77 per cent from engineering; and three, an average of 37 per cent from other technical fields.

The importance of the cooperative education program for the low-income minority is emphasized by the findings of this study with respect to family income levels. Nineteen of the colleges indicated a family income level of $7,500 or less, and only six indicated more than $7,500. Even in the absence of information regarding the number of siblings in the families represented by these students, it is clear that there is little money available to them for a college education from the limited family resources. In view of this fact, the cooperative education program again stands out as a boon to the disadvantaged student.

The respondents to the questionnaire were asked to list the advantages they saw in the cooperative education program, both from the viewpoint of the black college and that of the student.

Many of the advantages listed are applicable to all colleges and students regardless of sociological background. Nevertheless, the benefits enumerated are of special significance to the colleges and personnel of the disadvantaged minority because of the extra problems these face due to their sociological identity.

The advantages the respondents listed for students in the cooperative education program may be classified under four headings: (1) broadened learning experience, (2) personal development, (3) interpersonal relations, and (4) financial rewards. Many of the comments listed under "broadened learning experience" emphasize that black students have had little acquaintance with the variety of vocational choices open to them and that the cooperative education program provides an opportunity for the student to widen his career options and to get into the mainstream of American life. In connection with "personal development," respondents generally agreed that the cooperative education programs contributed greatly to arousing new hope and motivation on the part of the student, to the inculcation of confidence, independence, responsibility, and the acceleration of maturity. Under "interpersonal relations," some respondents emphasized how the cooperative education program results in cultural broadening by exposure to new or different life styles and learning how to cope with the non-black society. The advantages listed under "financial rewards" included the usual observations regarding the need on the part of most black students for monetary assistance in getting into and completing college work.

The advantages of the cooperative education program for the predominantly black college are listed in the following categories: (1) better rapport with the business community, (2) stimulation of curriculum revision, (3) increase of student enrollment, (4) keeping faculty members informed about the business world, and (5) more efficient use of college facilities.

This study of the present status of cooperative education among the predominantly black colleges indicates that an effective beginning has been made in involving minority students in this different approach to higher education. It is apparent now that more of these institutions will be adopting this program as part of their departmental and curriculum offerings. In May 1971, after the preceding statistics were tabulated, the Department of Health, Education, and Welfare granted forty-four predominantly black colleges approval of their applications for assistance in inaugurating or strengthening programs of cooperative education. Thirty of the grantees were colleges which had previously had no cooperative education program. In addition, two colleges serving other low-income minority groups, American Indians and Mexican Americans, received grants in this program (U.S. Department of HEW, 1971—b).

Special Problems

Colleges serving minority students and seeking to adopt cooperative education find they have many problems to solve—such as business and industrial contacts, programs of study which lead to specific careers—in order to properly operate a cooperative education program.

FINANCIAL LIMITATIONS. For a long time both private and public colleges for blacks have had a continuous struggle for funds adequate to meet their basic needs. Not until the Supreme Court anti-school-segregation decision of 1954 did the states with dual school systems begin to finance the predominantly black colleges with some degree of adequacy. Large sums have been spent on capital improvements. Salaries have been sharply increased. Curricula have been expanded and enriched. Compared with the prior situation, the material progress has been considerable. But compared with capital provisions for the predominantly white institutions, the black colleges have still a long way to go.

The situation in the private and church-related minority colleges is much more severe. In the early days of the formal education of blacks, these institutions established strong traditions and standards of leadership, which attracted the more economically secure members of the black community; in contrast, the state institutions were generally treated as stepchildren. In recent years, however, the private and church-related colleges have yielded some of their attractiveness and leadership to the tax-supported institutions. On the whole, their facilities are not as modern and extensive, and their student bodies are considerably smaller. Most of them are not able to compete for the top instructors through salaries and related fringe benefits. Because of this situation, several of these colleges have had to close their doors, some merging with one or another of the better-established private institutions.

STUDENT PREPARATION. The lack of adequate financial support for the education of low-income minorities is reflected in the poor preparation some students exhibit as they enter college. For many of them remedial work is needed in certain skill subjects. These students must be brought up to standard in communication skills and general cultural level for effective participation in the world of work. In addition, the admission policies of some institutions have been liberalized, with the result that a number of students are admitted who have a greater adjustment to make to college than their more academically able peers. The cooperative education counselor must be prepared carefully to determine through interview and examination of academic performance the suitability of a student for placement in certain types of employment.

For many black students fortunate enough to get into college, the primary goal is to complete their work in the minimum amount of time and begin earning a living as soon as possible. It is understandable that some of these students do not look with favor upon an educational program which requires their remaining in college five years rather than four. The cooperative education counselor is called upon to sell such students the advantages of participating in a work-study program involving a career type of occupation. To the determined student, however, the advantages of the cooperative education program are easily made clear.

OFF-CAMPUS PLACEMENT. The placement of low-income minority students in some cooperative education positions sometimes presents special problems. One of these problems is that of securing the cooperation of employers who, for some reason, have not previously given work to blacks in upgraded positions. These employers may be skeptical about the black's ability to perform effectively in a traditional white-collar position, the facility with which black and white employees will adjust to each other, and the effect of black employees upon the general public relations of the enterprise. Experience has shown that, as regards each of these areas of skepticism, the employment of black students in predominantly white businesses has generally been a positive rather than a negative value for all concerned.

Another problem area with which the coordinator must deal has to do with the student's conception of himself and of his ultimate role in society. Some students need considerable guidance in their efforts to find themselves and to establish a sense of significance. Some students who apply for a cooperative education assignment have made no definite decisions about their career objective. The coordinator will need to use his best judgment before assigning such a student in order to place him in the kind of situation likely to be meaningful to him.

Still another problem is that some students who live in the city where the college is located may object to going out of town for employment. Some students wish to avoid the extra expense of living away from home. Sometimes the student is simply fearful of having to make adjustments in a strange location, uprooted from the protective environment of home. Others are reluctant to leave their friends and make new ones.

Sometimes an employer will hire a black person primarily to give the impression that his company does not discriminate. Such "tokenism" is not happily accepted by the black person, although he may tolerate it in the hope that his presence on the job will make similar opportunities possible for other blacks.

Moreover, students are not always used appropriately. Some employers use cooperative education students for menial and repetitive tasks, which are not challenging and do not offer an opportunity for the students to use effectively the knowledge and skills they have acquired at school. Again, sometimes employers themselves have complained that students are not far enough along in their program adequately to handle complex and challenging jobs, and, at the same time, are inappropriately placed in job situations much too routine.

The overemphasis of some students on the financial rewards of cooperative employment often presents a problem to the coordinator. Some students are reluctant to take cooperative jobs which are low-paying, despite the fact that the jobs might offer great educational value. Closely related to this problem is one of orienting students to view their cooperative employment as an integral part of their total education. Often students view their employment solely as a means of securing financial aid for their education, or they become so involved in details of their job that they are unable to relate it effectively to their total education plan.

Another problem is related to emotional difficulties or personality adjustment growing out of the job situation. Sometimes a student unexpectedly is confronted with fellow workers who resent his presence and seek to make it hard for him. In some instances this resentment grows out of racial bias; in other instances it is traceable to the superior preparation and performance of the student. A student needs to have some understanding of why and under what conditions such resentments are likely to occur, so that he may be able to make a satisfactory adjustment. Emotional problems may also arise when a student does not feel quite competent to do the job to which he is assigned.

Finally, the Center for Cooperative Education at Northeastern

University, one of the pioneer and most influential institutions operating in the area of cooperative education, reports the following pertinent information on the placement of black students:

The Center's experience indicates that blacks in the South who are interested in cooperative education programs are eager for placement in business and industry to raise their economic status and to enter professions and careers that will give them greater economic security and a better standard of living. Many blacks in the North, however, who are in cooperative institutions and who come primarily from the ghettos, are torn by the desire to remain with their own people to help them as opposed to embarking on a program of placement and work which would lead to a career or profession which might take them out of their present environment. This is true of some blacks on our own campus. Many feel an obligation to spend their work periods with the blacks in the Roxbury and Cambridge areas and, particularly, help their brothers and sisters get prepared for colleges rather than taking a job at a bank or insurance company, etc. [*A. S. Knowles, personal letter, May 5, 1971*].

PART SIX

DEVELOPMENT OF NEW PROGRAMS

The Adoption of Cooperative Education

Asa S. Knowles, Roy L. Wooldridge

Many colleges and universities adopting cooperative education find that it provides a unique education which is relevant, which permits experimentation in a variety of ways, and which can provide additional revenue. (The advantages of cooperative education are set forth in more detail in Chapters 2, 18, and 19.) A new college may choose a coop plan as part of its basic design; an existing college may adopt it to provide students with an innovative option for learning or to achieve financial advantages by converting one or more programs. One men's college adopted a system which sends all sophomores and juniors to off-campus assignments for two quarters each year. The otherwise empty dormitory space will be used to enroll female students.

Financial Advantages

The financial advantages possible are in direct proportion to the magnitude of the commitment to the program. The greatest gain occurs when the program involves all students in a four- or five-year college or in one or more colleges of a university and when the plan is mandatory for all upper-class students with regular alternating periods of on-campus study and off-campus experience. Under this system enrollments may be increased substantially. Moreover, a uniform calendar permits economies in the use of faculty, avoids extra costs due to trailer courses, and makes the most efficient use of the physical plant.

If its objective is to provide educational alternatives, the college may find that the added costs of coordinators, placement, and faculty compensation and promotion exceed income from enrollees. However, if the optional program is substantial, a placement fee can be established which enables the program to operate on a basis of excess of income over expenses. This choice becomes wholly a matter of policy to be determined by the administration.

A public institution completely committed to cooperative education may still achieve no great financial advantage because of low or nominal tuition rates, even though a fee is charged to cover the added costs. Most public institutions adopt cooperative education to provide an innovative option for students, since the taxpayer supplies funds for operating budgets. However, the on- and off-campus feature allows the institution to serve more students with less expense to the taxpayer. A cooperative program in which all students leave campus for a specific period each year will not produce any financial advantage unless a special charge is made for the off-campus experience. On the contrary, having all students off campus at one time may increase the cost of operation, since coordination and placement will require faculty and staff time.

Two-year and community college programs which operate on parallel calendars (students work in the morning or afternoon each day) do not enhance income unless the complete academic program is offered in the morning for half the enrollees and repeated in the afternoon for the other half. Theoretically this plan would permit a double usage of the physical plant. Any financial advantages would depend upon economies in the use of faculty and staff time. Two-year cooperative programs of alternating periods of work and study based on a quarter or semester system will produce financial gain only if the calendar is carefully chosen and the on- and off-campus enrollments are arranged to make maximum use of faculty and staff. The high attrition rates of most two-year and community colleges make difficult the balancing of on- and off-campus enrollments.

First Procedures

Every institution considering a cooperative plan must have some faculty or administrators or both who accept the philosophy of cooperative education without reservation and who can spearhead the investigation and development of the program. The established college will encounter a variety of reactions on the part of students, faculty, administration, and governing boards. Therefore, it becomes very important to inform all parties of the philosophy and objectives—whether the program is to be optional for a few students or mandatory for all students. This work is best done by consultants qualified to give advice on the possible effects of adopting cooperative education. Several organizations now provide consulting service: the National Commission for Cooperative Education in New York City, the Center for Cooperative Education at Northeastern University in Boston, the Southeastern Center for Cooperative Education at the University of South Florida in Tampa; other centers are in the process of being established. Advice may be sought also from any institution that directs a well-established and successful program.

Planning Committee

If after preliminary consideration of cooperative education and its probable impact the institution decides to explore further, a planning committee should be appointed. The committee can be created by relieving two or more faculty members and an administrator of their regular duties so they may devote approximately half their time to committee work. If possible, a full-time staff member should be available to search for student placement opportunities off campus. The committee should have a secretary and other necessary staff assistance.

The resulting expenses become a part of the total cost of planning and conversion.

The work of the planning committee will be in two stages: to examine all factors involved in adopting the cooperative plan and then to initiate implementation. In the first stage, the committee must make some basic policy decisions, arrange for a preliminary survey of available off-campus placements, and determine the financial feasibility of adopting the plan.

Basic Policy Decisions

The planning committee must seek answers to questions in the following areas.

CALENDAR AND CURRICULUM. Should a four-year college adopt a program designed to lead to the bachelor's degree in five years or four years? Should a two-year college adopt a parallel calendar or one which permits alternating on-campus study and off-campus experience? Will the basic calendar be a quarter plan, semester plan, or some special term length? Should students spend their entire first year on campus before having periods of off-campus assignments? What will be the impact on the curriculum and how will necessary modifications be made?

STUDENT PARTICIPATION. Will there be a demand for such a program by the student clientele served by the college or university? Should transfer students be admitted to the program? Is the program to be optional or mandatory? If optional, should the institution select which students will have it? Should cooperative education be offered in all colleges or divisions of the institution? Should it be limited to professional programs? What would programs of various sizes cost? How many students are needed to insure financial success? Will there be any effect on total enrollment with such a program? Should the program give students in-depth exposure through a series of experiences with a minimum number of employers? Is it better to plan a variety of experiences with different employers? Will enrolled students be allowed to complete their program in a conventional manner if they decide to do so? If the program is to be offered only to new entrants, how can they be phased into the existing calendar of the institution?

EMPLOYER PARTICIPATION. What kind of employers should be contacted? How wide a geographic distribution of work opportunities should be sought? Should off-campus assignments be controlled by the institution? Should students be paired for assignment to off-campus experiences so that potential employers will have continuous job coverage?

COORDINATION STAFF. Should the program be coordinated by faculty members on a part-load basis or by a central staff devoting full time to coordination? Should coordinators have faculty rank? What is the place in the institution's organization of the director of the program? To whom should the director report and on what committees does he serve?

RULES AND REGULATIONS. How can the cooperative program be made a degree requirement? Should academic credit be given for off-campus periods? What procedure is to be followed when students fail on assignments? Is there a means for students to appeal unfavorable decisions? What types of reports are required from the employers and students? Are the rules firm but fair in allowing an orderly administration of the program? Is there sufficient flexibility to allow for the unusual cases? If the program is to be optional, is there control over a student's transfer to a conventional program at an inopportune time?

Finally, after essential basic decisions have been made, the committee must establish target dates for the installation of the program. If possible, a full year of planning is recommended before beginning the program. Sufficient time is needed for announcing the program, hiring and training the coordinator, publishing the necessary materials, contacting the employers, and interviewing and counseling students.

Curriculum Modifications

Curriculum modification and revamping of courses should not be begun until adoption is certain and there is agreement on the type of calendar to be used. In general, final modifications and course remodeling can best be done as the program develops. In any event, some faculty members of all colleges and departments concerned should be released from regular duties to guide changes in the length and content of courses. Individual faculty members must be responsible for rearranging the content of courses which they teach. If a four-year institution adopts a five-year cooperative plan and moves from a two-semester calendar to a four-quarter system, it will be a considerable undertaking to rearrange the curriculum and alter the length and content of courses. The cost of faculty time devoted to this project should be included as part of the expense of conversion.

Colleges and universities which have selective or optional programs may have additional costs for trailer courses—courses that are repeated because students cannot take them at the normal time they are offered. If there are sufficient coop students returning to the school after an off-campus experience to form a new section, a particular course may be offered for this special group. Trailer courses are not needed when college programs are mandatory, with regular alternating periods of work and study, or when all courses are repeated for the benefit of those students in school and those returning from off-campus assignments. If the university is large enough to repeat courses regularly for all students and offers a wide range of courses from which students may select substitutes to meet degree requirements, the need for trailer courses may be eliminated.

Preliminary Survey of Off-Campus Placement Opportunities

The number of students available for off-campus placement determines the job opportunities needed to operate the program. In the first stage of its work, the planning committee must make some preliminary inquiries regarding the availability of outside work. It must make contacts with business, industry, and health, social, and government agencies. This task will not be difficult if the college is located in or near a metropolitan area. However, if the college is in a rural area, the survey will be more arduous and time consuming.

If the program provides alternating on- and off-campus periods, the committee should plan to have each off-campus assignment held consecutively by two students. The committee must also consider allowing students to find their own jobs or undertake other kinds of activities which may not be related to their fields of study. At this stage the committee should make use of the advice of consultants. If the placement survey is favorable, the committee should then develop a model of conversion to determine the financial feasibility of proceeding with adoption.

Financial Feasibility

The new institution planning to "go coop" may not be too concerned about the financial advantages or disadvantages because cooperative education will be part of the overall cost of the development of the institution itself. Some colleges or universities adopting a cooperative program as an alternative means of study may also not care too much about operational costs. Most colleges converting to cooperative education, however, are very much concerned about conversion costs and possible financial advantages because most of them seek to improve their financial situation. These data can be determined only by developing models showing the required alterations in organization and operation. Models of conversion delineate changes in enrollment, changes in faculty and staff, and changes in expenses and income, year by year, after the cooperative program has developed. The models show also the financial picture when the program is in full operation, which is not until the seventh year in a four-year college converting to a five-year program.

To develop a model of conversion the following steps must be taken.

1. Determine the expected enrollments each year while the program is being installed and when it reaches full operation. (Enrollment figures are needed in order to know just how many placement opportunities must be provided.)

2. Decide on tuition and fees to be charged and calculate the total income during each of the years of conversion to cooperative education.

3. Determine additional faculty required to teach additional students and added faculty compensation (including fringe benefits) resulting from adoption of the plan.

4. Calculate the added costs of administration.

5. Determine the number and cost of additional clerical personnel.

6. Determine additional library expenses.

7. Calculate other expenses, including additional costs of gen-

eral and academic administration—deans of academic programs, registrar's office, computer services; changes in general expenses—catalogs, admissions office expense; and added costs of maintenance.

8. Determine costs of coordination and placement—department of cooperative education.

9. Consider added costs of athletics and student services.

10. Determine extra costs of student financial aid.

11. Estimate planning and conversion costs.

12. Develop a model of income and expenses showing preconversion income and expenses, changes during each year of conversion to cooperative education, and the projected post-conversion income and expenses (a summary of the data compiled in items 1 to 11).

ENROLLMENT. The optimum size of enrollment in programs with alternating periods of off-campus experience and on-campus study is achieved when the program is mandatory for all students. The on-campus enrollment will be the combined total of freshman enrollment and upperclassmen who are on campus. Total enrollment would include those on off-campus assignments. Therefore, in a four- or five-year college the overall figure may be 50 to 75 per cent greater than would be possible if all students were on campus. The higher enrollment which results from added freshmen and those on off-campus assignments is the source of the additional tuition and fees which derive from conversion to the cooperative plan. If the program is small, the cost of placing students may exceed additional revenues and the financial result will be a more costly operation. This result is likely in optional or selective programs until they are large enough to produce income in excess of the costs of operation.

Table 26 shows how enrollment calculations are made when converting from a college operating on a traditional calendar to a college operating on the cooperative plan with alternating periods of work and off-campus assignments. As the conversion to the cooperative plan is made, the size of the freshman class is increased. At the end of the first year, this class is divided into two divisions so that one group of students may return to the campus in the fall of the sophomore year for study, and the other undertakes off-campus assignments. As each class of students progresses, at the end of the freshman year and in each of the upper-class years, there will be an attrition of students. This attrition must be taken into account in determining the size of succeed-

Table 26. NUMBER OF STUDENTS NEEDED AT FRESHMAN LEVEL TO UTILIZE PLANT TO FULL CAPACITY WHEN STUDENTS ARE DIVIDED INTO TWO COOP DIVISIONS

Class Year	*Division*	*Pre-Coop Plan*	*1st Yr. Conv.*	*2nd Yr. Conv.*	*3rd Yr. Conv.*	*4th Yr. Conv.*	*5th Yr. Conv.*	*6th Yr. Conv.*	*7th Yr. Conv.*
1	f	325f	**400f**	450f	500f	500f	500f	500f	500f
2	f	250f	250f						
	a			**154a**	173a	192a	192a	192a	192a
	b			**154b**	173b	193b	193b	193b	193b
3	f	225f	225f	225f					
	a				**138a**	155a	173a	173a	173a
	b				**139b**	156b	173b	173b	173b
4	f	200f	200f	200f	200f				
	a					**124a**	139a	155a	155a
	b					**125b**	140b	156b	156b
5	f								
	a						**118a**	132a	147a
	b						**119b**	133b	148b
Total		1000	1075	1183	1323	1445	1747	1807	1837
Total Enrollment		1000	1075	1183	1323	1445	1747	1807	1837
Total f		1000	1075	875	700	500	500	500	500
Total a		—		154	311	471	622	652	667
Total b		—		154	312	474	625	655	670
Total Coop				308	623	945	1247	1307	1337
Total on Campus		1000	1075	1029	1011	972	1123	1153	1168

f = full time
a = 1st coop division
b = 2nd coop division
NOTE: Traditional 4 year to 5 year coop

ing freshman classes. Each institution must apply attrition rates which are realistic for it. If more students remain in school than planned and the physical plant has a fixed capacity, the freshman enrollments must be adjusted accordingly. Colleges that have excess classroom and laboratory capacity can enroll commuting students to the limit of this unused capacity provided they can place these students in off-campus assignments.

If the total number of on-campus students enrolled in the cooperative program is too large for the existing facilities, a decision must be made either to increase the size of those facilities or to adjust on-campus enrollments to the number which the physical plant can accommodate.

TUITION AND FEES. In order to determine properly the added income which will result from the cooperative plan of education, careful thought must be given to the tuition and fees to be charged those enrolled in the coop program. This income will vary according to the type and size of the program and the number of years in which students may undertake alternating periods of off-campus and on-campus assignments. The same, or larger, annual tuition should be charged upper-class cooperative students as is charged freshmen enrolled on a full-time basis. For example, if a program is operated on a quarter plan with three quarters on campus for all students in the freshman year and alternating periods of off-campus experience and study in the four upper-class years, the tuition rate should be the same each year—one-third of the total tuition payable each quarter in the freshman year and one-half of the annual tuition payable at the beginning of each on-campus quarter in the upper-class years. Charging the same tuition for three on-campus quarters in the first year and for two in the upper-class years is justified because students must be advised and placed. The college must also keep extensive records on off-campus experiences. Moreover, the off-campus experience is recognized as a specific requirement for the degree, or credit hours, which may be counted instead of course credits toward the degree, are awarded. Frequently coordinators must read reports on off-campus experiences. For more information on academic credit for off-campus experience, see Chapter 15.

Care must be taken to keep total tuition costs for the degree in line with those of traditional four-year institutions operating on a regular (traditional) academic calendar. Many students compare total tuition costs of the four-year traditional private college with those of the private cooperative college operated on a five-year basis.

Some cooperative institutions, particularly those with optional and selective programs, charge a fee for the student's work experience. Usually this fee is separate from the regular tuition charge. A few require a special cooperative registration fee. Only general guidelines can be used to determine these charges. For the most part, the fees for off-campus experience are determined by the nature and value of the experience and by the expense incurred by the institution in administering and arranging the off-campus period.

The following random examples illustrate how widely the amounts of these charges vary from institution to institution: $350 for each sequence of one academic quarter and one off-campus period; $11 for one semester hour of credit earned, the charge being determined in the same way as for any regular academic course; $60 for each off-campus period in the upper-class years; $136 of the normal tuition rate per term; $40 per off-campus experience (with a refund provision of up of $30 for courses taken at any accredited college or university).

In some instances the amount of the charge to students depends upon their place of residence. For example, one large university charges $75 per four-month off-campus period for its state residents and $245 for students from out of state. If credit is given for off-campus experience, charges can be in proportion to credits earned. Most colleges and universities do not require fees to record academic credits earned by students during off-campus periods by means of independent study, part-time study, projects, and the like. A few, however, do require transfer-credit fees or credit-hour fees, usually at the regular rate of tuition.

FACULTY COMPENSATION. Changes in enrollment and calendar naturally require additional faculty to teach during the conversion period and after the program is in complete operation. A realistic student-faculty ratio must be adopted as a basis for calculating the resulting costs.

When a college converts from a traditional calendar to a cooperative program with alternating periods of work and study throughout each calendar year in the upper-class years, faculty will be needed to take care of additional students enrolled in the freshman year and throughout the calendar year including the summer months in the upper-class years. The appointment of additional faculty to teach during the fourth quarter or summer term gives rise to some special considerations in determining compensation. Two basic methods are generally used to calculate faculty salaries for summer-term teaching: by a percentage of the annual compensation or by the number of credit hours, or units, taught. The policy of one college may be of little practical value to other institutions. It is interesting, however, to note just how widely these policies vary.

Among institutions that use the percentage of annual compensation (including fringe benefits) as a basis for pay for faculty teaching a fourth term during the summer months, the following formulas are applied: 33⅓ per cent of base annual compensation (three quarters contract) for teaching fourth quarter; 22 per cent of base annual compensation (nine-month contract) for those teaching eight-week summer session; 30 per cent of base annual compensation (nine-month contract) for those teaching eleven-week summer session; 50 per cent of base annual compensation (eight-month contract) for third term.

Obviously, compensation rates depend upon the basic salary structure of institutions at the various academic levels, on the length of base annual contracts, on the length of the summer term itself, and, in some cases, on the number of credit hours earned or taught in the summer program. One college compensates faculty at the rate of 1/42 of the base annual salary for each credit hour taught; another at the rate of 1/36. Still another offers 10 per cent of base rate for every three credit hours taught. Some of the contracts are quite involved. At one university, faculty are contracted to teach during one or both of two five-week summer sessions and are compensated on the basis of the total number of semester hours assigned. A maximum of six semester hours may be assigned in any one five-week period for 15 per cent of the faculty member's salary for the previous academic year. An assignment of fewer semester hours results in a correspondingly lower compensatory rate.

Hard and fast rules for establishing compensation rates for

summer-term teaching are impossible to determine. A personal agreement is usually reached between the faculty member and his department head, with appropriate further authorization as required by the institution. Developing institutions whose summer-term programs are similar to those of more established schools might be well advised to seek advice on general guidelines in this area.

ADMINISTRATIVE COMPENSATION. As a result of the adoption of cooperative education, additional staff may be needed in numerous offices and departments including public relations, publications, central information and telephone services, food services, housing, and the student center. For purposes of the conversion model, a ratio such as one administrative staff member to every ten faculty will provide a good basis for making projected calculations.

CLERICAL COMPENSATION. Additional clerical staff will be required as conversion progresses. A ratio of one additional clerical person to every five faculty and administrators is recommended.

LIBRARY COSTS. Extra expenses of operating the library result primarily from hiring additional staff to serve the increase in total enrollment and the students during the fourth quarter or summer months. The number of books purchased and other expenses also will be increased.

OTHER EXPENSES. As the program develops, there may be need for added persons in the central administration (office of the president, business manager, and so on). There will also be need for additional staff in the academic services departments (registrar's office, computer services, admissions office). Such expenses as new admissions literature, new catalogs, and promotional booklets will also be added to the cost of operation. Maintenance and housekeeping costs will be higher because of operation of the physical plant throughout the entire year. If a university is located in a warm climate, there may be extra costs for air conditioning.

DEPARTMENT OF COOPERATIVE EDUCATION. The costs of coordination and placement must be calculated and projected for each of the years of conversion. If the program is small, these costs may be merely a fraction of the salary of a faculty member, part-time clerical assistance required, and office expense, travel, telephone, printing, and so on. If the program is going to be one of substantial size, it will be necessary to project the added costs of establishing a cooperative education department with a director and as many coordinators as needed for the size of the program. The number of new staff will depend upon the number of students an individual coordinator is expected to counsel, place, and supervise. A coordinator who is developing a new program must find opportunities for off-campus placements in advance of the beginning of the first cooperative year. Initially a coordinator might counsel and place a total of 50 to 75 students, including those on campus and those off campus. As experience is gained and placement opportunities are both established and extended, this total can be increased to as many as 150. A long-established cooperative program will develop over the years many opportunities for off-campus experiences and placement. Many employers will expect to reserve places for cooperative students in their organizations and will tend to accept students referred to them by coordinators. Where such relationships exist, the coordinator may counsel and place a much larger number of students, ranging from 200 to 300 or more per term.

The number of students who can be assigned to a coordinator is also affected by the type of program to be offered and the geographic location of the school. Loads must be lightened when the emphasis of the program is experiential and each student requires considerable counseling to develop his own tailor-made program. When the institution is located in a rural area away from the job market, coordinators must be allowed more travel time for the development of suitable positions. The coordinator's effectiveness can be increased if he has competent clerical and secretarial staff.

A director of a cooperative program will be paid according to the size of the program. In a college with a program of substantial size his salary should be the same as that paid deans or directors of other major programs. Salary rates for coordinators should be commensurate with the rates for faculty of equal rank, adjusted to a twelve-month basis; that is, if the salary of an assistant professor is $10,000 for nine months of teaching, the coordinator holding the rank of assistant professor would have a salary of $12,500.

The costs of operating the department of cooperative education are set forth in the following list of items normally included in a department budget.

Salaries

1. Director
2. Coordinators—coop faculty
3. Administrative assistants
4. Secretarial staff
5. Clerical staff
6. Additional help—overtime or part-time student help

Office Expenses

1. Supplies
2. Repairs to typewriters
3. File folders
4. Stationery
5. Postage

Telephone and Telegraph

Printing

1. Handbook for students
2. Forms—records
3. Newsletters
4. Internal photocopying expenses
5. Wall calendars
6. Publications for coop employers

Travel and Entertainment

1. Public transportation for coop faculty
2. Automobile expenses—mileage for coop faculty
3. Cost of meals away from home
4. Insurance—extra coverage on personal cars
5. Trip insurance—public transportation
6. Entertainment—prospective employers

Staff Training and Development

1. Workshop attendance
2. Consultants' fees and expenses

Memberships

Conferences

1. On campus
2. Local, regional, national

Subscriptions—Publications

1. Occupational services
2. Guidance literature

Social Security—Staff

Major Medical—Staff

Group Life Insurance—Staff

Unemployment Insurance—Staff

Overhead—total administration and overhead costs assigned to department based on allotted space used

Capital

1. New typewriters
2. Alterations
3. Office equipment—furniture
4. File cabinets

Rental of Keypunch Machine

ATHLETICS AND STUDENT SERVICE COSTS. Operation during the summer months will increase the costs of the departments of athletics and health. Professional staff members must be retained and compensated and athletic equipment and medical supplies kept at a level commensurate with student needs. At many institutions part-time help must also be brought in to assure coverage for those full-time staff members who will be on vacation.

STUDENT FINANCIAL AID. As the conversion to cooperative education progresses, it will be necessary to revise the total amount of funds made available for student financial aid. Students holding paid jobs as off-campus assignments will have funds to meet a substantial portion of their college costs. Despite this, the increase in enrollments in the first year resulting from the adoption of a coop program will increase the total demand for financial aid by first-year students. (For further discussion of financial aid policies, see Chapter 14.)

PLANNING AND CONVERSION COSTS. These costs will include compensation of faculty whose time has been made available to the committee on a release-time basis, salaries for any additional staff, clerical, and secretarial assistance used by the committee, the cost of making a survey of placement opportunities, the cost of modifying the curriculum and revamping courses, the cost of consulting services, costs of attending workshops, and the cost of implementing the program.

Presidents of colleges and universities that are installing cooperative education should use their contacts with various foundations to seek financial support for conversion. In recent years several major foundations have been interested in giving total or partial support for cooperative education programs. In most cases their aid has covered the direct costs of establishing the coordination staff and the cost of consulting services, while the institution was responsible for hiring extra faculty.

Recently the federal government, through the Office of Education in the Department of Health, Education, and Welfare, has given some financial aid for the installation of cooperative programs in developing institutions under Title III of the Higher Education Act of 1965. Information concerning application procedures can be obtained by contacting the Director of the Division of College Support in the U.S. Office of Education. Title IV D of the Amendment to the Higher Education Act of 1965 authorizes grants to institutions of higher education to expand and strengthen student programs which alternate periods of full-time study and full-time employment. Interested parties should contact the Director of the Division of College Support for information about application procedures.

Conversion of Two-Year Programs

The conversion of a two-year junior college into a college with alternating periods of on-campus study and off-campus experience may not produce the financial advantages derived from the conversion of a traditional four-year college to the cooperative plan. The primary drawback is the high rate of attrition experienced by many two-year colleges and the fact that much of the dropout occurs between terms rather than at the end of a year, as in four-year colleges. This attrition results in an imbalance of students and faculty in some terms. When there is an excess of faculty total faculty compensation may exceed added income from increased enrollments.

The calculations required for converting a traditional two-year college to programs with alternating periods of work and study should follow the pattern recommended for four-year colleges. Traditional community colleges located in metropolitan areas planning to adopt parallel or concurrent calendars (see Chapter 4) will have conversion costs which include planning costs, added costs of instruction which may result from this type of program, particularly if classes are conducted during the summer months, and the cost of establishing and operating a department of cooperative education.

Conversion of Traditional Four-Year College to Four-Year Cooperative Program

Colleges making this conversion will need to make a choice of calendars. One popular system provides for off-campus experience during the sophomore and junior years. Students receive four off-campus experience periods on the cooperative plan. This type of calendar brings all students together in the freshman and senior years. Another plan provides alternating periods of work and study during all of the upper-class years. The adoption of this calendar makes possible only nine on-campus periods in which to earn academic credit and six off-campus periods. If the program is developed on the quarter system students will find it difficult to earn the traditional number of quarter hours required for graduation during their on-campus periods. The granting of credit for the off-campus experience then becomes necessary. If 160 quarter hours are required to receive a degree and if students earn 15 quarter hours during the nine on-campus periods, the total academic quarter hours earned would be 135, requiring that 25 quarter hours be granted for off-campus experience.

Conversion of Graduate Programs

Few graduate schools have thus far adopted cooperative education, although great interest is being shown currently. In programs registering only a few students, the institution often can work out the cooperative program on an individual basis and not incur any of the usual added costs. When enrollments are small, faculty members can adjust their time to meet student needs and can also handle the arrangements for off-campus experience. If undergraduate programs of cooperative education exist at the institution desiring to adopt graduate cooperative education, the existing coordinators can handle the placements. A college planning to establish a sizable graduate program with regular alternating periods of on- and off-campus assignments should make the same types of calculations to determine financial feasibility as are recommended for undergraduate programs. Discussion of the types of graduate programs and calendars which may be considered are presented in Chapter 6.

Model of Conversion

The model of conversion presented in Table 27 demonstrates how to calculate the financial feasibility of adopting cooperative education. The compensation figures and other cost figures have been chosen as average or typical and not as actual for any individual institution. The model shows enrollments prior to the adoption of cooperative education, enrollments expected during the period of conversion, and student population when the conversion is completed. It also shows estimated costs of operation before and after conversion. Therefore, the model is not only a basis for determining the financial feasibility of adopting cooperative education but also a source of information on the additional financing needed to make the conversion. Faculty compensation rates, including fringe benefits, student-faculty ratios, rates of attrition of students, administrative costs, and other expenses vary greatly from college to college. Each institution, therefore, must establish its own appropriate student-faculty ratios, attrition rates, and so forth.

The model describes a four-year college enrolling 1,000 commuting students which is changing into a five-year cooperative plan college and which expects to operate all programs for all students on a mandatory basis. Total enrollments increase from 1,000 to 1,837 students with a maximum of 1,168 students on campus at any one time. The result of this conversion is an excess of operating income over expenses. Increases in compensation and other costs have been estimated and included. Every institution making a conversion must consider the probable increase in tuition and fees and increases in compensation and other costs of operation. Failure to do so is merely to deceive oneself as to the probable outcome of adopting cooperative education.

Some colleges may find that the development of a model reveals

Table 27. MODEL OF CALCULATIONS TO DETERMINE FINANCIAL FEASIBILITY OF CONVERTING A TRADITIONAL FOUR-YEAR COLLEGE OF 1,000 COMMUTING STUDENTS TO FIVE-YEAR COOPERATIVE COLLEGE ENROLLING 1,837 COMMUTING STUDENTS

	Pre-Coop Plan	*1st Year Conversion*	*2nd Year Conversion*	*3rd Year Conversion*	*4th Year Conversion*	*5th Year Conversion*	*6th Year Conversion*	*7th Year Conversion*
Income								
Tuition and fees	$1,875,000	$2,015,625	$2,283,190	$2,553,390	$2,868,325	$3,467,795	$3,586,895	$3,646,445
Expenses								
Faculty compensation	750,000	837,000	874,672	929,516	969,032	1,125,875	1,200,052	1,233,394
Administrative staff compensation	75,000	77,500	80,000	82,500	85,000	87,500	108,000	111,000
Clerical compensation	72,000	75,600	79,200	82,800	86,400	90,000	109,200	113,400
Library costs	100,000	107,500	117,200	136,300	146,800	155,000	177,500	186,250
Other expenses	475,000	500,000	525,000	550,000	575,000	625,000	605,000	660,000
Department of coop educ.	—	27,000	117,275	229,425	238,375	262,850	272,375	281,900
Athletics	72,000	77,400	87,542	97,902	109,820	132,772	137,332	139,612
Student services	75,000	80,625	94,640	105,840	122,825	148,495	153,595	156,145
Finan. aid @ 15% of tuition	270,000	290,250	328,282	367,132	411,825	497,895	514,995	523,545
Planning and conv. cost	25,000[a]	50,000[b]	25,000[b]	12,500[b]	12,500[b]	—	—	—
Total Costs and Expenses	$1,914,000	$2,122,875	$2,328,811	$2,593,915	$2,757,577	$3,105,387	$3,298,049	$3,405,246
Net Gain (Loss)	($39,000)	($107,250)	($45,621)	($40,525)	$110,748	$362,408	$288,846	$241,199

[a] Advance planning

[b] Conversion costs

SCHEDULE A: ENROLLMENTS

Class Year	Pre-Coop Plan	1st Year Conversion	2nd Year Conversion	3rd Year Conversion	4th Year Conversion	5th Year Conversion	6th Year Conversion	7th Year Conversion
1	325f	400f	450f	500f	500f	500f	500f	500f
2 77% of yr. 1	250f	250f	308c	346c	385c	385c	385c	385c
3 90% of yr. 2	225f	225f	225f	277c	311c	346c	346c	346c
4 90% of yr. 3	200f	200f	200f	200f	249c	279c	311c	311c
5 95% of yr. 4	—					237c	265c	295c
Total	1,000	1,075	1,183	1,323	1,445	1,747	1,807	1,837
On Campus = f + ½ of c	1,000	1,075	1,029	1,011	972	1,123	1,153	1,168

c = coop students
f = full-time students

SCHEDULE B: TUITION AND FEE INCOME

Year	Total Enrollment[a]	Tuition Rate	Tuition Income	Fees	Fee Income	Total Income
Pre-Coop	1000	$1800	$1,800,000	$75	$ 75,000	$1,875,000
1st year conversion	1075	1800	1,935,000	75	80,625	2,015,625
2nd year conversion	1183	1850	2,188,550	80	94,640	2,283,190
3rd year conversion	1323	1850	2,447,550	80	105,840	2,553,390
4th year conversion	1445	1900	2,745,500	85	122,825	2,868,325
5th year conversion	1747	1900	3,319,300	85	148,495	3,467,795
6th year conversion	1807	1900	3,433,300	85	153,595	3,586,895
7th year conversion	1837	1900	3,490,300	85	156,145	3,646,445

[a] See Schedule A

SCHEDULE C: FACULTY COMPENSATION

	Pre-Coop Plan	*1st Year Conversion*	*2nd Year Conversion*	*3rd Year Conversion*	*4th Year Conversion*	*5th Year Conversion*	*6th Year Conversion*	*7th Year Conversion*
No. of faculty (3 quarters)[a]	50	54	52	51	49	56	58	58
No. of faculty (4th quarter)[b]	0	0	8	16	24	25	26	26
Faculty compensation (3 quarters)[c]	$750,000	$837,000	$832,000	$841,500	$833,000	$ 980,000	$1,044,000	$1,073,000
Faculty compensation (4th quarter)[d]	0	0	42,672	88,016	136,032	145,875	156,052	160,394
Total Compensation	$750,000	$837,000	$874,672	$929,516	$969,032	$1,125,875	$1,200,052	$1,233,394

[a] Faculty/student ratio 1:20 of on-campus students

[b] Faculty/student ratio 1:20 of one half coop students not seniors

[c] $15,000 average salary pre-coop; average compensation increases @ $500 per year

[d] $15,000/3 = $5,000; average compensation per quarter; increase $500/3 = $167 per year

SCHEDULE D: ADMINISTRATIVE STAFF COMPENSATION

	Pre-Coop Plan	*1st Year Conversion*	*2nd Year Conversion*	*3rd Year Conversion*	*4th Year Conversion*	*5th Year Conversion*	*6th Year Conversion*	*7th Year Conversion*
Staff[a]	5	5	5	5	5	5	6	6
Total Cost[b]	$75,000	$77,500	$80,000	$82,500	$85,000	$87,500	$108,000	$111,000

[a] Admin./faculty ratio 1:10

[b] $15,000 average salary pre-coop; average salary increase $500 per year

SCHEDULE E: CLERICAL COMPENSATION

	Pre-Coop Plan	*1st Year Conversion*	*2nd Year Conversion*	*3rd Year Conversion*	*4th Year Conversion*	*5th Year Conversion*	*6th Year Conversion*	*7th Year Conversion*
Clerical Personnel[a]	12	12	12	12	12	12	14	14
Total Cost[b]	$72,000	$75,600	$79,200	$82,800	$86,400	$90,000	$109,200	$113,400

[a] Ratio 1:5 clerical to faculty plus admin.
[b] Salary $6,000 per year pre-coop; average salary increase $300 per year

SCHEDULE F: LIBRARY COSTS

	Pre-Coop Plan	*1st Year Conversion*	*2nd Year Conversion*	*3rd Year Conversion*	*4th Year Conversion*	*5th Year Conversion*	*6th Year Conversion*	*7th Year Conversion*
No. of staff (4 quarters)	5	5	5.2	6.2	6.4	6.4	7.5	7.5
Staff compensation[a]	$ 50,000	$ 52,500	$ 57,200	$ 71,300	$ 76,800	$ 80,000	$ 97,500	$101,250
Books and other expenses	50,000	55,000	60,000	65,000	70,000	75,000	80,000	85,000
Total	$100,000	$107,500	$117,200	$136,300	$146,800	$155,000	$177,500	$186,250

[a] $10,000 average compensation pre-coop; $500 average compensation increase per year (includes fringe benefits)

SCHEDULE G: OTHER EXPENSES

	Pre-Coop Plan	*1st Year Conversion*	*2nd Year Conversion*	*3rd Year Conversion*	*4th Year Conversion*	*5th Year Conversion*	*6th Year Conversion*	*7th Year Conversion*
General and academic admin. and general expense	$325,000	$350,000	$365,000	$385,000	$395,000	$425,000	$435,000	$470,000
Maintenance expense	150,000	150,000	160,000	165,000	180,000	180,000	190,000	190,000
Total	$475,000	$500,000	$525,000	$550,000	$575,000	$605,000	$625,000	$660,000

SCHEDULE H: DEPARTMENT OF COOPERATIVE EDUCATION

	Pre-Coop Plan	*1st Year Conversion*	*2nd Year Conversion*	*3rd Year Conversion*	*4th Year Conversion*	*5th Year Conversion*	*6th Year Conversion*	*7th Year Conversion*
Administration[a]	0	1	1	1	1	1	1	1
Coordinators[b]	0	0	6	13	13	14	14	14
Clerical staff[c]	0	1	2	3	3	3	3	3
Admin. compensation[d]	0	$18,000	$ 18,500	$ 19,000	$ 19,500	$ 20,000	$ 20,500	$ 21,000
Coordinators compensation[e]	0		72,000	162,500	169,000	189,000	196,000	203,000
Clerical compensation[f]	0	6,300	13,200	20,700	21,600	22,500	23,400	24,300
Coordinator expense[g]	0	2,700	13,575	27,225	28,275	31,350	32,475	33,600
		$27,000	$117,275	$229,425	$238,375	$262,850	$272,375	$281,900

[a] One
[b] Ratio coordinators to coop students: first year—0, 2nd—1:50, 3rd—1:50, 4th—1:75, 5th—1:90, 6th—1:100, 7th—1:100
[c] Ratio staff to admin. and coordinators 1:5
[d] $18,000 1st conversion year increasing @ $500 per year (includes fringe benefits)
[e] $11,000 1st conversion year increasing @ $500 per year (includes fringe benefits)
[f] $6,000 pre-coop year increasing @ $300 per year (includes fringe benefits)
[g] 15% of administrator and coordinator compensation

SCHEDULE I: ATHLETICS

	Pre-Coop Plan	1st Year Conversion	2nd Year Conversion	3rd Year Conversion	4th Year Conversion	5th Year Conversion	6th Year Conversion	7th Year Conversion
Total costs[a]	$72,000	$77,400	$87,542	$97,902	$109,820	$132,772	$137,332	$139,612

[a] Assume 4% of total tuition

SCHEDULE J: STUDENT SERVICES

	Pre-Coop Plan	1st Year Conversion	2nd Year Conversion	3rd Year Conversion	4th Year Conversion	5th Year Conversion	6th Year Conversion	7th Year Conversion
Total costs	$75,000	$80,625	$94,640	$105,840	$122,825	$148,495	$153,595	$156,145

NOTE:

Pre-coop and 1st year—$75 per student per year
2nd year conversion and 3rd year conversion—$80 per student per year
4th year conversion through 7th year conversion—$85 per student per year

Table 28. Comparison of Cost of Living Away from Home While Attending a Public College and a Private Cooperative Plan College

Public College (Quarter System)		*Coop Plan Private College* (Mandatory Five-Year Plan, Quarter System)	
Tuition	$100 for each 12-week quarter	Tuition	$500 per (12-week) quarter for freshman year; $750 per on-campus quarter upper-class years, including two 12-week quarters on campus and two 13-week quarters on work assignments[a]
Fees	$100 per year	Fees	$100 per year
Travel[b]	$100 per year	Travel[b]	$100 per year
Dorm. cost	$ 32 per week	Dorm. cost	$ 32 per week
Books	$300 per year	Books	$300 per year
Clothes and personal expense	$250 per year	Clothes and personal expense	$250 per year
Estimated Cost of Attending Public College for Four Years		*Estimated Cost of Attending Five-Year Coop College*	
Tuition	$1,200 (12 qtrs. x $100)	Tuition	$ 7,500 (3 × $500 + 4 × $1,500)
Fees	400 (4 × $100)	Fees	500 (5 × $100)
Travel	400 (4 × $100)	Travel	500 (5 × $100)
Dorm. cost	4,608 (36 wks. @ $32 × 4 years)	Dorm. cost	1,152 (36 weeks @ $32) 3,072 (24 weeks @ $32 = $768 × 4)
Books	1,200 (4 × $300)	Books	1,500 (5 × $300)
Clothing and personal expense	1,000 (4 × $250)	Clothing and personal expense	1,250 (5 × $250)
Total	$8,808	Total	$15,474
Earnings	$3,000 (3 summers of 10 weeks each @ $100)	Earnings	$10,400 (4 years, 26 weeks @ $100 per week)
Net Cost	$5,808	Net Cost	$ 5,074

[a] Cooperative students live at home while on work assignments.

[b] Students of both colleges must travel from home to the campus.

Table 29. COST TO COMMUTING STUDENTS OF ATTENDING PUBLIC COLLEGE VS. COOPERATIVE PLAN COLLEGE

Public College		*Private Cooperative College (Mandatory Five-Year Plan)*	
Tuition	$100 for each 12-week quarter	Tuition	$500 per 12-week quarter for freshman year; $750 per on-campus quarter upper-class years, including two 12-week quarters on campus and two 13-week quarters on work assignments[a]
Fees (health ins. and other)	$100 per year	Fees (health ins. and other)	$100 per year
Travel (carfare)	50¢ per day	Travel (carfare)	50¢ per day
Books	$300 per year	Books	$300 per year
Clothing and personal expense	$250 per year	Clothing and personal expense	$250 per year
Estimated Cost of Attending Public Four-Year College (Four Years of Three Quarters Each)		*Estimated Cost of Attending Five-Year Cooperative College*	
Tuition	$1,200 (12 qtrs. × $100)	Tuition	$ 1,500 (3 quarters @ $500) 6,000 (8 quarters @ $750)
Fees	400 (4 × $100)	Fees	500 (5 × $100)
Travel (carfare)[b]	435	Travel (carfare)	590 (including coop assignment)[c]
Books	1,200 (4 × $300)	Books	1,500 (5 × $300)
Clothing and personal expenses	1,000 (4 × $250)	Clothing and personal expenses	1,250 (5 × $250)
Total	$4,235	Total	$11,340
Earnings	$3,000 (3 summers, 10 wks. @ $100 per week)	Earnings	$10,400 (26 weeks per year @ $100 per week)
Net Cost	$1,235	Net Cost	$ 940

[a] Cooperative assignments are within commuting distance of college.
[b] 720 school days, 150 work days
[c] 660 school days, 520 work days

Table 30. COST OF ATTENDING PUBLIC UNIVERSITY WITH OPTIONAL FIVE-YEAR COOPERATIVE PROGRAM (Quarter System)

Expenses	*Unit Cost*	*Cost for Five Years*
Tuition	$100 per qtr. (11 qtrs. on campus)	$ 1,100
Placement fee	$100 per quarter (4 × 2 quarters @ $100)	800
Travel	50¢ per day	590
Books	$300 per year	1,500
Personal expense	$250 per year	1,250
	Total Cost	$ 5,240
Average coop earnings (8 qtrs. off-campus)	$100 per week, 26 wks. × 4 upper-class yrs.	$10,400
	Net earnings	$ 5,160[a]

[a] This excess of earnings over expenses is used by many students enrolled in cooperative programs of public colleges and universities to meet the costs of accepting a coop job assignment away from home. The funds help pay for transportation to and from the assignment, housing, utilities, food, and miscellaneous expenses. In addition, it may be possible to retain some earnings as savings, depending upon the total amount received and the expenses incurred as a result of the off-campus assignment.

NOTE: Students attend on a commuting basis, live at home, and coop assignments (paid jobs) are within commuting distance of home.

little or no financial advantage in converting existing programs to cooperative education. Perhaps special costs which cannot be avoided are offsetting the advantages that might be achieved by conversion. No institution should at any time adopt cooperative education on either an optional or mandatory basis unless the administration is confident that it can recruit enough qualified students required to operate the program efficiently and that it can provide the number and types of off-campus placement opportunities needed for all students enrolled. Recognizing this problem, some colleges which were uncertain of their ability to meet these requirements have begun cooperative programs by experimenting with optional programs. Experience has shown that once optional programs are begun there is a tendency to continue them indefinitely. If the college is confident that cooperative education is desirable or necessary, it should proceed immediately to mandatory programs.

Comparative Costs to Students

Students who enroll in cooperative colleges should do so because they want this type of education, recognizing that the off-campus experience related to their fields of study makes for a superior quality of education. For many students and their parents, however, the opportunity for off-campus experience in the form of paid employment makes cooperative education very desirable. Moreover, for students from low-income families, the cooperative plan may provide the only way they can obtain an education, unless they are able to attend a low-cost public institution near their homes on a commuting basis. When cooperative work earnings are taken into account, some cooperative plan private colleges require less out of pocket expenditure than do most traditional four-year private colleges which have relatively high tuition rates. The student with limited financial means who is trying to determine the net cost of getting an education, therefore, will probably compare the cost of attending an inexpensive public college and the cost of attending either a private or public college offering cooperative education.

Looking at the total cost of an educational program (four academic years and five calendar years), many students will find that there is a financial advantage in attending cooperative programs of study. Tables 28 and 29 illustrate the cost of attending public colleges and private cooperative plan colleges while living away from home and as commuting students. As salary rates for cooperative students tend to increase and the tuition at state colleges tends to increase, the cooperative plan college may have an even greater financial advantage to the prospective student. Table 30 depicts the cost to the student commuter of attending an optional cooperative program at a public university while he lives at home and works on a cooperative assignment also within commuting distance. The financial advantage to the student is considerable. In many instances, however, this advantage is used to pay travel and living costs while he is on assignments located at some distance from the local campus.

Students on the coop plan can expect that some of their wages will be withheld for taxes. This deduction is omitted from the following tables since the amount withheld varies considerably according to the dependency status of the individual, the total amount earned in a given year, and the regulations of various states. In some cases all monies withheld are refunded by the state and federal governments to students when tax returns are filed and refunds requested. In other cases students may be paying approximately 10 per cent of their gross incomes in taxes.

For many students the opportunity to earn while learning is an important feature of cooperative education. More significantly, a student gains a superior education by performing work related to his field of study and by pursuing other activities which enrich the more formal on-campus educational program.

Promotion and Exchange of Information

George E. Probst

Cooperative education has promotion and communication problems of intense difficulty. Consider the case of an innovation in higher education that ten years ago was utilized by only twenty thousand students and forty-five institutions. Despite its growth to more than five times these figures, how many can be expected to know about cooperative education today? Consider an innovation that cuts against the grain of the traditional elitist concept of higher education. Consider further that even the name of this innovation makes for an easy confusion with the common concept of "just working his way through college" and for confusion with the comparatively recent federally subsidized work-study program of student financial aid for part-time work.

A large number of cooperative institutions have successfully solved such problems. There are answers to be obtained from institutions that have successful working models of cooperative education programs. It is important to emphasize that cooperative education is both an innovation in traditional higher education and an innovation with sixty-five years of history and development.

National Commission for Cooperative Education

Since cooperative education has successful models, it is possible to carry through a successful public-information effort in its behalf. The National Commission for Cooperative Education has demonstrated this.

The National Commission since 1962 has been drawing on the experience and leadership of the institutions with long-established programs of cooperative education. It has successfully used these resources to carry out the recommendations of the Study of Cooperative Education and the Princeton Conference in 1961 that cooperative education be substantially expanded.

The National Commission is composed of members having long experience with cooperative education in colleges and universities, and with its operation in business and industry. They have joined in establishing the commission as a means of increasing understanding and information about cooperative education, because there are educational and economic benefits for both students and institutions, as well as advantages to employers and the overall society.

The original ten-year goals of the commission were reached and far surpassed when, by 1971, a total of over 100,000 cooperative students were enrolled in 225 colleges and universities; these students earned $220,000,000 in the work phases of their programs. These are significant figures for communicating the growing importance of cooperative education.

The National Commission's purpose is to forward the expansion of cooperative education. It tries to achieve this purpose in a number of ways: by sponsoring conferences designed to inform leaders about cooperative education; by providing consultants to institutions that need advice in developing, organizing, and setting up programs; by providing a continuing public-information program; by encouraging the development of new forms of cooperative education; by interesting colleges and universities, as well as industry, labor, government, and other employers, in cooperative education; and by assisting in the formulation of national policy in support of cooperative education.

In accomplishing these purposes the commission has used many important tools of communication. It has taken advantage of the knowledge gained in the two-year research study of cooperative education accomplished by James Wilson and Edward Lyons. It has used insights into the problems of modern education that are to be found in Alfred North Whitehead's *The Aims of Education*. Whitehead has said that the problem of adapting education "to the needs of a democratic community is very far from being solved." "For successful education there must always be a certain freshness in the knowledge dealt with. It must either be new in itself or it must be invested with some novelty of application to the new world of new times. Knowledge does not keep any better than fish. You may be dealing with knowledge of the old species, with some old truth; but somehow or other it must come to the students, as it were, just drawn out of the sea and with the freshness of its immediate importance."

The National Commission has been actively and successfully performing since 1962. Progress has taken place despite the fact that traditional institutions are often manned by administrators and faculties who tend to feel that cooperative education is too vocational. This general feeling exists even though cooperative education successfully answers some of the legitimate complaints of students: the depersonalization of the individual in our educational system and the matter of the relevancy of the subject matter.

Sources of Information

Effective administration of a cooperative education program requires the acquisition of a great deal of background and current information. Since the entire field is only now in the process of developing adequate professional literature, much of the necessary information can be gained only through direct face-to-face communication with those who have had successful experience in carrying forward active responsibility for administering cooperative education programs. Therefore, membership in the Cooperative Education Division of the American Society for Engineering Education, 1 Dupont Circle, Washington, D.C., 20036, is essential for an opportunity to gain information through the publications and the annual meeting of this organization.

Second, the Cooperative Education Association, which the National Commission assisted in getting started in 1963 by providing headquarters during its first few years, is a national professional association for all those engaged in all phases of cooperative education. It has presently approximately one thousand members divided about equally between education and various kinds of employers. A membership can be arranged by writing to the Cooperative Education Association, Drexel University, 32nd and Chestnut Streets, Philadelphia, Pa., 19104. The annual Cooperative Education Association meeting offers an invaluable means of meeting those with critical expertise in various facets of cooperative education for all types of curricula. The Cooperative Education Association publishes an informative journal, which is the largest single source of current written reports about the field.

Joining these two organizations and attending the annual conferences will enable those new to cooperative education to meet several hundred employer representatives from the largest corporations in the nation, U.S. Civil Service representatives, and coordinators and administrators of every type of institution and cooperative education programs.

Not to be neglected are the different regional associations and frequent workshops on cooperative education that are organized and offered by Northeastern University and the University of South Florida, and planned at Virginia Polytechnic Institute, the University of Detroit, and the University of Houston. Announcements concerning workshops at institutions throughout the nation are provided in the newsletters regularly issued by the Cooperative Education Association and the Cooperative Education Division of the American Society of Engineering Education. Further, the U.S. Office of Education is annually funding institutes on cooperative education which pay an allowance for the living costs of the participants.

New institutions entering cooperative education should acquire sample items of the informational materials that are used to promote and organize a program. Sample college and university newsletters issued to serve the cooperative students in the institutions; brochures for employers, catalogs, coop handbooks, leaflets distributed to high schools, press releases describing the accomplishments of coop students —all of these should be acquired from five to ten institutions with long-established successful programs. The choice can then be made of the best information program to fit the needs of the particular institution.

Those without an acquaintance with cooperative education will find it useful to spend several days at a cooperative education institution with a curriculum and a type of student body comparable to their own institution's. The experience of the National Commission has revealed that this is the most effective way for those from traditional institutions to acquire a realization of the multifaceted values of cooperative education for the student, the institution, and the society. Conversations with professional peers and with cooperative students invariably communicate the vitality of the process of mixing experience with education. Seeing the living reality of an institution where the faculty and the students are engaged in the process of education is more persuasive than all written descriptions.

Public Relations Programs

For the National Commission, the goal of increasing the number of students and colleges committed to cooperative education involved an intensive program of persuading educational and political leaders of the instructional, social, and economic validity of this form of higher learning. The routine or commonplace devices of public relations were judged to be inadequate to gain the approbation and support of decision makers for an idea that had acquired a sudden pertinence to the educational needs of the nation. Although newspapers, magazines, and the broadcast media were exposed to the meaning and content of cooperative education, and began devoting columns and time to reporting it, this kind of coverage was not sufficient to impress either the political or the intellectual communities. Newsletters and pamphlets published by the National Commission were more impressive in their impact, but they too did not succeed in dramatically breaking down the preconceptions of the conventional education establishment. For, in fact, although cooperative education was first installed in the University of Cincinnati in 1906, in the 1960s it had taken on the appearance of a new social invention that, if widely adopted, would upset fixed positions and attitudes of college administrators and faculties. It became apparent then that attitudes at the top had to be changed if cooperative education was to be embraced by many more colleges and students.

It was easy to communicate with students. The National Commission arranged for articles in *Reader's Digest,* for example. The students read the newspaper and magazine articles and heard the radio and television reports; and to many of them (particularly those from low-income families and those with only average grades) cooperative education offered an almost miraculous opportunity to go forward from high school to higher learning. It also offered relevance. Thousands wanted to know how and where to enroll in cooperative education colleges. Northeastern University, for example, arrived at the point of having four applicants for each place in the freshman class.

But many educators were not so eager to learn or to test the idea—at least, not until 1967, when President Johnson delivered his Education Message to the Congress and, for the first time in history a President made specific reference to the national importance of a specific kind of education. On February 28, President Johnson stated: "A number of our colleges have highly successful programs of cooperative education which permit students to vary periods of study with periods of employment. *This is an important educational innovation that has demonstrated its effectiveness. It should be applied more widely in our schools and universities.*"

This was a triumphant acknowledgment of the validity of cooperative education, but this too came after a long and arduous process of education of those in government and education who brought their influence to bear upon the White House. The necessary communication relied less on the printed word than on verbal communication, talking head to head across conference tables. Much of it resulted from well-documented material presented verbally to the Senate and House Subcommittees on Education.

Revelations of the results attained by cooperative education schools and their students presented to the Secretaries of Health, Education, and Welfare and of Labor led them to endorse and sponsor cooperative education. Indeed, Secretary of Labor Willard Wirtz declared after one meeting on the subject, "This is important enough to be taken up by the Cabinet." Later, in January 1970, in a public address, the U.S. Commissioner of Education declared that the national need for an expansion of cooperative education had been expressed eloquently by Ralph Tyler, Chairman of the National Commission, and that the National Commission must be accorded public acknowledgment for its leadership and unrelenting diligence in helping to push this cooperative education legislation through to enactment.

A lesson to be noted from the experience of the National Commission is that at each institution adopting cooperative education there must be a program to reach and inform the top decision makers in business, industry, and government in their local region if the cooperative education program is to grow and flourish.

The basis, in large part, of the endorsement by the White House and the gaining of a specific line-item budget classification for cooperative education in the federal budget was a series of five statewide conferences on cooperative education, which the National Commission organized to carry the message to leaders of education, business, and industry in New Mexico, Indiana, Oregon, Texas, and California. With imagination and effectiveness, M. B. Zerwick, Chairman of the Board of Commco PR Inc., designed the concept and organized the first two statewide conferences in New Mexico and Indiana. In each state the conference leadership was assumed by the president of the state university and the senior U.S. Senator from that state. In each of these conferences business and industrial leaders actively urged more colleges and universities to adopt cooperative education.

The final passage of the legislation for cooperative education by the Senate, on October 1, 1968 (following House action in the previous week), authorized the Commissioner of Education

to make grants to institutions of higher education for the planning, establishment, expansion, or carrying out by such institutions of programs of cooperative education that alternate periods of full-time academic study with periods of full-time public or private employment that will not only afford students the opportunity to earn through employment funds required toward continuing and completing their education but will, so far as practicable, give them work experience related to their academic or occupational objective.

The federal government appropriated $1,700,000 for the fiscal year 1972 to carry out the purposes of this legislation.

The passage of this federal legislation has added enormous impetus to the public interest, understanding, and support for developing new programs in cooperative education. It is now a settled matter of public policy to favor its expansion.

Epilogue

Future of Cooperative Education

Asa S. Knowles

Many new terms have become popular in the field of higher education—off-campus experience, interlude, field experience, university without walls, external degree, internship, experiential education, foreign travel/study, independent study and research, collateral reading project, and others. Methods of developing, administering, and evaluating programs represented by them vary from institution to institution, and of course from student to student. They are all patterns of cooperative education, and reflect a recognition on the part of many educators of the tremendous values provided by a partnership between the academic and actual life-learning experience.

With the national spotlight now strongly focused on off-campus experience as a way toward relevance in education, the future of cooperative education appears brighter than ever. The number of cooperative institutions is growing at an unprecedented rate (from 35 in 1960 to 225 in 1971), both at the senior and junior college levels.

The major goal of higher education is not merely to prepare a student to effect a smooth transition into an unfamiliar and often alien workaday world. On the contrary, the goal should be to eliminate that transition period before the student completes his college career. The proper use of a relevant academic background in a real-life experience beyond the confines of the campus can be a major step in accomplishing this goal. Cooperative education is the best means of uniting the world of the campus and the world beyond it. (See Chapters 1 and 2.)

Traditionalism and Innovation

Although traditionalism has always been the watchword in education, these are times when innovation is desperately needed. This is exactly what the various forms of cooperative education provide, although there are some who will undoubtedly continue to resist it. Furors were raised when high schools were first established in this country, when the way was paved for the land-grant colleges in 1862, when graduate education was introduced at Johns Hopkins, and even when junior and community colleges began to grow and expand in the 1920s. If historical examples are reliable, resistance will be met regarding expansion of the various forms of cooperative education as well.

The resistance, on the other hand, may be futile, for relevance is a quality inherent in cooperative education. By exposing the student to the working world of business, industry, the professions, and social services, cooperative education breaks the lockstep traditionalism (and often the boredom) of a system too long set apart from the realities of post-education life experiences. (See Chapters 18 and 19.)

In any event, cooperative education—whose name some educators would change to "experiential" education, for some reason—is not exactly a radical innovation. It has a 65-year history of background and experience. Its policies and principles in coordination and placement of students have been soundly developed and, most important, have been proved successful. Regardless of the type of off-campus experience an institution may try, it should recognize the validity of application of time-tested methods. (See Chapters 10 and 11.)

Accreditation

The origins of cooperative education lie deep in business and industry, health and government agencies, and the professions, all of which provided paid employment to cooperative students. Now the use of the off-campus experience is broadening and includes self-study, travel abroad, and volunteer service. This expansion creates many problems, especially as they concern accreditation of programs. Take self-employment as just one example. Is it educationally sound? Who determines this? How are the accrediting agencies to be convinced that minimum standards are being met by the program—standards which must be met in order to protect the general public, which exercises degree-granting powers through the state?

The best way toward relevance in education—through combined classroom experience and off-campus experience—is through the proven principles of cooperative education. Programs must be unquestionable from the point of educational value, and they must stand the test of accreditation. Cooperative education has already stood that test. Institutions that are seriously considering a changeover to the cooperative system should consult with schools that have successfully applied this educational principle for a number of years, preferably in a variety of academic disciplines. (See Chapters 14 and 20.) Many "frill" programs are being established today in the name of cooperative education. Their lives will be short indeed if they are not based upon proven principles and methods of operation.

At the risk of repetition, any program that leads to a degree and includes a form of off-campus experience in its curriculum must have educational value, and this educational value *must* be proved to the accrediting agencies. They may accept as educationally sound a history major's viewing and reporting in detail the many monuments and items of interest along Boston's Freedom Trail, but they probably would not make a similar decision about a student engineer's viewing of the Golden Gate Bridge.

Admittedly, cooperative education had its beginnings in an almost strictly "vocational" setting, and many educators therefore would not even consider the concept. Times have changed. Cooperative education has expanded into virtually all academic disciplines, including the liberal arts and more than thirty professional fields, such as nursing, pharmacy, architecture, and law. Northeastern University's new cooperative program in law, for example, based on time-tested and proven cooperative policies and principles and offering credit for the off-campus legal experience, recently received national accreditation from the American Bar Association and the American Association of Law Schools.

In programs where licensing is involved, the off-campus experience must be especially sound and viable, since these programs are particularly vulnerable to scrutiny by licensing boards. The off-campus experience aspect of Northeastern's College of Nursing serves as a good example. Solid cooperative experience has been gained by many of its students, not only in hospitals and other health agencies in this country, but in health service agencies for the indigent in such places as Venezuela, Jamaica, and Africa. These students are learning their profession and at the same time are gaining valuable experience in healing, assisting, and counseling those who need it most.

Flexibility of Cooperative Education

One of the greatest assets of cooperative education is its flexibility. (See Chapters 3, 4, and 5.) It can be employed in programs running from two years in length to five, and in some cases even longer. In many instances, large universities need hardly alter their regular academic calendar at all to accommodate cooperative students, provided they offer enough substitution or "trailer" (repeat) courses. No set pattern of work and study alternation must be followed by any institution, regardless of the length of its cooperative program. It is the individual institution, with the cooperation of the employer or employing agency, that establishes the calendar pattern to best serve the interests of its particular student clientele.

The flexibility of cooperative education, plus its inherent relevance and financial-aid features, has been a prime factor in its relatively recent expansion into the graduate level (both master's and doctoral programs) of higher education (see Chapter 6). Most graduate cooperative programs are in engineering or business administration, although some are offered in liberal arts, science, and a few various other programs. This development is quite significant, since it very closely follows the development of undergraduate cooperative programs. First engineering, then business administration, and then a branching out into other academic disciplines. A continuation of this pattern could result in a tremendous growth in graduate cooperative education in the years ahead. (See Chapter 7 for examples of cooperative programs that are completely sponsored and supported by a single corporation; of special programs sponsored by industry or government at existing institutions; and of a graduate program sponsored by a single corporation or industry.)

For a description of how the cooperative plan has been adopted in Canada, and how a form of it (the sandwich plan) has been successfully operated in England for many years, see Chapters 8 and 9. Many visitors from other parts of the world, particularly from Russia, India, and the Far East, continue to visit American cooperative institutions to study the possibilities of adopting a form of the system in their home lands.

Attitudes toward Cooperative Education

FACULTY. As was mentioned, resistance to change is inherent in our educational system. And some faculty members—particularly those who come to cooperative institutions from more traditional schools—have been resistant to cooperative education (see Chapter 15). Some do not understand the system; some do not appreciate its values; some are simply unwilling or very reluctant to become involved in a year-round academic program. However, as pointed out in Chapter 15, many of these faculty become the most ardent supporters of cooperative education once they understand its philosophy and objectives. Those who do not totally commit themselves to the philosophy of cooperative education are certainly better off (as are their students) at other types of institutions, although experience has shown that this type of teacher is in a very small minority. It is a minority which should shrink even further, incidentally, in light of the recommendations recently made by the three national higher education study groups to be referred to subsequently.

STUDENTS. Cooperative students themselves are—understandably—among the first to extol cooperative education. The financial self-help feature notwithstanding, they are finding relevance, innovation, and life experience on the job, not to mention development of important human relations skills. Cooperative students have a different perspective, being more vocationally and professionally oriented than most of their counterparts at traditional institutions. Although we are aware of no formal studies as yet made, observation alone indicates much less student unrest on campuses of cooperative institutions. Where there has been unrest on those campuses, observation again tells us that those students in optional cooperative programs have generally not been a part of it. They are much less susceptible to political "sways" stemming from classroom discussions than are many less positively directed full-time students.

Admittedly, many cooperative assignments are routine at the outset, just as they are for any recent college graduates. A surprising number of students, however, have held what many would consider "unusual" job experiences. The following are examples of jobs held by several Northeastern University students.

An electrical engineering sophomore participated in the redesigning of fire-control systems on submarines while employed at the U. S. Naval Underwater Ordnance Station in Newport, Rhode Island.

A mechanical engineer, employed by the Singer Company of New York, assisted in the development of a physical distribution program and traveled to Venezuela, Japan, Singapore, and Malaysia.

A senior political science major wrote a 230-page book now in use as a training manual and reference for land court certificate writers. He was employed at the Middlesex South Registry of Deeds in Cambridge, Mass.

Two women seniors, one in sociology and the other in journalism, alternated assignments in educational television as production assistants at WGBH-TV in Boston.

A biology major employed by the Department of Retina Research of the Retina Foundation in Boston designed a glare recovery test which was incorporated into a commercial vision tester.

A finance and insurance major spent his upper-class terms at the Pan

American Airways Corporate headquarters in New York City, where he worked in the passenger reserve and maintenance cost areas, and then was promoted to the internal audit staff investigating cargo operations in London, Panama, and Guatemala.

A student of nursing recently returned from a cooperative term in an Israeli kibbutz, and another from the Jamaican Hanson Leprosarium in the British West Indies in preparation for a career of missionary service.

Although the above examples are admittedly exceptional cooperative assignments, cooperative education is relevant, exciting, and challenging to any student who applies himself to whatever job he or she may have.

Finally, the earning power of students is one of the major attractions of the cooperative plan, and in numerous cases has provided the major portion of the funds necessary for students to enter college initially. Without this plan, many of them would never have been able to do so.

EMPLOYERS. Most employers of cooperative students have enthusiastically endorsed the cooperative system. (See Chapters 12 and 13.) Some employers rely entirely on cooperative students for manpower and do not recruit at the senior level at all. Also, many have supported cooperative education in a very generous financial manner, some assisting the efforts of the National Commission for Cooperative Education in its self-appointed task to help institutions adopt the cooperative system.

A large insurance company employer has said that it is much less expensive to bring in cooperative students during their college years than to recruit seniors at the end of their college years. Training costs can run very high with recent graduates, and there is no assurance that they will stay with the company. A study has also revealed that cooperative students tend to remain with their employers much longer than those who come to a company from another type of institution.

Also, the introduction of cooperative students into company departments "hung up" on one way of doing things can infuse new ideas into the operation and many times be prime factors in increasing a company's profits.

The cooperative student is no less critical than any other student. On the contrary, he is likely to be more mature in his criticism because of his work experience. Employers know this. They also know that cooperative graduates realize that there are no push-button answers to our many problems. Companies which employ cooperative students as trainees and bring them into the organization with relevant orientation can avoid many of the unreasonable extremist attitudes and difficult problems which may otherwise arise.

Conversion to Cooperative Education

Institutions considering conversion to one or more of the various patterns of cooperative education must recognize immediately that the process is not always simple. (See Chapters 14, 15, 16, and 20.) Furthermore, with any other type of educational institution, cooperative colleges and universities have their "bad times," particularly during periods of recession and depression. Stamina and fortitude are necessary during such periods, when business and industry are not always waiting eagerly for cooperative students. One protection is to spread the geographic base for cooperative assignments as widely as possible, just in the event a recessive period should strike a particular city or part of the country. (See Chapter 14.)

There seems to be little question of the need for a study (or studies) of the further expansion of cooperative education in this country. There are 225 active schools now. Hundreds of others have applied for federal assistance to establish new cooperative programs. How many colleges *should* there be? Should there be one for each large urban area, which on the surface seems an extremely practical and workable concept? How many jobs would be available, or even desirable, in these areas? How many cooperative students would be available? These are vital questions, desperately in need of answers.

Regardless of the results of such a study, if it is ever forthcoming, it is certainly among the purposes of this handbook to encourage the further expansion of the various forms of cooperative education at this point in time—particularly in new academic areas such as law, the health sciences (such as nursing and pharmacy) and the many disciplines within liberal arts, education, and other fields. Cooperative education opportunities already exist to a large degree in such areas as engineering and business administration.

It is also hoped that cooperative education will continue to expand in our two-year junior and community colleges. These institutions perform a particular function for a particular clientele, and most of them do it very well. They could do their job even better by adopting the cooperative plan of education.

Much attention has been paid to the financial aspects of converting from a traditional to a cooperative program. (See Chapter 20.)

Costs are generally high during the initial stages of conversion, whether it is entered into by the institution as a whole or by one or more programs within the institution. Advance planning must be carried out, and a careful survey made of the potential placement opportunities for students in a particular area. Curricula have to be modified and courses repackaged, which is a considerable expense in terms of a faculty member's time. Also, particularly in optional and selective programs, there are additional costs of adding a sufficient number of repeat or "trailer" courses to the curriculum. Initial costs of setting up a new cooperative education department also run quite high, staff salaries and equipment being the major capital outlays.

Once these initial steps have been completed, however, the successful institution stands to realize many financial benefits and advantages from the cooperative system. This is especially true of institutions that establish mandatory cooperative programs, as opposed to the optional and selective. Many cooperative institutions that offer only optional and selective programs never fully realize the financial advantages of the system, and often incur continuing additional expenses.

Some of the financial advantages to cooperative institutions (especially those offering mandatory programs) are as follows:

Much more efficient use of the *physical plant* can be realized in a cooperative institution, particularly during summer months, when freshmen are on vacation and the plant is only in partial operation—thus allowing time and space for any necessary remodeling or modernization.

It is a great advantage for the cooperative institution's physical plant to be able to accommodate large numbers of students. However, the school cannot automatically double its upper-class enrollments and still use the same facilities. The freshman class has to be increased in size to provide full occupancy of the plant in each of the two alternating upper-class divisions.

Also, a cooperative institution which can house students who have been placed on jobs in the immediate vicinity, as well as those who are attending classes, has still another financial advantage—additional income for the institution, since the planned operation of dormitories generally is not based on full occupancy.

The advantage of a *dual student body* ties in with the advantage of more efficient use of the institution's physical plant. It also means more efficient use of the faculty, and tuition receipts are obviously substantially increased. Furthermore, the cooperative system opens the doors for institutional fund raisers with many employers of cooperative students. This has proved to be very advantageous.

Other special features of administration relevant to cooperative programs are also discussed in detail in Chapter 14. Chapter 15 pays particular attention to such matters as faculty personnel policies, academic credit, accreditation, and R.O.T.C. administration. Chapter 20 covers costs of conversion.

To repeat the opening thought of this section, the future of cooperative education appears brighter than ever. It is being recommended as a major force in breaking the lock-step traditionalism of higher education (four years of full-time study with summers off for vacations or part-time jobs). The three national studies which recommended, in effect, "an integration of some form of work experience with academic study" were the Carnegie Commission Report, *Less Time, More Options*; The Report of the Assembly on University Goals and Governance of the National Academy of Arts and Sciences; and the so-called "Newman Report on Higher Education," strongly endorsed by the Department of Health, Education, and Welfare.

The Carnegie Commission Report specifically recommended that "opportunities be expanded for students to alternate employment and study" and that "programs at American colleges that combine work experience and formal study are increasing in number and should be encouraged."

The National Academy of Arts and Sciences Report also supported cooperative education, stating that such programs are "needed nonacademic experiences."

Finally, to quote the *Congressional Record* of June 17, 1971:

Most recently, the Newman Task Force has cautioned us further about the need for reform, and that the simple expansion of the present system of higher education "will not provide meaningful education for the ever broader spectrum of students gaining entrance." Thus, while this report adamantly supports and encourages the federal government to increase access for disadvantaged students and to make it easier for these students to go to school, it likewise warns us that our present system of higher education is not adequate for this task and that we must encourage diversity of public and private institutions. Higher education must become more sensitive to public concern and public needs for education.

The Newman Report also recommends intensive development of off-campus programs and urges that academic credit toward degrees be awarded for "appropriate" experiences outside the classroom. (See Chapter 15.)

The trend is unmistakable, and it is growing rapidly. Some of the nation's largest private universities, including several Ivy League schools, are looking into the off-campus experience aspect of higher education as an avenue toward more relevance for their students. Dartmouth, for example, has already announced plans for its students to spend time off campus.

Colleges and universities wishing to adopt the cooperative plan of education are encouraged to do so by use of federal funds provided by the 1968 amendments to the Higher Education Act of 1965. A total of $1,700,000 has been appropriated for the fiscal year 1972 for this purpose—one of the very few times when the federal government has put its stamp of approval on a particular type of education.

Seventy colleges and universities are now in various stages of planning, developing, or implementing new cooperative education programs utilizing federal funds. Recently, when the Office of Education invited institutions to submit proposals to receive grants to study the feasibility of adopting or to implement the adoption of a cooperative education program, 345 institutions responded, asking for over $12,000,000. This is only one of the many indicators of current interest in cooperative education. For this unique system, in existence for more than 65 years, the time and the idea have met.

Those of us who have been close to cooperative education for many years, who know of its early struggles, but who also have seen it survive and expand to its present unparalleled level, applaud and commend those who now see in its wider application a major vehicle for transforming higher education into a much more relevant experience for all men and women.

Every aspect of the cooperative plan of education as we know it has been touched upon in this handbook. Disadvantages and potential problems have been openly discussed, as have the advantages and the positive aspects of this unique educational system. Cooperative education has survived, and prospered because of that very uniqueness. It is relevant, it is innovative, and it is student oriented, not only through its built-in financial-aid feature but through its individualization of the educational process as a whole. No other type of higher education in the world can make those claims.

APPENDICES

A

Colleges and Universities Offering Cooperative Education Programs[1]

ALABAMA
Alabama A & M College
Alabama, University of
Auburn University
Gadsden State Junior College
Jefferson State Junior College
Southern Alabama, University of
Tuskegee Institute

[1] The following sources were used in compiling this information: *Cooperative Education Newsletter,* issue of April 1971, published by the State University System of Florida; *Newsletter,* issue of Spring 1971, published by the National Commission for Cooperative Education; *List of Colleges and Universities Offering Cooperative Education Programs,* issue of June 1970, published by the National Commission for Cooperative Education; *A Directory of Cooperative Education,* edition of March 1970, prepared under the auspices of the Cooperative Education Association; *Cooperative Education,* copyright 1971, by the American Association of Junior Colleges.

ARIZONA
Arizona, University of
Maricopa Technical College
Phoenix College

ARKANSAS
Arkansas, University of

CALIFORNIA
California State College—Dominguez Hills
California State College—Fullerton
California State College—Los Angeles
California State College—San Jose
California, University of—Berkeley
California, University of—Davis
Cañada College
Cerritos College
Chabot College
Chaffey College
Foothill College
Fresno City College
Fullerton Junior College
Golden Gate College
Golden West College
Grossmont College
Long Beach City College
Los Angeles City College
Los Angeles Harbor College
Los Angeles Pierce College
Los Angeles Trade-Technical College
Los Angeles Valley College
Marin, College of
Moorpark College
Mt. San Antonio College
Northrop Institute of Technology
Orange Coast College
Pacific, University of
Pasadena City College
Sacramento City College
San Bernardino Valley College
San Diego Junior College
San Mateo, College of
Santa Monica City College
Skyline College

COLORADO
Denver, University of

CONNECTICUT
Central Connecticut State College
Wesleyan University

DISTRICT OF COLUMBIA
George Washington University
Howard University
The American University

FLORIDA
Bethune-Cookman College
Broward Junior College
Florida, University of
Florida A & M University
Florida Atlantic University
Florida Institute of Technology
Florida State University
Florida Technological University
Gulf Coast Junior College
Hillsborough Junior College
Indian River Junior College
Manatee Junior College
Miami-Dade Junior College—North Campus
Miami-Dade Junior College—South Campus
Miami, University of
Okaloosa-Walton Junior College
Palm Beach Junior College
Pensacola Junior College
Polk County Junior College

Santa Fe Junior College
Seminole Junior College
South Florida Junior College
South Florida, University of
St. Johns River Junior College
West Florida, University of

GEORGIA
Abraham Baldwin Agricultural College
Berry College
Georgia Institute of Technology

HAWAII
Hawaii Pacific College

IDAHO
Idaho, University of

ILLINOIS
Bradley University
Chicago City College—Loop
DuPage, College of
Illinois, University of
Illinois Institute of Technology
Northwestern University
Rock Valley College
Roosevelt University
Sangamon State University
Southern Illinois University
Triton College

INDIANA
Evansville, University of
Indiana Institute of Technology
Indiana Northern University
Indiana State University
Purdue University—Lafayette
Purdue University—Indianapolis
St. Joseph's College
Tri-State College

IOWA
Iowa State University

KANSAS
Friends University
Kansas State College
Kansas State University

KENTUCKY
Alice Lloyd College
Lees Junior College
Louisville, University of
Western Kentucky University

LOUISIANA
Louisiana Polytechnic Institute
Louisiana State University
Tulane University

MARYLAND
Maryland, University of
Morgan State College

MASSACHUSETTS
Grahm Junior College
Massachusetts, University of
Massachusetts Institute of Technology
Northeastern University
Worcester Industrial Technical Institute

MICHIGAN
Central Michigan University
Delta College
Detroit, University of
Detroit Institute of Technology
Ferris State College
General Motors Institute
Grand Rapids Junior College
Henry Ford Community College

Kalamazoo College
Macomb County Community College
Michigan, University of
Michigan Technological University
Northwood Institute of Midland
Wayne State University
Western Michigan University

MINNESOTA
Concordia College
Minnesota, University of

MISSISSIPPI
Jackson State College
Mary Holmes College
Mississippi State University

MISSOURI
Missouri, University of—Columbia
Missouri, University of—Rolla
Rockhurst College
St. Louis University
Washington University

NEW JERSEY
Bloomfield College
Rider College
Rutgers University

NEW MEXICO
New Mexico Institute of Mining & Technology
New Mexico Highlands University
New Mexico State University

NEW YORK
Adelphi University
Bard College
Cornell University
Elmira College
Insurance, College of
Keuka College
Mohawk Valley Community College
New York, City University of
City College
Manhattan Community College, Borough of
New York, State University of
Agricultural & Technical College—Alfred
Agricultural & Technical College—Morrisville
Bronx Community College
Broome Technical Community College
Fashion Institute of Technology
Monroe Community College
Nassau Community College
New York City Community College
Westchester Community College
New York Institute of Technology
Pratt Institute
Rensselaer Polytechnic Institute
Rochester Institute of Technology
Union College

NORTH CAROLINA
East Carolina University
Holding Technical Institute, W.W.
North Carolina State University
Shaw University

OHIO
Akron, University of
Antioch College
Applied Science, Ohio College of
Bowling Green State University
Cincinnati, University of
Cincinnati Technical Institute

Cuyahoga Community College
Kent State University
Ohio University
Sinclair Community College
The Cleveland State University
Wilberforce University
Wilmington College

OKLAHOMA
Oklahoma, University of

OREGON
Lane Community College
Oregon, University of
Oregon State University
Portland State University
Southern Oregon College

PENNSYLVANIA
Drexel Institute of Technology
Lehigh University
Pennsylvania State University
St. Joseph's College
Temple University Technical Institute

RHODE ISLAND
Roger Williams College

TENNESSEE
Tennessee, University of—Knoxville
Tennessee, University of—Martin
Tennessee State University
Tennessee Technological University

TEXAS
Houston, University of
Lamar State College of Technology
Le Tourneau College
Pan American College
Southern Methodist University
St. Thomas, University of
Texas, University of—Arlington
Texas, University of—Austin
Texas A & M University

VERMONT
Bennington College
Goddard College

VIRGINIA
Hampton Institute
Norfolk State College
Virginia Polytechnic Institute
Virginia State College

WASHINGTON
Puget Sound, University of
Seattle University
Washington, University of
Washington State University

WEST VIRGINIA
Alderson-Broaddus College
West Virginia Institute of Technology
West Virginia University

WISCONSIN
Beloit College
Marquette University
Milwaukee School of Engineering
Stout State University
Wisconsin, University of—Milwaukee
Wisconsin State University—Platteville
Wisconsin State University—River Falls

Summary

Figures based on this list show that 225 colleges and universities offer cooperative education programs in the United States, on 235 different campuses. Six institutions in Canada also offer cooperative education programs:

Mohawk College of Applied Arts and Technology
Newfoundland, Memorial University of
Nova Scotia Technical College
Saskatchewan, University of
Sherbrooke, University of
Waterloo, University of

There is little doubt that the figures above are, or soon will be, inaccurate. For example, we already know that the City University of New York (CUNY) has undertaken to establish cooperative education programs in each of nine community colleges. One of these, Fiorello H. La Guardia Community College, will open in 1971 as a fully cooperative institution. Also, the State University System of Florida has announced that the following schools will begin cooperative education programs in the fall of 1971:

Central Florida Junior College[2]
Edward Waters College
Florida Junior College[2]
Florida Keys Community College
Florida Presbyterian College
Lake City Junior College[2]
Lake Sumter Community College[2]
North Florida Junior College
Tampa, University of

The following institutions in Florida also are planning cooperative education programs, although the opening dates have yet to be established:

[2] These institutions have submitted a consortium proposal to USOE, specifying that they be under the leadership of Central Florida Junior College.

Emery-Riddle Aeronautical University
Florida International University
North Florida, University of
St. Petersburg Junior College
Valencia Junior College
Webber College

B

Colleges and Universities Supported Under the Cooperative Education Program, Fiscal 1970[1,2]

ALABAMA

Alabama, University of (planning)
- Program Coordinator for:
  - Huntingdon College
  - Stillman College

Alabama State University (planning)

Daniel Payne College (planning)

Huntingdon College (planning)

Miles College (planning)
- Program Coordinator for:
  - Alabama State University
  - Daniel Payne College
  - Oakwood College
  - Talladega College

Oakwood College (planning)

Stillman College (planning)

Talladega College (planning)

[1] Authorized under the Higher Education Act of 1965, as amended by the Labor-HEW Appropriations Act of 1970.

[2] Type of grant in parentheses.

Tuskegee Institute (expansion and strengthening)

CALIFORNIA
Merritt College (strengthening)
Pacific, University of (implementation)
Pasadena City College (strengthening)

COLORADO
Fort Lewis College (planning)

CONNECTICUT
Manchester Community College (planning)

DISTRICT OF COLUMBIA
Federal City College (planning)
Washington Technical Institute (planning)

FLORIDA
Florida A & M University (planning and implementation)
Florida Memorial College (planning)
South Florida, University of (planning, implementation, strengthening, and expansion) Grant will be administered in behalf of the nine junior and community colleges and the thirteen private institutions of higher education within the State of Florida.

GEORGIA
Abraham Baldwin Agricultural College (planning)
Clark College (implementation, planning, and strengthening)
Program Coordinator for:
Spelman College
Spelman College (planning and implementation)

IOWA
Ottumwa Heights College (planning)
Simpson College (planning)

KENTUCKY
Alice Lloyd College (strengthening)
Jefferson Community College (planning)
Lees Junior College (strengthening)

LOUISIANA
Dillard University (planning)
Southern University (strengthening and expanding)
Tulane University (planning)
Xavier University (planning)
Program Coordinator for:
Dillard University
Jackson State College
Tulane University

MAINE
Maine, University of (planning)

MARYLAND
Bowie State College (planning and implementation)
Program Coordinator for:
Cheyney State College
Federal City College

Maryland, University of
(planning)

MASSACHUSETTS
Merrimack College
(implementation)

MICHIGAN
Detroit, University of
(implementation, strengthening, and expansion)
Michigan Lutheran College
(planning)
Wayne State University
(strengthening)

MINNESOTA
Minnesota State Junior College System (planning and implementation)
Grant will be administered in behalf of the following institutions:
Anoka-Ramsey State Junior College
Inver Halls State Junior College
Lakewood State Junior College
Metropolitan State Junior College
Normandale State Junior College
Northland State Junior College
North Hennepin State Junior College
Willmar State Junior College

MISSISSIPPI
Jackson State College (planning)
Mary Holmes College
(strengthening and expansion)
Meridian Junior College
(planning)
Rust College (planning)
Tougaloo College (planning and implementation)
Program Coordinator for:
Rust College

MONTANA
Carroll College (planning)

NEW JERSEY
Bloomfield College
(implementation, strengthening, and expansion)

NEW YORK
City College of the City University of New York (planning)
Hostos Community College
(planning and implementation)
Hunter College (planning)

NORTH CAROLINA
Bennett College (planning)
Program Coordinator for:
Saint Paul's College
Virginia Union University
Winston-Salem State University
Kittrell College (planning and implementation)
North Carolina A & T State University—unilateral (strengthening and expansion)
North Carolina A & T State University (planning)
Program Coordinator for:
Alabama A & M State University
Albany State College

Bethune-Cookman College
Grambling College
Kentucky State College
Langston University
Mississippi Valley State College
Morgan State College
North Carolina Central University
Prairie View College
South Carolina State College
Southern University
State Agricultural Mechanical and Normal College
Tennessee State University
Tuskegee Institute

Saint Augustine's College (planning)
Winston-Salem State University (planning)

NORTH DAKOTA
Lake Region Junior College (planning)

OHIO
Baldwin-Wallace College (planning)
Cleveland State University (strengthening and expansion)
Wilberforce University (strengthening and expansion)

OKLAHOMA
Seminole Junior College (planning)

OREGON
Oregon, University of (planning and implementation)

PENNSYLVANIA
Cheyney State College (planning)
Pennsylvania State University (planning, expansion, and strengthening)
Temple University (planning and expansion)

SOUTH CAROLINA
Clemson University (planning)
Morris College (planning)

RHODE ISLAND
Rhode Island, University of (planning)

TENNESSEE
LeMoyne-Owen College (planning)
Tennessee Technical University (planning)

TEXAS
Houston-Tillotson College (planning)
Texas Southern University (planning, strengthening, and expansion)

VIRGINIA
Saint Paul's College (planning)
Virginia State College (strengthening and expansion)
Virginia Union University (planning)

WEST VIRGINIA
Alderson-Broaddus College (planning)

Summary

The total amount of the grants for the fiscal year 1970 was $1,540,000. Although 74 institutions were direct recipients of the grants, 142 institutions were either primary or secondary beneficiaries. This is due to the fact that some of the grantee schools are serving as program coordinators in cooperative arrangements with those awarded smaller grants; still others are serving as consortium coordinators for planning programs which include institutions desiring such an arrangement.

The average grantee award was $20,811. Fifty-nine grants went to four-year institutions, and fifteen to two-year institutions. The programs supported were selected from 206 applications.

C

Fields of Study Offered by Cooperative Colleges and Universities[1]

Accounting
Actuarial Science
Advertising & Advertising Design
Administration
Administrative & Engineering Systems
Aero, Aerospace Engineering & Aeronautics
Agriculture, Agriculture Engineering & Farming
Animal Husbandry and Science
Anthropology
Architecture and Architecture Design
Art
Astronomy-Mathematics
Automotive Engineering & Technology

Bacteriology
Behavioral Science
Biochemistry
Biology and Biological Engineering
Bio-Medical Engineering

[1] As listed in Collins (1970).

Bio-Physics
Building Construction Engineering & Technology
Business & Business Administration

Cabinetmaking, Carpentry, & Furniture Manufacturing
Ceramic Engineering & Ceramics
Chemical Engineering
Chemical-Electrical Engineering
Chemical Technology
Chemistry
Civil Engineering
Civil Engineering Technology & Civil Technology
Clinical Technology
Communications
Community Planning
Computer Science & Technology
Construction Technology
Criminal Justice

Dairy Science
Data Processing
Die Design
Dietetics
Drafting & Drafting Technology

Economics
Education (all fields)
Electrical Engineering
Electrical Engineering Technology
Electronics & Electronics Technology
Engineering Administration
Engineering Mathematics
Engineering Mechanics
Engineering Physics
Engineering Science
Engineering Unspecified
English
Environmental Science

Fashion Design & Fashion Merchandising
Finance & Banking
Fine Arts
Fluid Power
Food Distribution, Management, & Technology
Forestry & Forestry Technology
Fire Protection Engineering & Science
French
Geography
Geology, Geological Engineering, & Geophysics
German
Graphic Design & Graphic Technology

Health Safety
History
Home Economics
Hospital Management
Hotel & Restaurant

Industrial Administration
Industrial Design
Industrial Electronics
Industrial Engineering
Industrial Management
Industrial Relations
Industrial Technology
Instrument Technology
Insurance
Interior Design
International Relations

Journalism
Juvenile Correction

Language, Literature, & Philosophy
Liberal Arts
Life Sciences

Machine Design & Machine Design Technology
Management
Manufacturing Technology
Marine Biology
Marketing
Masonry
Materials Engineering & Materials Science
Mathematics
Mechanical Engineering
Mechanical-Chemical Engineering
Mechanical-Electrical Engineering
Mechanical Engineering Technology
Mechanical-Industrial Engineering
Mechanical Technology
Mechanics
Medical Science & Technology
Merchandising
Metallurgical Engineering, Metallurgy, & Metals
Meteorology
Metrology
Microbiology
Mineral Engineering
Mining Engineering
Music

Natural Gas Engineering
Nuclear Engineering
Nursing

Oceanography & Ocean Engineering
Office Occupations
Optical Technology
Petroleum Engineering
Pharmacy
Philosophy
Physical Therapy
Physics & Applied Physics
Plastics Technology
Police Science
Political Science
Poultry Science
Pre-Engineering
Pre-Law
Pre-Medical
Pre-Medical–Zoology
Pre-Veterinarian
Printing, Printing Management, & Printing Technology
Production
Psychology
Public Administration
Purchasing Management

Quality Assurance
Quantitative Analysis

Radiology Technology
Real Estate
Religion
Retail Management & Retailing

Safety
Science–Applied Science
Secretarial
Sheet Metal
Social Science
Social Service & Social Welfare
Sociology
Spanish
Speech & Drama
Systems Engineering
Statistics
Surveying & Surveying Technology

Textiles—Administration, Design, Chemistry, & Engineering
Tool Fixture Design
Traffic, Transportation

Upholstering

Visual Design

Vocational Rehabilitation

Welding
Wholesaling Management
Wood Utilization

Zoology

D

Cooperative Calendars at Northeastern University

Colleges of Engineering, Business Administration, Liberal Arts, Nursing, and Criminal Justice.

CLASS SCHEDULED TO GRADUATE IN AN ODD YEAR					CLASS SCHEDULED TO GRADUATE IN AN EVEN YEAR			
Sept. | Oct. | Nov.	Dec. | Jan. | Feb.	Mar. | Apr. | May	June | July | Aug. | Sept.		Sept. | Oct. | Nov.	Dec. | Jan. | Feb.	Mar. | Apr. | May	June | July | Aug. | Sept.
Quarter 1	Quarter 2	Quarter 3	Vacation	FRESHMAN	Quarter 1	Quarter 2	Quarter 3	Vacation
Quarter 4	Work	Quarter 5	Work	SOPHOMORE *Division A*	Work	Quarter 4	Work	Quarter 5
Work	Quarter 4	Work	Quarter 5	SOPHOMORE *Division B*	Quarter 4	Work	Quarter 5	Work
Work	Quarter 6	Work	Quarter 7	MIDDLER *Division A*	Quarter 6	Work	Quarter 7	Work
Quarter 6	Work	Quarter 7	Work	MIDDLER *Division B*	Work	Quarter 6	Work	Quarter 7
Quarter 8	Work	Quarter 9	Work	JUNIOR *Division A*	Work	Quarter 8	Work	Quarter 9
Work	Quarter 8	Work	Quarter 9	JUNIOR *Division B*	Quarter 8	Work	Quarter 9	Work
Work	Quarter 10	Quarter 11		SENIOR *Division A*	Quarter 10	Work	Quarter 11	
Quarter 10	Work	Quarter 11		SENIOR *Division B*	Work	Quarter 10	Quarter 11	
Sept. | Oct. | Nov.	Dec. | Jan. | Feb.	Mar. | Apr. | May	June | July | Aug. | Sept.		Sept. | Oct. | Nov.	Dec. | Jan. | Feb.	Mar. | Apr. | May	June | July | Aug. | Sept.

College of Education and Boston-Bouve College. Boston-Bouve College offers baccalaureate programs in Physical Therapy, Physical Education, and Recreation Education. Calendar for the four-year Physical Therapy program appears on the following page.

CLASS SCHEDULED TO GRADUATE IN AN ODD YEAR

Class	Sept. | Oct. | Nov.	Dec. | Jan. | Feb.	Mar. | Apr. | May	June | July | Aug. | Sept.
FRESHMAN	Quarter 1	Quarter 2	Quarter 3	Vacation
SOPHOMORE *Division A*	Quarter 4	Work	Quarter 5	Work
SOPHOMORE *Division B*	Work	Quarter 4	Work	Quarter 5
MIDDLER *Division A*	Work	Quarter 6	Work	Quarter 7
MIDDLER *Division B*	Quarter 6	Work	Quarter 7	Work
JUNIOR *Division A*	Quarter 8	Work	Quarter 9	Work
JUNIOR *Division B*	Work	Quarter 8	Work	Quarter 9
SENIOR *Division A*	Practice Teaching	Quarter 10	Quarter 11	
SENIOR *Division B*	Quarter 10	Practice Teaching	Quarter 11	

CLASS SCHEDULED TO GRADUATE IN AN EVEN YEAR

Class	Sept. | Oct. | Nov.	Dec. | Jan. | Feb.	Mar. | Apr. | May	June | July | Aug. | Sept.
FRESHMAN	Quarter 1	Quarter 2	Quarter 3	Vacation
SOPHOMORE *Division A*	Work	Quarter 4	Work	Quarter 5
SOPHOMORE *Division B*	Quarter 4	Work	Quarter 5	Work
MIDDLER *Division A*	Quarter 6	Work	Quarter 7	Work
MIDDLER *Division B*	Work	Quarter 6	Work	Quarter 7
JUNIOR *Division A*	Work	Quarter 8	Work	Quarter 9
JUNIOR *Division B*	Quarter 8	Work	Quarter 9	Work
SENIOR *Division A*	Quarter 10	Practice Teaching	Quarter 11	
SENIOR *Division B*	Practice Teaching	Quarter 10	Quarter 11	

Boston-Bouve College (four-year Physical Therapy program) Work Periods in the Sophomore Year Only.

CLASS SCHEDULED TO GRADUATE IN AN EVEN YEAR (Sept.–Nov.)	(Dec.–Feb.)	(Mar.–May)	(June–Sept.)	Class	CLASS SCHEDULED TO GRADUATE IN AN ODD YEAR (Sept.–Nov.)	(Dec.–Feb.)	(Mar.–May)	(June–Sept.)
Quarter 1	Quarter 2	Quarter 3	Vacation	FRESHMAN	Quarter 1	Quarter 2	Quarter 3	Vacation
Quarter 4	Work	Quarter 5	Work	SOPHOMORE *Division A*	Work	Quarter 4	Work	Quarter 5
Work	Quarter 4	Work	Quarter 5	SOPHOMORE *Division B*	Quarter 4	Work	Quarter 5	Work
Quarter 6	Quarter 7	Quarter 8	Vacation	JUNIOR	Quarter 6	Quarter 7	Quarter 8	Vacation
Quarter 9	Quarter 10	Quarter 11		SENIOR	Quarter 9	Quarter 10	Quarter 11	

Sept. | Oct. | Nov. | Dec. | Jan. | Feb. | Mar. | Apr. | May | June | July | Aug. | Sept.

College of Pharmacy

CLASS SCHEDULED TO GRADUATE IN AN ODD YEAR					CLASS SCHEDULED TO GRADUATE IN AN EVEN YEAR			
Sept. | Oct. | Nov.	Dec. | Jan. | Feb.	Mar. | Apr. | May	June | July | Aug. | Sept.		Sept. | Oct. | Nov.	Dec. | Jan. | Feb.	Mar. | Apr. | May	June | July | Aug. | Sept.
Quarter 1	Quarter 2	Quarter 3	Vacation	FRESHMAN	Quarter 1	Quarter 2	Quarter 3	Vacation
Quarter 4	Work	Quarter 5	Work	SOPHOMORE *Division A*	Work	Quarter 4	Work	Quarter 5
Work	Quarter 4	Work	Quarter 5	SOPHOMORE *Division B*	Quarter 4	Work	Quarter 5	Work
Quarter 6	Quarter 6A	Work	Quarter 7	MIDDLER *Division A*	Quarter 6	Quarter 6A	Quarter 7	Work
		Quarter 7	Work	MIDDLER *Division B*			Work	Quarter 7
Quarter 8	Work	Quarter 9	Work	JUNIOR *Division A*	Work	Quarter 8	Work	Quarter 9
Work	Quarter 8	Work	Quarter 9	JUNIOR *Division B*	Quarter 8	Work	Quarter 9	Work
Quarter 10	Quarter 10A	Quarter 11		SENIOR	Quarter 10	Quarter 10A	Quarter 11	
Sept. | Oct. | Nov.	Dec. | Jan. | Feb.	Mar. | Apr. | May	June | July | Aug. | Sept.		Sept. | Oct. | Nov.	Dec. | Jan. | Feb.	Mar. | Apr. | May	June | July | Aug. | Sept.

Five-Year Quarter-System Cooperative Program (with sixth-year option to continue to master's degree)[1]

Class	Odd year: Sept.–Nov.	Odd year: Dec.–Feb.	Odd year: Mar.–May	Odd year: June–Aug.	Even year: Sept.–Nov.	Even year: Dec.–Feb.	Even year: Mar.–May	Even year: June–Aug.
FRESHMAN	Quarter 1	Quarter 2	Quarter 3	Vacation	Quarter 1	Quarter 2	Quarter 3	Vacation
SOPHOMORE *Division A*	Quarter 4	Work	Quarter 5	Work	Work	Quarter 4	Work	Quarter 5
SOPHOMORE *Division B*	Work	Quarter 4	Work	Quarter 5	Quarter 4	Work	Quarter 5	Work
MIDDLER *Division A*	Work	Quarter 6	Work	Quarter 7	Quarter 6	Work	Quarter 7	Work
MIDDLER *Division B*	Quarter 6	Work	Quarter 7	Work	Work	Quarter 6	Work	Quarter 7
JUNIOR *Division A*	Quarter 8	Work	Quarter 9	Work	Work	Quarter 8	Work	Quarter 9
JUNIOR *Division B*	Work	Quarter 8	Work	Quarter 9	Quarter 8	Work	Quarter 9	Work
SENIOR *Division A*	Work	Quarter 10	Quarter 11	Work	Quarter 10	Work	Quarter 11	Work
SENIOR *Division B*	Quarter 10	Work	Quarter 11	Work	Work	Quarter 10	Quarter 11	Work
GRADUATE	Quarter 12	Work	Quarter 13		Quarter 12	Work	Quarter 13	

Left: CLASS SCHEDULE TO RECEIVE B.S. DEGREE IN AN ODD YEAR. Right: CLASS SCHEDULE TO RECEIVE B.S. DEGREE IN AN EVEN YEAR. (Month scale: Sept. | Oct. | Nov. | Dec. | Jan. | Feb. | Mar. | Apr. | May | June | July | Aug. | Sept.)

[1] This unique cooperative program, pioneered and currently in effect at Northeastern University in Boston, Mass., is in power systems engineering.

E

Cooperative Agreement (Northeastern University)

As previously stated, continuity is the key to a successful cooperative program from the employer's viewpoint. Usually the greatest objection to initiating a program is the employer's fear of a rapid turnover, which means that he will be constantly training new persons for the job. To overcome this, the University must be able to assure an employer that even though he must initially train two students for one job, he can expect a minimum of two work quarters of service from each student placed on a cooperative assignment. For this reason, the student is asked to sign an agreement before he is placed on a cooperative assignment to insure an understanding of the terms of employment.

I, the undersigned, agree to work for the company named on the reverse side of this card as my regular cooperative assignment, in accordance with the regulations of the Department of Cooperative Education as outlined in the CO-OP HANDBOOK. I also agree to accept the rate of pay stated, this amount to be increased as my ability and other conditions may warrant. I understand that this agreement becomes effective upon my acceptance of the position offered.

The agreement covers two basic policies: (1) The student must continue on the job assignment until released by the coordinator. Theoretically, this could extend over the entire length of the Cooperative Program. (2) The student may not expect a change of assignment until he has completed a minimum of two quarters with the employer. Only under unusual circumstances will the coordinator consider a change in less than that time, and the change may not be granted even after the minimum period has expired.

Some training programs require the student to undertake a commitment of a minimum period of employment of more than two work quarters. When this occurs, the student must give careful consideration to the commitment before accepting the assignment.

The agreement is strictly between the student and the University. The employer is not an active participant in the agreement. The University believes that contracts with employers to retain students in their employ are neither necessary nor desirable. To promote mutual confidence and assure the maintenance of higher standards, employers are advised to discharge any student who, after a fair trial period, performs unsatisfactorily, is judged incompetent or incapable of performing tasks expected of him, is irregular in attendance or punctuality, or fails to cooperate in every reasonable way.

An employer cannot be expected to retain cooperative students any longer than is practical from a sound business standpoint. Moreover, it is not conducive to sound cooperative relations for students to expect priority considerations over other regular employees. It is believed than an employer who sincerely demonstrates an interest in training cooperative students may be trusted to judge when business conditions make it advisable to terminate the employment of cooperative students.

TIME OFF. *A student must be on the job regularly and punctually. He has only the privileges allowed other regular employees of the company. He* must not ask the employer for or take time off *from work for any college requirements without first obtaining the consent of the Department of Cooperative Education.*

Students will not be allowed to take academic work for credit through daytime classes during the regular work hours. In addition, ROTC summer camp requirements for cooperative students in that program must be completed during the summer following graduation and not during a cooperative work period.

ABSENCE FROM WORK. *The tasks performed by students on their cooperative jobs are part of a carefully planned and scheduled program of work. A student's absence from work immediately necessitates replanning and rescheduling of performances expected of him. Therefore, in case of sickness or other emergency necessitating a student's absence from work, the employer should be notified by telephone as early as possible. If an absence will cause the student to miss a full week or more, then his coordinator should also be notified.*

LAYOFF. *Any student who is permanently or temporarily laid off must notify the Department of Cooperative Education at once.*

DISCHARGE OR DESERTION. *A student who leaves his cooperative job without prior approval of the Department of Cooperative Education, or who so conducts himself on the job as to cause his discharge, will be subject to disciplinary action which could result in suspension from the University.*

FAILURE ON JOB. *Any student who, although not discharged immediately by the employer, fails to perform in a satisfactory manner on a maximum of two cooperative assignments shall be brought before the proper academic committee for appropriate action.*

OWN JOBS. *Under certain conditions, a student may be permitted to work on a job of his own finding. He must petition his coordinator for approval of such work before accepting the job. Petitions are obtained from the coordinator and, if approved, remain in effect for one work period. If conditions warrant the student's continuance on his own job beyond one work period, a new petition must be submitted for approval.* The student is expected to conduct himself on this job in the same manner as on any cooperative assignment. All cooperative education rules and regulations apply. *Approval of the petition is based on the following considerations: (1) The job of the student's own finding must be the equivalent (in training potentialities and application to the student's field of study) of any job that the Department can provide for the student. (2) Existing assignments with cooperative employers must be given priority. (3) The employer must be informed that the student is attending Northeastern on the cooperative program and that he will be returning to school at the end of the work period.*

EXPERIENTIAL PROGRAM. *One or more times during his participation in the cooperative program, a student may wish to engage in an activity other than paid employment, such as travel, independent study, or volunteer services. The Department of Cooperative Education recognizes the educational value of this type of experience and may allow the student to participate in the Experiential Program. Any student anticipating participation in the Experiential Program should discuss the possibility with his coordinator or the Director. He must petition his coordinator for approval of this activity before he makes any commitment. If approved, a petition remains in effect for one work period. Petition forms may be obtained from the coordinator concerned.*

SOCIAL SECURITY AND UNEMPLOYMENT COMPENSATION. *Social Security numbers* are required *of cooperative students before they may start work on cooperative jobs. Federal and State laws require that employers pay taxes based upon the amount of their payroll to provide funds for Old Age Retirement Annuities and Unemployment Compensation Benefits. The administration of these laws necessitates the registration of all employees of employers subject to these laws. Practically all workers are now included. This registration is evidenced by a Social Security number. The Social Security number may be obtained in one of two ways: (1) The number may be obtained without any delay by applying* in person *at the Regional Office of the U.S. Social Security Office. (2) Application blanks may be obtained at any U.S. Post Office. These blanks must then be taken or sent to the local regional headquarters, and the Social Security card bearing the number will be issued immediately or mailed to the address given on the application. There are two separate taxes, one for Old Age Assistance, the other for Unemployment Compensation. The law requires contributions by the workers as well as by the employers. The employer is required to de-*

duct the worker's share from his pay envelope or check. The amount deducted is ordinarily made known to the worker either on the check or on a slip accompanying the pay in the envelope. The deductions from the student's pay are for Old Age Assistance; the employer pays all of the Unemployment Compensation Tax. The Massachusetts Unemployment Compensation Law, Section 7, reads: "The term 'employment,' except as used in the definition of 'payroll' in subsection 'n' of section one, shall not include: (1) "Services performed by an individual while registered for a prescribed course at any educational institution on a cooperative plan of education and industrial training. (2) Services performed during customary vacation periods by an individual who was registered for full attendance at and regularly attending an established school, college, or university, in the most recent school term and who intends to return thereto or to enter another school, college, or university as a student for the next regular term." Therefore, Northeastern students are not eligible to receive Unemployment Compensation Benefits. *Other states have similar laws.*

WORKING CERTIFICATES. *The laws of the Commonwealth of Massachusetts require that, on certain kinds of work, minors under 18 years of age may not be employed without first obtaining a working certificate. Employers are fined if this certificate is not posted in accordance with the law. Therefore, because the student is the only one who can procure this certificate, he should assume the responsibility of getting it immediately after he has been accepted for the job and present it to his employer when he starts work. Certificates are available at the office of the superintendent of schools of the student's residential community or, for graduates of Boston schools, at the Continuation School Headquarters, 45 Myrtle Street, Boston.*

HEALTH PROBLEMS. *A student may occasionally have a health problem which will have a significant effect on his placement on a cooperative assignment. It may be a physical defect which will hurt his placement possibilities, or it may be a condition requiring extensive or unusual medical or surgical treatment. In some cases, it will require removal from a particular cooperative job or a leave of absence for all or part of a work term. Regulations require that the student discuss the prob-*

lem with his coordinator and fill out a petition requesting appropriate action. The coordinator may refer the student to the University Health Department, where, after an exchange of information with the family physician, a judgment will be made with respect to the legitimacy of the request. In most cases, the student will be asked to sign a statement releasing the health information so that the Health Department may disclose the necessary facts to the coordinator. Also the coordinator is given permission, through the signed statement, to use the information with potential or existing employers to the best advantage of the student. Whenever surgical or medical treatment is elected, the student must petition in advance. When emergency conditions prevail, the petition must be filed with the coordinator as soon as possible after the emergency.

Bibliography

American Academy of Arts and Sciences. *A First Report: The Assembly on University Goals and Governance.* Cambridge, Mass.: Assembly on University Goals and Governance, 1971.

American Association of Junior Colleges. *Selected Papers.* Washington, D.C., 1967.

American Society for Engineering Education, Committee on Aims and Ideals of Cooperative Engineering Education. "The Cooperative System—A Manifesto." *Journal of Engineering Education,* 1946, *37,* 117–134.

————, Committee Report of Cooperative Education Division. "Goals for Cooperative Education in Engineering Baccalureate Programs." *Journal of Engineering Education,* 1968, *59,* 236–238.

ARMSBY, H. *Cooperative Education in the United States.* Bulletin No. 11. Washington, D.C.: Office of Education, Department of Health, Education, and Welfare, 1954.

AYER, F. E. "Some Unsung Aspects of Cooperative Training." *Journal of Engineering Education,* May 1931, 625–626.

BASKIN, S. "The Graduate of the College Work-Study Program: A Study of His Career Planning and Later Work Adjustment." Unpublished doctoral dissertation, New York University, 1954.

Beloit College Catalogue. Beloit, Wis., 1968.

BONNELL, A. T. "The Academic Soundness of Cooperative Education." *Journal of Cooperative Education,* 1964, *1*(1), 19–27.

BORMAN, A. K. "Cooperative Education Moves Up to Graduate Study." *Journal of College Placement,* 1967, *28,* 97–98.

BROWN, C. "Cooperative Education: The Extended Classroom." *Junior College Journal,* 1960, *31,* 22–24.

BURNS, G. W. "Effect of the Present Economic Dislocation on our Cooperative Program." *Journal of Engineering Education,* 1934, 557–561.

CADDY, D. " 'Working My Way through College' Different at Nation's Second Largest Private University." *NAM Reports,* 1965, *10*(38). Washington, D.C.: National Association of Manufacturers.

"Careers for Negro Students: Northeastern University's Pilot Program." *School and Society,* 1965, *93,* 364.

Carnegie Commission on Higher Education. *Less Time, More Options.* New York: McGraw-Hill, 1971.

COLEMAN, P. E. "A New Appraisal of the Cooperative Plan." *Journal of Business Education,* 1934, 913–914.

College Entrance Examination Board. *College Credit by Examination through the College Level Examination Program.* New York, 1970.

COLLINS, S. B. *A Directory of Cooperative Education: Its Philosophy and Operation in Participating Colleges in the United States and Canada.* Philadelphia: Cooperative Education Association, Drexel University, 1970.

CONNERY, R. H. *The Corporation and the Campus.* New York: Praeger Publishers, 1970.

Cooperative Education Association. *Cooperative Education Programs* (Directory). Philadelphia: Cooperative Education Association, Drexel University, 1970.

Cooperative Education Association and Cooperative Education Division of the American Society for Engineering Education. *Guidelines for Employers Considering the Use of Cooperative Students.* Philadelphia: Cooperative Education Association, Drexel University, 1970.

Chrysler Corporation. *The Chrysler Institute of Engineering Graduate Program.* Detroit, n.d.

DAWSON, J. D. "New Directions for Cooperative Education." *Journal of Cooperative Education,* 1971, *7,* 1–12.

Directory of Predominantly Negro Colleges and Universities in the United States of America. Washington, D.C.: Government Printing Office, 1969.

DIXON, J. P., and D. BUSH, "College and the World of Work." *Educational Leadership,* 1966, *23,* 326–329.

DOWDEN, A. L., ed. *Hand in Hand Book Committee.* Medford, Mass.: Gordon & Co., 1958.

Engineering Education, Cooperative Engineering Education. 1971, *61* (7).

Executive Office of the President of the United States, Office of Science and Technology. *Catalogue of Federal Laboratory-University Programs and Relationships.* Washington, D.C.: Government Printing Office, 1969.

"Expansion of Cooperative Education: Work-Study Plan." *School and Society,* 1963, *91,* 102.

FARRELL, J. T. "Job That Buys a Dream: Work-Study Programs." *American Education,* 1965, *1,* 1–4.

FRAM, E. H. "An Evaluation of the Work-Study Program at the Rochester Institute of Technology." Ed.D. diss., State University of New York at Buffalo, 1964.

General Motors Institute. *Engineering and Industrial Administration Programs.* Flint, Michigan, 1971–72.

HARRIS, M. R. *Five Counter-Revolutionaries in Higher Education.* Corvallis: Oregon State University Press, 1970.

HENDERSON, A. D., and D. HALL. *Antioch College: Its Design for Liberal Education.* New York: Harper & Row, 1946.

HODNETT, E. *Industry-College Relations.* New York: World Publishing Co., 1955.

HUNT, D. C. "And It Happened This Way." *Journal of Cooperative Education,* 1964, *1* (1), 3–4.

HUNT, M. B. *A Remarkable Instrument for Learning.* Yellow Springs, Ohio: Antioch College, 1965.

HUTKINS, R., and R. W. STADT. "Understanding Cooperative Education." *Educational Forum,* 1970, *34* (4), 541–545.

Industry Aid to Education. New York: National Industrial Conference Board, 1965.

Industry's Stake in the Changing Engineering Curriculum. Washington, D.C.: American Society for Engineering Education, 1969.

JOHNSON, B. L. *Islands of Innovation Expanding (Changes in Community Colleges).* Beverly Hills, Calif.: Glencoe Press, 1969.

Kalamazoo College Bulletin, 1969. Kalamazoo, Michigan.

KAPP, C. A. "The Effect of Unions upon the Placement of Cooperative Students." *Journal of Engineering Education,* 1935, 263–265.

KLAURENS, M. K. "Distributive Education for the Future: Job Satisfaction in Cooperative Distributive Education." *Business Education Forum,* 1968, *22,* 9–10.

KNOWLES, A. S. *A College President Looks at Cooperative Education.* New York: National Commission for Cooperative Education, 1963.

———. "Colleges on the Co-op Plan." *American Youth,* 1966, *7* (1), 14–16.

———. "The Cooperative College." *College and University Journal,* 1965, *4*(3), 45–49.

———. "Co-op Education, Boon to Health and Allied Medical Sciences." *Business Topics,* 1966, *4*(2), 1–3.

———. *Education under the Cooperative Plan.* Management Bulletin 73. New York: American Management Association, 1965.

———. "Is Cooperative Education the Answer?" *The Conference Board Record,* 1971, *8*(1), 48–51.

———. "Partnership between Business and Education." *The Purple and Gold,* 1965, *82*(3), 39–42.

LAPP, P. A., J. W. HODGINS, and C. B. MACKAY. *Ring of Iron—A Study of Engineering Education in Ontario.* Toronto, Canada: Committee of Presidents of Universities of Ontario, 1970.

LARKIN, J. A. *Work Study.* New York: McGraw-Hill, 1969.

LINDENMEYER, R. S. "A Comparison of the Academic Progress of the Cooperative and Four-Year Student." *Journal of Cooperative Education,* 1967, *3*(2), 8–18.

LUPTON, D. K. "The Employer Role in Cooperative Education." *Journal of Cooperative Education,* 1969, *6*(1), 51–56.

———. *The Student in Society.* Totawa, N.J.: Littlefield, Adams and Co., 1969.

LYONS, E. H., and D. C. HUNT. "Cooperative Education: Evaluated." *Journal of Engineering Education,* 1961, *51,* 436–444.

MARKS, M. V. "Improving Occupational Experiences." *Business Education Forum,* 1963, *17,* 5–7.

MASON, R. E. *Cooperative Occupational Education and Work Experiences in the Curriculum.* Danville, Ill.: Interstate Printers, 1965.

———. "Effective Cooperative Business Education Programs." *Business Education Forum,* 1962, *16,* 21.

Massachusetts Civil Service Law. Chapter 30, Section 60, of the General Laws, Amended by Chapter 203 in 1968.

———. Chapter 31 of the General Laws, Amended by Chapter 7 in 1970.

MC MILLION, M. B. "Supervision and Coop Education." *Agricultural Educational Magazine,* 1967, *39,* 276–277.

MEACHAM, C. "Cooperative Education: An Answer?" *Liberal Education.* 1969, 571–575.

MINEAR, L. P. "Piece of the Action; Work-Study Program." *American Education,* 1969, *5,* 4–6.

MOSBACKER, W. "Women Graduates of Cooperative Work-Study Programs on the College Level." *Personnel and Guidance Journal,* 1957, *35,* 508–511.

National Commission for Cooperative Education. *Colleges and Universities Offering Cooperative Education Programs.* New York: National Commission for Cooperative Education, 1970.

New Careers and Curriculum Change. Atlanta: Southern Regional Education Board, 1968.

NEWMAN, F., Chairman. *Report on Higher Education.* Washington, D.C.: Department of Health, Education, and Welfare, 1971.

Northeastern University. *The Co-op Handbook, 1970–71.* Boston, Mass. *Graduate School of Actuarial Science.* Boston, n.d.

———. *Introducing Northeastern University, Freshman Programs, 1971–72.* Boston, Mass.

OSBORN, C. R. *The Company-Owned Cooperative College: General Motors Institute.* Management Bulletin 73. New York: American Management Association, 1965.

PARK, C. W. *Ambassador to Industry—the Idea and Life of Herman Schneider.* Indianapolis and New York: Bobbs-Merrill, 1943.

PLOSKI, H. A., and R. C. BROWN, eds. *The Negro Almanac.* New York: Bellwether Publishing Co., 1967.

PROBST, G. E. "Cooperative Education Is First-Rate Education." *PTA Magazine,* 1963, *58,* 26–28.

Public Law 90–575, 90th Congress, S.3769, Title 1, Part D, Section 451, 1968.

SANTORA, A. C. "Industry Faces STEP to Find Training Solutions." *American Vocational Journal,* 1967, *42,* 22–23.

SANTORA, P. "Co-op Colleges: All Work Makes Jack for Jack." New York *Daily News,* June 30, 1965, p. 14c.

———. "From the University Prexy on Down, the Spirit Is Up." New York *Daily News,* July 1, 1965, p. 14c.

———. "The Go Go Students Keep Profs Up to Snuff." New York *Daily News,* July 2, 1965. p. 14c.

SCOTT, N. T. "Higher Education for Life; Linking Study and Work." *New York Times Educational Supplement,* 1965, *2615,* 21.

SEAVERNS, C. F., JR. *A Manual for Coordinators of Cooperative Education.*

2nd ed. Boston: Center for Cooperative Education, Northeastern University, 1970.

"Selection and Placement of Students in Cooperative Programs." *Business Educational Forum,* April 1970, 21–22.

SEULBERGER, F. G. "Cooperative Education and the Business Depression." *Journal of Engineering Education,* March 1932, 611–612.

SMITH, H. S., JR. "The Influence of Participation in the Cooperative Program on Academic Performance." *Journal of Cooperative Education,* 1965, *3*(1), 7–20.

SMITH, L. F. "Cooperative Work Programs." *Journal of Higher Education,* 1944, *15*(4), 207–212.

————. "Effects of the War on Cooperative Education." *Higher Education,* 1946, *2*(14), 1–3.

"Society for the Promotion of Engineering Education [SPEE] Report." *Journal of Engineering Education,* April 1930, 841.

"Society for the Promotion of Engineering Education [SPEE] Division Report." *Journal of Engineering Education,* Nov. 1937, 174–176.

STARK, M. H. "An Appraisal of the Work-Study Program at Wilmington College and the Cooperative Industry." Ph.D. diss., Colorado State College, 1965.

STIRTON, W. E. "My Meat and Drink." *Journal of Cooperative Education,* 1968, *4*(2), 24–34.

"Support for Collegiate Cooperative Education Program." *School and Society,* 1970, *98,* 399.

"Support for Work-Study Projects." *School and Society,* 1967, *95,* 512.

TONNE, A. A. "Apprenticeship as One Answer to Job Training." *Journal of Business Education,* 1966, *41,* 142–143.

TUNLEY, R. "Work-Study Route to a College Degree." *PTA Magazine,* 1968, *63,* 14–16.

TYLER, R. W. "Introduction to the Study; Conclusions and Recommendations." In James W. Wilson and Edward H. Lyons, *Work-Study College Programs.* New York: Harper & Row, 1961.

————, and A. L. MILL. *Report on Cooperative Education: Summary of the National Study.* Detroit: Thomas Alva Edison Foundation, 1961.

U.S. Civil Service Commission. *Cooperative Work Study.* Bulletin N.330–15. Washington, D.C., 1970.

U.S. Department of the Air Force. *Cooperative Education Programs.* Supplement 29, AFM 40.1. Washington, D.C., 1964.

U.S. Department of the Army. *Cooperative Education Program.* DA Pam 350–4. Washington, D.C., 1967.

U.S. Department of Commerce, Bureau of the Census. *Population Characteristics.* Series No. 145. Washington, D.C.: Government Printing Office, 1965.

U.S. Department of Health, Education, and Welfare. "Report of Special Task Force on Higher Education." As reported in *The Chronicle of Higher Education,* March 1971 (a).

———, Federal Interagency Committee on Education. *Federal Agencies and Black Colleges.* Washington, D.C.: Government Printing Office, 1971 (b).

———, Office of Education. *Handbook: Organization and Functions.* OE11002–B, Rev. Washington, D.C., 1968.

———, Office of Education. *Notification to Members of Congress.* Washington, D.C.: Bureau of Higher Education, 1971.

———, Office of Education, National Center for Educational Statistics. *Education Directory,* 1969–1970, Part 3, Higher Education. Washington, D.C.: Government Printing Office.

U.S. Department of Labor, Bureau of Labor Statistics. *The U.S. Economy in 1980.* Bulletin 1673. Washington, D.C.: Government Printing Office, 1970.

———, Bureau of Labor Statistics, Middle Atlantic Region. *Women in the World of Work.* Washington, D.C.: Government Printing Office, 1970.

———, Wage and Labor Standards Administration, Women's Bureau. *Fact Sheet on the Earnings Gap.* Washington, D.C.: Government Printing Office, 1970.

———, Wage and Labor Standards Administration, Women's Bureau. *1969 Handbook on Women Workers.* Bulletin 394. Washington, D.C.: Government Printing Office, 1969.

———, Wage and Labor Standards Administration, Women's Bureau. *Trends in Educational Attainment of Women.* Washington, D.C.: Government Printing Office, 1969.

———, Workplace Standards Administration, Women's Bureau. *Underutilization of Women Workers.* Rev. ed. Washington, D.C.: Government Printing Office, 1971.

University of Cincinnati Bulletin, College of Business Administration. Cincinnati, Ohio, 1971.

WANDMACHER, C. "Values of Cooperative Education." *Journal of Engineering Education,* Dec. 1969, 326.

WHITE, W. C. "The Cooperative Plan in the Depression." *School and Society,* 1933, *37*(942), 65–67.

WILLIAMS, G. L. "Beyond the Classroom: Life Experiences in the Field." *Clearinghouse,* 1970, *45,* 81–85.

WILSON, J. W. "Growth and Current Status of Cooperative Engineering Education." *Journal of Engineering Education,* 1971, *61*(7), 790–794.

WILSON, J. W. "On the Nature of Cooperative Education." *Journal of Cooperative Education,* 1970, *6*(2), 1–10.

———. "Study of Cooperative Education." *School and Society,* 1960, *88,* 399.

———. "Survey of Cooperative Education, 1969." *Journal of Cooperative Education,* 1969, *6,* 5–15.

———. "Survey of Cooperative Education, 1970." *Journal of Cooperative Education,* 1970, *7*(1), 31–45.

———, and E. H. LYONS. *Work-Study College Programs: Appraisal and Report of the Study of Cooperative Education.* New York: Harper & Row, 1961.

WINKIE, J. D. "Responsibility and Cooperative Education," in C. W. Havice (Ed.), *Campus Values.* New York: Scribners, 1971.

WOHLFORD, J. G. "The Cooperative Education Division of ASEE—A Brief History." *Engineering Education,* 1971, *61*(7), 785–789, 824.

WOOLDRIDGE, R. L. *Analysis of Student Employment in a Cooperative Education Program.* Report for the National Commission for Cooperative Education. Boston: Center for Cooperative Education, Northeastern University, 1970.

———. "Cooperative Education." In Asa S. Knowles, ed., *Handbook of College and University Administration,* Vol. 2. New York: McGraw-Hill, 1970.

———. *Cooperative Education and the Community Colleges in New Jersey.* New York: National Commission for Cooperative Education, 1966.

———. *Student Employment and Cooperative Education: Its Growth and Stability.* New York: National Commission for Cooperative Education, 1964.

YENCSO, W. R. "A Comparative Analysis of Engineering Graduates from Cooperative and Regular Programs." Ph.D. diss., University of Michigan, 1970.

Index

A